DATA PROTECTION BEYOND BORDERS

This timely book examines crucial developments in the field of privacy law, efforts by legal systems to impose their data protection standards beyond their borders and claims by states to assert sovereignty over data.

By bringing together renowned international privacy experts from the EU and the US, the book provides an accurate analysis of key trends and prospects in the transatlantic context, including spaces of tensions and cooperation between the EU and the US in the field of data protection law.

The chapters explore recent legal and policy developments both in the private and law enforcement sectors, including recent rulings by the Court of Justice of the EU dealing with Google and Facebook, recent legislative initiatives in the EU and the US such as the CLOUD Act and the e-evidence proposal, as well as ongoing efforts to strike a transatlantic deal in the field of data sharing.

All of the topics are thoroughly examined and presented in an accessible way that will appeal to scholars in the fields of law, political science and international relations, as well as to a wider and non-specialist audience. The book is an essential guide to understanding contemporary challenges to data protection across the Atlantic.

Data Protection Beyond Borders

Transatlantic Perspectives on Extraterritoriality and Sovereignty

Edited by
Federico Fabbrini
Edoardo Celeste
and
John Quinn

•HART•
OXFORD • LONDON • NEW YORK • NEW DELHI • SYDNEY

HART PUBLISHING
Bloomsbury Publishing Plc
Kemp House, Chawley Park, Cumnor Hill, Oxford, OX2 9PH, UK
1385 Broadway, New York, NY 10018, USA
29 Earlsfort Terrace, Dublin 2, Ireland

HART PUBLISHING, the Hart/Stag logo, BLOOMSBURY and the Diana logo are trademarks of Bloomsbury Publishing Plc

First published in Great Britain 2021

A catalogue record for this book is available from the British Library.

Library of Congress Cataloging-in-Publication data

Names: Fabbrini, Federico, 1985- editor, author. | Celeste, Edoardo, editor, author. | Quinn, John, 1949- editor, author.

Title: Data protection beyond borders : transatlantic perspectives on extraterritoriality and sovereignty / edited by Federico Fabbrini, Edoardo Celeste and John Quinn.

Description: Oxford, UK ; New York, NY : Hart Publishing, an imprint of Bloomsbury Publishing, 2021. | Includes bibliographical references and index.

Identifiers: LCCN 2020052027 (print) | LCCN 2020052028 (ebook) | ISBN 9781509940660 (hardback) | ISBN 9781509946778 (paperback) | ISBN 9781509940677 (pdf) | ISBN 9781509940684 (Epub)

Subjects: LCSH: Data protection—Law and legislation—European Union countries. | Data protection—Law and legislation—United States.

Classification: LCC K3264.C65 D373 2021 (print) | LCC K3264.C65 (ebook) | DDC 343.2409/99—dc23

LC record available at https://lccn.loc.gov/2020052027

LC ebook record available at https://lccn.loc.gov/2020052028

ISBN: HB: 978-1-50994-066-0
ePDF: 978-1-50994-067-7
ePub: 978-1-50994-068-4

Typeset by Compuscript Ltd, Shannon

ACKNOWLEDGEMENTS

This book collects the proceedings of the annual Conference of the Law Research Centre of Dublin City University (DCU), convened in Dublin, Ireland on 5–6 March 2020 and hosted by Grant Thornton. The event, which occurred just on the eve of the outburst of the Covid-19 pandemic, offered a unique opportunity for authors to get together and debate their draft chapters – and we are very grateful to Mike Harris at Grant Thornton for supporting this and other initiatives undertaken by DCU in the field of data protection and privacy law, and for giving a speech at the book conference.

We are also pleased to acknowledge that the preparation of this book received financial support from the DCU Faculty of Humanities and Social Sciences Book Publication Scheme.

Dublin, July 2020

CONTENTS

PART III
COOPERATION

PART IV
PROSPECTS

LIST OF CONTRIBUTORS

Angela Aguinaldo is Researcher at Max Planck Institute for the Study of Crime, Security and Law, Freiburg, Germany.

Dana Burchardt is Senior Research Fellow at Freie Universität Berlin.

Edoardo Celeste is Assistant Professor of Law, Technology and Innovation at the School of Law & Government of Dublin City University (DCU).

Paul De Hert is Full Professor of Privacy Law at the Free University of Brussels.

Federico Fabbrini is Full Professor of EU Law at the School of Law & Government of Dublin City University (DCU), where he is the Director of the Law Research Centre and the Founding Director of the Brexit Institute.

Jordan Fischer is Assistant Teaching Professor of Law at Drexel University Kline School of Law, Philadelphia.

Orla Lynskey is Associate Professor of Law at the London School of Economics and Political Science, and Visiting Professor at the College of Europe, Bruges.

TJ McIntyre is Associate Professor of Law at the University College Dublin Sutherland School of Law.

John Quinn is Assistant Professor of Corporate Law at the School of Law & Government of Dublin City University (DCU).

Oreste Pollicino is Full Professor of Constitutional Law at Bocconi University Milan and a member of the management board of the EU Fundamental Rights Agency.

Stephen Smith is Director of Fourth Amendment & Open Courts, Center for Internet and Society, Stanford Law School, and former US Magistrate Judge for the Southern District of Texas, Houston Division.

Maria Tzanou is Associate Professor in Law at Keele University.

Vincenzo Zeno-Zencovich is Full Professor of Comparative Law at University of Rome III.

TABLE OF CASES

European Court of Justice / Court of Justice of the European Union

European Court of Human Rights

Permanent Court of International Justice

Australia

Austria

Belgium

Canada

France

Germany

Ireland

Italy

United Kingdom

United States of America

TABLE OF LEGISLATION

EU Legislation

Other EU Material

Brazil

Canada

China

Germany

Ireland

Japan

Spain

United Kingdom

United States

Federal

State

California

International Conventions

Other Material

1

Introduction

FEDERICO FABBRINI, EDOARDO CELESTE,
AND JOHN QUINN

The purpose of this book is to examine the protection of personal data from a transatlantic perspective. Personal data are the backbone of the contemporary digital society. Data, by its nature, is unterritorial, yet law has traditionally been limited by territorial boundaries. Therefore, a tension emerges between data and the laws which regulate it. As a result of this tension, a serious question has emerged regarding how to protect personal data rights across borders. Data flows across jurisdictions for commercial purposes, as digital companies transfer data from subsidiaries to their headquarters for processing purposes. Moreover, data flow occurs in the context of law enforcement, as national authorities increasingly seek access to personal data stored in foreign countries in order to prevent and fight serious crimes. The issues that arise from this situation have been mostly developed in the transatlantic context between the European Union (EU) and the United States (US), which are at the vanguard of technological innovation.

Over the past few years, significant legislative and jurisprudential developments in the field of data privacy have taken place on both sides of the Atlantic. In 2016 the EU adopted a new pan-European data protection law – the General Data Protection Regulation (GDPR)[1] – while, in the US, at state level, California passed a new piece of data privacy legislation,[2] and, at federal level, the CLOUD Act has introduced the possibility for law enforcement authorities to request data stored in third countries.[3] In both jurisdictions, moreover, seminal judicial decisions have been recently adopted, such as judgments by the EU Court of Justice (CJEU) involving the American tech giants Facebook[4] and Google,[5] and the much-discussed US Supreme Court *Carpenter* case, which applies constitutional

[1] Regulation (EU) 2016/679, OJ 2016 L 119/1.

[2] California Consumer Privacy Act, Cal Civ Code §§ 1798.100-.199 (West 2018) (effective 1 January 2020).

[3] Clarifying Lawful Overseas Use of Data (CLOUD) Act, HR 1625, 115th Cong div V (2018).

[4] Case C-18/18, *Eva Glawischnig-Piesczek v Facebook Ireland Ltd*, ECLI:EU:C:2019:821.

[5] Case C-507/17, *Google LLC v Commission Nationale de l'Informatique et des Libertés (CNIL)*, ECLI:EU:C:2019:772.

protections against law enforcement agencies accessing cell location data.[6] These developments have produced, occasionally, convergence and cooperation between the two regimes, but at times, also amplified pre-existing areas of divergence and tensions. The recent July 2020 CJEU judgment in *Schrems II*,[7] declaring invalid the European Commission's decision establishing the adequacy of the EU-US Privacy Shield, is a paradigmatic example of how, after years of intense debate and failed reforms, there is still a significant divergence between the EU and the US in the field of data privacy.

These developments, as this book explains, are further complicated by the emergence of two conflicting dynamics in the digital environment. On the one hand, on both sides of the Atlantic and beyond, jurisdictions increasingly endeavour to apply their legislation extraterritorially. In particular, the EU applies data protection law outside its borders in order to ensure effective protection of European fundamental rights and limit the risk of circumvention. The US, instead, has recently adopted new legislation to access data stored in foreign data centres managed by US-based companies. On the other hand, both jurisdictions also endeavour to claim, with ever-greater assertiveness, their sovereignty over data and digital infrastructures. The EU is investing significantly in a project to build a cloud 'made in the EU' that could compete against the American tech giants. The US, as a response, is considering strengthening its position by adopting competing federal legislation, which would favour business and foster innovation.

These trends are further blurred by fast-changing technological transformations and by the fluidity of longer-term processes that are currently subverting pre-existing economic and political equilibria. In particular, Brexit – the United Kingdom (UK) withdrawal from the EU – will change the status of the UK from EU Member State, to which data can be freely transferred, to third country, which will require specific arrangements similar to those that the European Commission has for years attempted to put in place with the US. In parallel, the increasing EU quest for digital sovereignty, which seeks to reattract data into the orbit of the EU, clashes with the technological superiority of US technology companies, and risks generating an arm-wrestling match in a context already in turmoil because of the economic war currently under way between the US and China.

This book therefore aims to analyse these ongoing dynamics, shedding light on the EU and US developments in the field of data protection, the areas of tension and cooperation between these jurisdictions, and the future prospects for the protection of data across borders.

The book, which brings together contributions by leading legal scholars from across Europe and the US, is structured in four parts. Part I sets the scene, presenting the latest legal developments in the field of data protection both in the EU and the US. Part II critically examines the emerging tensions in the protection of

[6] *Carpenter v United States*, 138 S Ct 2206, 2220 (2018).

[7] Case C-311/18, *Data Protection Commissioner v Facebook Ireland Ltd and Maximillian Schrems* ECLI:EU:C:2020:559.

personal data beyond borders and analyses recent judgments dealing with issues of extraterritorial application of EU data protection law and their challenges. Part III analyses a series of scenarios where transatlantic cooperation in the data protection field is already present or advocated, with a particular focus on the law enforcement sector. Finally, Part IV reflects on the future prospects of the tension between extraterritoriality and sovereignty in the data protection field.

In Chapter two, Edoardo Celeste and Federico Fabbrini map the legal architecture for the protection of personal data in the EU, examine its resilience in the context of Covid-19, and explore the question of the extraterritorial application of EU data protection law. The chapter explains that there are good arguments for the EU to apply its high data protection standards outside its borders. As data is un-territorial, only a global application of EU data protection law can guarantee effective enforcement of privacy rights. However, the chapter also highlights how such an extraterritorial application of EU data protection law faces challenges, as it may clash with duties of international comity and the need to respect diversity of legal systems, and could ultimately be nullified by contrasting rulings delivered by other courts in other jurisdictions. As the chapter points out from a comparative perspective, the protection of privacy in the digital age increasingly exposes a tension between efforts by legal systems to impose their high standards of data protection outside their borders and claims by other legal systems to assert their own power over data. The chapter suggests that navigating these conflicting currents will not be an easy task, and that greater convergence in the data protection framework of liberal democratic systems worldwide appears to be the preferable – albeit far from easy – path to secure privacy in the digital age.

In Chapter three, Jordan Fischer investigates the US data privacy legal framework. She argues that, in contrast to the EU, the US adopted a radically different approach in the privacy field. The right to privacy was never enshrined in the US Constitution, but progressively recognised by the case law of state and federal courts. US data privacy legislation is sectoral and fragmented. Industry codes and standards play a significant role. Fischer contends that, despite the influence that the GDPR has exercised over the past few years, the US can still provide a crucial input to frame a global approach to privacy. The chapter explores how the US can develop new federal legislation, while resisting the GDPR effect and preserving the peculiarities of the US tradition. In particular, Fischer argues that a new federal privacy law should still rely on the mix of public authorities' oversight and private companies' self-enforcement that is common in the US. The chapter finally explains how developing a new federal privacy framework in the US presents a series of challenges, but also offers multiple opportunities.

In Chapter four, John Quinn analyses the 2019 CJEU decision in *Google v CNIL*, which directly addressed the territorial scope of a successful de-referencing request made under the right to be forgotten in Article 17 of the GDPR, and discusses the implications of this major case. The CJEU held that the default position of EU law was that search engines, following a successful de-reference request, must remove the relevant information from their EU domains only, and not across all versions of their search engine. Therefore, the case limited the territorial scope of a successful de-referencing request to within the EU. Quinn explains how the existence of geo-blocking technology influenced the ruling of the CJEU. However, he contends that because the right to be forgotten is not absolute the CJEU decision in *Google v CNIL* is a proportionate one in attempting to balance rights on a global scale.

In Chapter five, Dana Burchardt examines tensions within the EU by analysing the German Federal Constitutional Court's recent jurisprudence on the right to be forgotten. In two decisions delivered in late 2019, the Constitutional Court developed a framework of 'parallel applicability' which seems to reduce the scope of application of EU fundamental rights in Germany. The framework also allows the German Court to influence how the right to be forgotten under EU law is interpreted and applied within the German legal order. Burchardt argues that the framework significantly broadens the competence of the German Constitutional Court, thereby creating a significant risk of internal fragmentation in the protections offered by EU law as well as inconsistencies due to a diverging EU and German interpretation of EU law in the data protection field and beyond.

In Chapter six, Oreste Pollicino offers a comprehensive overview of the effects of the extraterritoriality of EU law, investigating to what extent the case law of the CJEU in the digital field has an impact on the digital sovereignty of third states. The chapter claims that the CJEU has turned privacy and data protection into a 'super' fundamental right and that this constitutes the theoretical justification for the extraterritorial effects of the EU legal system. Pollicino argues that the absence of a comprehensive privacy framework in the US, combined with the special status that EU legislation and case law have accorded to the rights to privacy and data protection, has fuelled a process of 'Europeanisation' at global level. The chapter analyses as a further example of this trend the recent CJEU decision in *Glawischnig-Piesczek v Facebook*, illustrating how the CJEU is explicitly authorising a global application of EU law if necessary to preserve European fundamental rights.

In Chapter seven, Maria Tzanou addresses the conditions on which the extraterritorial effects of EU law are grounded, focusing on the application of EU fundamental privacy rights to trans-border data flows. She analyses the *Schrems I* decision where the CJEU invalidated the EU administrative framework for data transfers to the US as incompatible with EU fundamental rights. She also analyses the July 2020 judgment of the CJEU in *Schrems II* where again the CJEU ruled to suspend the transfer of personal data from Facebook Ireland to its US parent company, on the basis that the data could be made available to American authorities in violation to EU privacy rights. She argues that the CJEU has failed to consider important theoretical and doctrinal considerations in these decisions and has neglected to meaningfully engage with the interpretation of EU fundamental rights in the context of their extraterritorial application.

In Chapter eight, Stephen Smith examines the CLOUD Act, a US federal statute which provides law enforcement authorities with significant power to obtain electronic data stored in foreign jurisdictions. Smith focuses on the provisions which authorise real-time surveillance of the activities of criminal suspects and others beyond US territory. He outlines the modes of surveillance explicitly and implicitly covered by the CLOUD Act and explains their potential extraterritorial impacts. One of Smith's concerns is that much of the Act contains ambiguous language that perhaps implicitly authorises numerous types of surveillance, including 'network investigative techniques', a term Smith believes to equivalent to hacking. Smith explores the implications of this piece of US legislation in the context of international law, and argues that, to the extent the CLOUD Act authorises US law enforcement to unilaterally engage in surveillance on foreign soil, it disregards international law.

In Chapter nine, TJ McIntyre analyses the system of voluntary disclosure by Irish-based online service providers to foreign law enforcement authorities. The chapter explains that digital companies established in the jurisdiction of the Irish state play a crucial role, by acting as controllers of the data of millions of European users. McIntyre argues that, despite this responsibility, the Irish state has not ratified the Cybercrime Convention and has failed to regulate cross-border access to data stored in Ireland. By virtue of vague provisions of Irish law, foreign law enforcement authorities regularly resort to companies based in Ireland to request personal data that otherwise could be obtained only through the lengthy and burdensome mutual legal assistance procedure. McIntyre argues that this practice has been made illegal by the entry into force of the GDPR, and shows that this circumstance may be regarded as a violation of the obligations owed by the Irish state by virtue of the ECHR, and considers options for challenging the status quo.

In Chapter ten, Angela Aguinaldo and Paul De Hert critically assess the last decade of direct cooperation, this time between EU law enforcement authorities and US technology companies. The chapter reconstructs the legal grounds justifying the use of direct transatlantic cooperation in the law enforcement context, and analyses the new opportunities offered by the adoption of the US CLOUD act and a series of proposals at European level, including the additional protocol to the Cybercrime Convention and the EU e-Evidence package. Aguinaldo and De Hert highlight the persistence of a series of public international law conundrums related to sovereignty and jurisdiction and the risks deriving from a burden shift from public authorities to private companies. The chapter concludes by analysing to what extent the new direct cooperation systems still fail to address significant data protection issues, and by highlighting the relevance of the recent *Schrems II* CJEU decision and the judgment of the German Federal Constitutional Court on the proportionality of domestic production orders in this field.

In Chapter eleven, Vincenzo Zeno-Zencovich investigates whether international trade law could be a solution to avoid conflicts of law and guarantee free-flow of data across borders. The chapter illustrates the complexities of applying international trade law to data flows. It highlights that data exchanges are not easily classifiable as either goods or services, often because they represent ancillary elements of a transaction. It critically appraises to what extent the same notion of data, and in particular that of a personal nature, may fit with the rules of international trade. Zeno-Zencovich explains that the international trade law principles of the 'Most Favoured Nation' (MFN) and 'National Treatment' (NT) do not offer practical solutions when applied in the context of data flows. As such, Zeno-Zencovich concludes by exploring alternative answers to the application of these international trade law principles, and illustrating potential fora that could successfully address the issue of free-flow of data.

In Chapter twelve, Orla Lynskey critically addresses the mechanisms through which EU law gains its extraterritorial effects. Firstly, by comparing EU data protection law with other areas of EU law, she argues that extraterritorial impact is not particular to EU data protection law, thereby rejecting claims of data exceptionalism. As she points out, environmental law and competition law are other examples where EU law operates beyond its borders. Lynskey then continues examining the rationale for EU law's extraterritorial impact, arguing that it flows from nascent principles of EU law such as mutual trust and the autonomy of the EU legal order. Finally, she concludes by using the question of cross-border data flows after Brexit to support the argument for the extraterritorial effect of EU law.

In Chapter thirteen, finally, Edoardo Celeste reconstructs the meaning of digital sovereignty, investigating its significance, rationale and challenges as a core value inspiring recent policy in the EU. The chapter surveys the historical evolution of the concept of sovereignty in general, and contextualises its application in the digital ecosystem, providing a definition of 'digital sovereignty'. Celeste then examines how this concept has been articulated in the EU, explaining that the rationale underlying this idea lies in the need to preserve the European 'DNA' of values and rights. European data are mostly processed by foreign companies and stored outside the EU. This circumstance poses serious risks in terms of potential fundamental rights violations. The chapter therefore summarises a number of initiatives that have been put forward to strengthen the EU digital sovereignty. However, Celeste also illustrates a series of risks associated with this tendency, warning that digital sovereignty can easily degenerate into forms of sovereigntism. Celeste finally contends that EU rights and values can continue to be upheld without resorting to counterproductive 'arm-wrestling' with foreign countries, by respecting the principles of international comity, peacefully cooperating and respecting pluralism.

Indeed, as the recent Covid-19 pandemic has highlighted, borders remain a porous concept, and cooperation trumps isolation as the way to deal with transnational problems like a pandemic. Yet, as this book explains, with specific reference to data, the protection of privacy across borders remains a work in progress – and we hope that this collective volume will contribute to the debate on how to advance in this effort, particularly in a transatlantic context.

PART I

Developments

2

EU Data Protection Law between Extraterritoriality and Sovereignty

FEDERICO FABBRINI AND EDOARDO CELESTE

I. Introduction

Writing in the *Harvard Law Review* in 1890, leading American jurists Louis Brandeis and Samuel Warren outlined the contours of a new right to privacy conceived as the right to be let alone.[1] Yet, 130 years later – and with the advent of the digital age – privacy is leaving this perimeter and entering new dimensions, with challenges of their own.[2] As the international newspaper *The New York Times* put it in launching 'The Privacy Project', a comprehensive months-long endeavour to explore how technology is altering conceptions of individual privacy, the terminology of privacy itself is changing, and crucially, new demands connected to privacy are emerging, especially in relation to the protection of personal data.[3]

The European Union (EU) has been at the forefront of the protection of the right to data privacy at the global level. The EU is currently endowed with an advanced constitutional and legislative framework for the protection of personal data. Moreover, the European Court of Justice (ECJ) has taken the lead as the most protective privacy court worldwide, developing a case law which has been taken as a model by courts also at the national level. In fact, recently, the EU legal framework for data protection has proved to be resilient also during the Covid-19 health crisis: in the context of the largest pandemic the world has experienced in a century, EU data protection law shaped and constrained government initiatives to track and trace individual movements and contacts, confirming the importance that privacy rights play even in a dramatic health scenario.

[1] Samuel D Warren and Louis D Brandeis, 'The Right to Privacy' (1890) 4 *Harvard Law Review* 193.

[2] See Federico Fabbrini, 'Human Rights in the Digital Age: The European Court of Justice Ruling in the Data Retention Case and Its Lessons for Privacy and Surveillance in the United States' (2015) 28 *Harvard Human Rights Journal* 65.

[3] See James Bennet, 'Opinion: Do You Know What You Have Given Up', *The New York Times* (10 April 2019), www.nytimes.com/2019/04/10/opinion/privacy-project-launch.html, accessed 13 July 2020.

Among the data privacy rights developed by the ECJ, and now explicitly codified in EU law, one of the most significant and innovative is the right to be forgotten, also known as the right to erasure: this right enables a data subject to request data controllers, including online digital platforms, to erase personal data concerning him or her – an entitlement which has grown in importance in the sprawling digital society.

However, the scope of EU data protection law in general, and the right to be forgotten in particular, has increasingly faced a question of jurisdictional boundaries. Indeed, one of the most debated features of EU data protection law is its capacity to apply beyond the borders of the EU.[4] Moreover, the recent introduction of harsher fines has led many foreign companies to comply with EU data protection law not only in relation to their European business, but on a global scale. Over the past few years, therefore, the scope of EU data protection law has not only expanded by virtue of a precise legislative choice, but also as a result of the economic and political influence of the EU – what Anu Bradford defined the 'Brussels effect'.[5]

The chapter maps the legal architecture for the protection of personal data in the EU, examines its resilience in the context of Covid-19, and explores the question of the extraterritorial application of EU data protection law.[6] The chapter explains that there are good arguments for the EU to apply its high data protection standards outside its borders. As data are un-territorial,[7] only a global application of EU data protection law can fully guarantee effective enforcement of privacy rights. However, the chapter also highlights how such an extraterritorial application of EU data protection law faces challenges, as it may clash with duties of international comity and the need to respect the diversity of legal systems, and could ultimately be nullified by contrasting rulings delivered by other courts in other jurisdictions.

As the chapter points out from a comparative perspective, however, this challenge is not unique to the EU legal system. Rather, it emerges in other jurisdictions as well, such as Canada and Australia. In fact, the protection of privacy in the digital age increasingly exposes a tension between efforts by legal systems to impose their high standards of data protection outside their borders – a dynamic which could be regarded as 'imperialist'[8] – and claims by other legal systems to assert their

[4] See Dan Jerker B Svantesson, 'Extraterritoriality and Targeting in EU Data Privacy Law: The Weak Spot Undermining the Regulation' (2015) 5 *International Data Privacy Law* 226.

[5] Anu Bradford, 'The Brussels Effect' (2012) 107 *Northwestern University Law Review* 1.

[6] See also Federico Fabbrini and Edoardo Celeste, 'The Right to Be Forgotten in the Digital Age: The Challenges of Data Protection Beyond Borders' (2020) 21 *German Law Journal* 55, on which this chapter draws.

[7] Jennifer Daskal, 'The Un-Territoriality of Data' (2015) 125 *Yale Law Journal* 326.

[8] See Oxford Learner's Dictionaries, 'Imperialism' (defining imperialism as '1. A system in which one country controls other countries […], 2. The fact of a powerful country increasing its influence over other countries through business, culture, etc.'), www.oxfordlearnersdictionaries.com/definition/american_english/imperialism, accessed 13 July 2020.

own power over data – a dynamic which one could name 'sovereigntist'.[9] As the chapter suggests, navigating between the Scylla of imperialism and the Charybdis of sovereigntism will not be an easy task – particularly when claims to control the digital realm are made by authoritarian regimes, which are eager to exploit digital technology for their illiberal missions.[10] In this context, greater convergence in the data protection framework of liberal democratic systems worldwide appears as the preferable – albeit far from easy – path to secure privacy in the digital age.

The chapter is structured as follows. Section II presents the EU constitutional framework for data protection and the expanding case law of the ECJ in the field. Section III highlights the resilience of EU data protection law during the Covid-19 pandemic. Section IV analyses the right to be forgotten afforded to data subjects – originally developed by the ECJ and then codified in EU legislation. Section V illustrates how the EU framework for data protection has progressively extended its reach outside the jurisdiction of the EU, looking in particular at the recent case law of the ECJ in the field of the right to be forgotten and removal of content from online platforms. Section VI, drawing a comparison with other jurisdictions, explores the rationale behind the extraterritorial application of EU data protection law and examines the challenges that this tendency poses. Section VII finally concludes suggesting that transnational cooperation among liberal democratic jurisdictions appears the preferable path to navigate the emerging tension between data protection imperialism and digital sovereignty and to guarantee an elevated standard of protection of data privacy in the digital age.

II. EU Data Protection Law and Jurisprudence

At the constitutional level, the EU abides by one of the most advanced standards for data privacy worldwide. The EU Charter of Fundamental Rights, adopted in 2000, introduced a constitutional recognition of the right to data protection in the EU legal order.[11] Whereas Article 7 of the Charter (entitled 'Respect for Private and Family Life') re-affirmed the content of Article 8 of the European Convention on Human Rights, proclaiming that 'Everyone has the right to respect for his or

[9] See Oxford Learner's Dictionaries, 'Sovereignty' (defining sovereignty as '1. Complete power to govern a country. 2. The state of being a country with freedom to govern itself'), www.oxfordlearners-dictionaries.com/definition/english/sovereignty?q=sovereignty, accessed 13 July 2020.

[10] See Yi-Zheng Lian, 'Opinion | Where Spying Is the Law', *The New York Times* (13 March 2019), www.nytimes.com/2019/03/13/opinion/china-canada-huawei-spying-espionage-5g.html, accessed 7 December 2019; US President, Executive Order on Securing the Information and Communications Technology and Services Supply Chain (*The White House*, 15 May 2019), www.whitehouse.gov/presidential-actions/executive-order-securing-information-communications-technology-services-supply-chain/, accessed 1 December 2019; cf Zak Doffman, 'Trump's Huawei Ban Rejected By New Ruling In Germany', *Forbes* (15 October 2019), www.forbes.com/sites/zakdoffman/2019/10/15/trumps-huawei-ban-rejected-by-surprise-new-report/, accessed 1 December 2019.

[11] See Maria Tzanou, 'Data Protection as a Fundamental Right Next to Privacy? "Reconstructing" a Not so New Right' (2013) 3 *International Data Privacy Law* 3.

her private and family life, home and communications', Article 8 of the Charter (entitled 'Protection of Personal Data') introduced a new explicit recognition of the rights to data privacy by stating that

1. Everyone has the right to the protection of personal data concerning him or her.
2. Such data must be processed fairly for specified purposes and on the basis of the consent of the person concerned or some other legitimate basis laid down by law. Everyone has the right of access to data which has been collected concerning him or her, and the right to have it rectified.
3. Compliance with these rules shall be subject to control by an independent authority.

With the entry into force of the Lisbon Treaty in 2009, the Charter has acquired full legal value.[12] Moreover, the Lisbon Treaty introduced another provision confirming the central role that the rights to data protection now play in the constitutional order of the EU.[13] Pursuant to Article 16 of the Treaty on the Functioning of the EU (TFEU), 'Everyone has the right to the protection of personal data concerning them.' The same provision empowers the European Parliament with the Council to

> lay down the rules relating to the protection of individuals with regard to the processing of personal data by Union institutions, bodies, offices and agencies, and by the Member States when carrying out activities which fall within the scope of Union law, and the rules relating to the free movement of such data. Compliance with these rules shall be subject to the control of independent authorities.

At the legislative level, then, the EU has been endowed with a comprehensive framework on data protection since the 1990s. The Data Protection Directive, adopted in 1995,[14] introduced a far-reaching obligation for the Member States to 'protect the fundamental rights and freedoms of natural persons, and in particular their right to privacy, with respect to the processing of personal data'[15] within their jurisdictions.[16] The principles codified in the Data Protection Directive were then expanded in 2001 to the EU institutions by a Regulation on the protection of individuals with regard to the processing of personal data by EU bodies, offices and agencies,[17] which also established the European Data Protection Supervisor (EDPS).[18] Moreover, selected pieces of EU legislation expanded the protection of data privacy in specific sectors, such as electronic communications,[19] and police and judicial cooperation in criminal matters.[20]

[12] See also Federico Fabbrini, *Fundamental Rights in Europe* (Oxford University Press, 2014).
[13] See also Stefano Rodotà, 'Data Protection as a Fundamental Right' in Serge Gutwirth et al (eds), *Reinventing Data Protection?* (Springer, 2009).
[14] Directive 95/46/EC, OJ 1995 L 281/31.
[15] Ibid, Article 1.
[16] Ibid, Article 4.
[17] Regulation 45/2001/EC, OJ 2001 L 8/1.
[18] See Hielke Hijmans, 'The European Data Protection Supervisor: The Institutions of the EC Controlled by an Independent Authority' (2006) 43 *Common Market Law Review* 1313.
[19] Directive 2002/58/EC, OJ 2002 L 201/37.
[20] Council Framework Decision 2008/977/JHA, OJ 2008 L 350/60.

Ultimately, in 2016, the European Parliament and the Council, on the basis of Article 16 TFEU, enacted the General Data Protection Regulation (GDPR),[21] and simultaneously adopted a Directive on the protection of natural persons regarding processing of personal data connected with criminal offences or the execution of criminal penalties.[22] The GDPR replaced the Data Protection Directive with measures that are directly and uniformly binding throughout the Member States of the EU, with the aim to provide an even more advanced framework for data protection, updated to meet the challenges of globalisation and rapid technological developments.[23]

At the jurisprudential level, finally, the ECJ, through its case law, has championed the protection of data protection, performing with confidence the role of a human rights court.[24] In particular, heavily drawing on the Charter of Fundamental Rights, the ECJ has expanded its prior jurisprudence[25] and enforced a high standard of data privacy protection: 1) vertically, ie vis-à-vis the Member States; 2) horizontally, ie vis-à-vis the EU political branches; as well as 3) diagonally, ie vis-à-vis private companies which hold relevant power in the processing of personal data. First, the ECJ ruled that Article 8 of the Charter and Article 16 TFEU implied a need for data protection authorities to be fully independent and ruled against Member States which had failed to secure this objective in their legislation,[26] and set aside national legislation introducing surveillance measures in breach of data protection rights.[27] Second, the ECJ found that Articles 7 and 8 of the Charter provided data subjects with a right to be protected from practices of systematic government surveillance and thus struck down, as incompatible with EU primary law both the EU Data Retention Directive, which required the retention of personal data for law enforcement purposes,[28] and an international agreement concluded between the EU and Canada, which foresaw the collection of passenger name record (PNR) data.[29] Third, the ECJ has also applied a high standard of data protection vis-à-vis tech companies, subjecting IT providers

[21] Regulation (EU) 2016/679, OJ 2016 L 119/1.

[22] Directive (EU) 2016/680, OJ 2016 L 119/89.

[23] See Viviane Reding, 'The Upcoming Data Protection Reform for the European Union' (2011) 1 *International Data Privacy Law* 3.

[24] Federico Fabbrini, 'The EU Charter of Fundamental Rights and the Right to Data Privacy: the EU Court of Justice as a Human Rights Court' in Sybe de Vries et al (eds), *The EU Charter of Fundamental Rights as a Binding Instrument* (Hart Publishing, 2015) 261.

[25] See e.g. Case C-101/01, *Criminal Proceedings against Lindqvist* [2003] ECR I-12971 (ruling that the placing of information on the internet constituted processing of personal data wholly or partially by automated means within the meaning of the Data Protection Directive).

[26] Case C-518/07, *Commission v Germany* [2010] ECR I-1885; and Case C-614/10, *Commission v Austria*, ECLI:EU:C:2012:631.

[27] Joined Cases C-203/15 and C-698/15 *Tele2 Sverige AB v Postoch telestyrelsen* and *Secretary of State v Watson*, ECLI:EU:C:2016:970.

[28] Joined Cases C-293/12 and C-594/12, *Digital Rights Ireland Ltd v Minister for Communication et al* and *Kärntner Landesregierung, Seitlinger, Tschohl et al*, ECLI:EU:C:2014:238.

[29] Opinion 1/15, judgment of 26 July 2017, ECLI:EU:C:2017:592.

offering services within the EU internal market to EU data protection laws, and expanding the protections afforded to data subjects.[30]

III. EU Data Protection Law and Covid-19

EU data protection law proved to be very resilient also in the context of one of the most dramatic crises that Europe, and indeed the world, ever faced: the recent coronavirus pandemic. The outburst of this new, severe acute respiratory syndrome, known also by its medical acronym Covid-19, resulted in the largest pandemic the world has experienced, at least since the 1918 Spanish influenza. Having originally emerged in China in the winter of 2019, the virus has slowly but steadily spread across the globe, leading in the spring of 2020 to unprecedented governmental action in the effort to stop the spread of contagion. Across the world, Covid-19 prompted state authorities to impose wartime-style lock-downs, closing schools, factories, and public facilities, banning the movement of persons, prohibiting public gatherings and requisitioning properties essential to address the health crisis.

In order to map infections and prevent the further spread of the virus a number of initiatives were proposed to use digital technology to combat Covid-19. In some countries, such as Taiwan and Israel, the satellite position of mobile phones was used to monitor people's observance of lockdown measures.[31] In Europe, similar measures were seen as fully incompatible with the right to privacy and data protection. Yet, an intense debate has emerged in relation to the adoption of contact-tracing apps. Contact-tracing aims to identify the network of people met by an individual who has tested positive for the virus. In this way, national health services can contain the further spread of the virus by asking the persons concerned to self-isolate. Contact-tracing is usually conducted manually, but use of mobile apps can make this process more efficient. By resorting to the technologies embedded in a mobile phone, it is possible to have a more accurate overview of the people who entered into close contact with a specific individual. The conundrum in the EU was therefore how to reconcile the ability to make contact-tracing more efficient with the need to preserve the respect of fundamental rights, and in particular the rights to privacy and data protection.

From an early stage, however, EU data protection law successfully shaped and constrained the type of initiatives that were proposed, and taken, to use contact-tracing apps in the fight against coronavirus. On 15 April 2020 the Presidents of the

[30] See also Edoardo Celeste, 'Digital Constitutionalism: A New Systematic Theorisation' (2019) 33 *International Review of Law, Computers & Technology* 76.

[31] See Tomas Pueyo, 'Coronavirus: Learning How to Dance' (*Medium*, 28 May 2020), medium.com/@tomaspueyo/coronavirus-learning-how-to-dance-b8420170203e, accessed 13 July 2020; cf 'Coronavirus: Israel Halts Police Phone Tracking over Privacy Concerns' (*BBC News*, 23 April 2020), www.bbc.com/news/technology-52395886, accessed 13 July 2020.

European Council and of the European Commission put forward a joint European Roadmap towards lifting Covid-19 containment measures, which indicated as a strategy toward the lifting of lock-down measures and the creation of 'a framework for contact tracing [...] which respects data privacy.'[32] Moreover, on 16 April 2020, the European Commission adopted comprehensive guidelines on apps supporting the fight against the Covid-19 pandemic in relation to data protection.[33] These emphasised the importance of adhering to the EU data protection framework even in the context of the responses to coronavirus. In particular, while the European Commission recognised that contact-tracing apps could be valuable to respond to Covid-19, it stressed that they had to be designed to fully comply with EU data protection law. The Commission required that the installation of the app had to be voluntary, that proper legislation had to be adopted to this end, and that criteria of data minimisation had to be put in place, with limitations on the disclosure and access to the data. The Commission stressed that both the GDPR and the ePrivacy Directive prohibit the bulk collection, access and storage of health data and location data. Contact-tracing apps are only allowed to process proximity data, ie information about the likelihood of virus transmission based on the epidemiological distance and duration of contact between two individuals. For this reason, the use of GPS tracking should be prohibited in the EU, while resorting to Bluetooth technology is recommended. Moreover, the Commission highlighted the importance of precisely setting the purpose for data use, ensuring the security of the data and setting precise time-limit on its use, so as to protect the individuals' trust into this instrument. A similar emphasis on the importance of protecting personal data was put also by the European Data Protection Board, which on 21 April 2020 disclosed its guidelines on the use of location data and contact tracing tools in the context of the Covid-19 outbreak.[34]

As a result of these multiple constraints set by the EU institutions as well as by national data protection authorities, all Member States' initiatives to develop contact-tracing apps turned into small-scale exercises, which seemed to gain limited traction among the population.[35] This is testament to the strength of EU data protection law, even during a pandemic. In fact, as the Commission pointed out in its first review of the GDPR – published on 24 June 2020, just over two years since its entry into force – the EU data protection framework has proved its worth also in the current Covid-19 pandemic and the effort to use digital technology to

[32] European Commission, 'Joint European Roadmap towards lifting Covid-19 containment measures', 2020/C 126/01, 15 April 2020, 7.

[33] European Commission, 'Guidance on Apps supporting the fight against Covid-19 pandemic in relation to data protection', 16 April 2020, COM(2020) 2523 final.

[34] European Data Protection Board, Guidelines 4/2020, 21 April 2020.

[35] See Ryan Browne, 'Why Coronavirus Contact-Tracing Apps Aren't yet the "game Changer" Authorities Hoped They'd Be' (*CNBC*, 3 July 2020), www.cnbc.com/2020/07/03/why-coronavirus-contact-tracing-apps-havent-been-a-game-changer.html, accessed 13 July 2020; see also Dan Sabbagh and Alex Hern, 'UK Abandons Contact-Tracing App for Apple and Google Model', *The Guardian* (18 June 2020), www.theguardian.com/world/2020/jun/18/uk-poised-to-abandon-coronavirus-app-in-favour-of-apple-and-google-models, accessed 13 July 2020.

fight it, because the 'GDPR is clear that any restriction must respect the essence of the fundamental rights and freedoms, and be a necessary and proportionate measure in a democratic society to safeguard a public interest, such as public health.'[36]

IV. The Right to be Forgotten

One of the most significant and innovative features of EU data protection law is the recognition of a right to be forgotten. The first step towards the recognition of such a right was taken by the ECJ in May 2014, in *Google Spain SL v Agencia Española de Protección de Datos (AEPD)*.[37] The case concerned the interpretation of the Data Protection Directive, which was then applicable in domestic proceedings between Google and the AEPD, the Spanish data protection agency. Pursuant to an application by a Spanish national, the AEPD had required Google to remove from its search engine links to information relating to the applicant, on the grounds that data protection law applied to it. Google had challenged the administrative decision in the Spanish courts, which decided to refer several questions to the ECJ.

In its judgment, the ECJ recognised a new right for data subjects to request removal of on-line content, and, correspondingly, an obligation for the operator of a search engine to remove such content from the list of results displayed.[38] As a preliminary matter, the ECJ ruled that a search engine like Google must be classified as a processor and controller of personal data within the meaning of the Data Protection Directive.[39] On the substance, then, the ECJ – after recognising that a name search through Google could provide a 'more or less detailed profile of [the data subject]'[40] – held that the operator of a search engine

> is obliged to remove from the list of results displayed following a search made on the basis of a person's name links to web pages, published by third parties [...], also in a case where that name or information is not erased beforehand or simultaneously from those web pages, and even, as the case may be, when its publication in itself on those pages is lawful.[41]

The judgment of the ECJ in *Google Spain* opened the door to a fully-fledged codification of the right to be forgotten in EU law. The GDPR, in fact, enshrined in Article 17 a 'Right to erasure (right to be forgotten)', stating in paragraph 1 that

[36] European Commission, 'Data Protection as a pillar of citizens' empowerment and the EU's approach to the digital transition – two years of application of the General Data Protection Regulation', 24 June 2020, COM(2020) 264 final, 3.

[37] Case C-131/12, *Google Spain v Agencia Española de Protección de Datos (AEPD)* [2014] ECLI:EU:C:2014:317.

[38] See for comments on the case: Eleni Frantziou, 'Further Developments in the Right to Be Forgotten' (2014) 14 *Human Rights Law Review* 761; and Herke Kranenbourg, 'Google and the Right to be Forgotten' (2015) 1 *European Data Protection Law Review* 70.

[39] *Google Spain* (n 37 above), at 41.

[40] Ibid, at 80.

[41] Ibid, at 88.

'The data subject shall have the right to obtain from the controller the erasure of personal data concerning him or her without undue delay and the controller shall have the obligation to erase personal data without undue delay.' The same provision clarifies that the right to erasure applies when:

(a) the personal data are no longer necessary in relation to the purposes for which they were collected or otherwise processed;
(b) the data subject withdraws consent on which the processing is based [...];
(c) the data subject objects to the processing [...]; and
(d) the personal data have been unlawfully processed.

Moreover, pursuant to Article 17(2) GDPR,

> Where the controller has made the personal data public and is obliged pursuant to paragraph 1 to erase the personal data, the controller, taking account of available technology and the cost of implementation, shall take reasonable steps, including technical measures, to inform controllers which are processing the personal data that the data subject has requested the erasure by such controllers of any links to, or copy or replication of, those personal data.

While Article 17(3) GDPR indicates that the right to erasure 'shall not apply to the extent that processing is necessary: (a) for exercising the right of freedom of expression and information; (b) for compliance with legal obligations [...] in the public interest' or for a number of other selected reasons related to public health, scientific or historical research and legal defence, the GDPR nevertheless seemed to follow the ECJ's view that the data subject's right to request the removal of on-line content 'override[s], as a rule, not only the economic interest of the operator of the search engine but also the interest of the general public in finding that information upon a search relating to the data subject's name.'[42]

V. Extraterritorial Application of EU Data Protection Law

Over the past few years, the EU framework for data protection has progressively extended its reach outside the jurisdiction of the EU. To begin with, the ECJ has reviewed the standard of data protection existing in specific third countries to decide whether this was sufficient to authorise the transfer of personal data from the EU to such third country – essentially pressuring the latter to raise its domestic standards to meet the EU benchmark. In the *Schrems*[43] and *Schrems II*[44] judgments, in particular, the ECJ reviewed the adequacy of the US privacy framework for the

[42] Ibid, at 97.

[43] Case C-362/14, *Maximillian Schrems v Data Protection Commissioner and Digital Rights Ireland Ltd*, ECLI:EU:C:2015:650.

[44] Case C-311/18, *Data Protection Commissioner v Facebook Ireland Ltd and Maximillian Schrems*, ECLI:EU:C:2020:559.

purpose of compliance with the EU data protection law, and concluded on both occasions that this fell short of EU standards.[45]

In particular, in *Schrems*, delivered in 2015, the ECJ reviewed the European Commission 2000 'Safe Harbour' decision – which recognised US data protection standards as providing an adequate level of protection, and therefore authorised private companies to transfer data across the Atlantic[46] – and struck that down, ruling that in light of the revelations of US mass surveillance, it appeared that law and practice in force in the US did not ensure adequate protection of personal data.[47] The ECJ ruling in *Schrems*, which was prompted by a Facebook user disgruntled with the limited protection that his data would receive in the US, forced the EU and the US to renegotiate further guarantees on the protection of personal data – including limitations on the access and use of personal data transferred for national security purposes, as well as oversight and redress mechanisms that provide safeguards for those data to be effectively protected against unlawful interference and the risk of abuse – which were codified in a new Commission adequacy decision called Privacy Shield.[48]

However, in the recent *Schrems II* judgment, delivered in 2020, the ECJ ruled that the 2016 Privacy Shield too was incompatible with the rights to privacy and data protection,[49] as well as with the essence of the right to an effective remedy,[50] enshrined in the EU Charter of Fundamental Rights. While in its judgment the ECJ upheld the European Commission decision on standard contractual clauses,[51] which creates a framework for business-to-business data exchange, it ruled that the level of privacy protection afforded to data subjects in the US was not adequate, given the ongoing ability of US national security agencies to undertake surveillance operations on the transferred data, and the limited right to judicial recourse against abuse under US law. In its two *Schrems* rulings, therefore, the ECJ leveraged EU data protection law to put incremental pressure on the US as a third country. In this way, the EU is seeking to raise US standards through international negotiations in order to secure unhindered flow of data beyond borders.[52]

Moreover, the ECJ has directly subjected economic operators incorporated outside the EU to EU data protection rules when they deal with data collected within the EU. The point was made first in *Google Spain*: here the ECJ ruled that in

[45] See also further Maria Tzanou, Chapter 7 of this volume.

[46] Commission Decision 2000/520, OJ 2000 L 215/7.

[47] See David Cole and Federico Fabbrini, 'Bridging the Transatlantic Divide? The United States, the European Union, and the Protection of Privacy across Borders' (2016) 14 *International Journal of Constitutional Law* 220.

[48] Commission Implementing Decision (EU) 2016/1250, OJ 2016 L 207/1.

[49] *Schrems II* (n 44 above), para 180.

[50] Ibid, para 187.

[51] Commission Decision 2010/87/EU of 5 February 2010 on standard contractual clauses for the transfer of personal data to processors established in third countries under Directive 95/46, OJ 2010 L 39/5.

[52] See David Cole and Federico Fabbrini, 'Transatlantic Negotiations for Transatlantic Rights' in David Cole et al (eds), *Surveillance, Privacy and Transatlantic Relations* (Hart Publishing, 2017) 197.

light of the objective of EU data protection law 'of ensuring effective and complete protection of the fundamental rights and freedoms of natural persons, and in particular their right to privacy, with respect to the processing of personal data, [the notion of establishment] cannot be interpreted restrictively'[53] – and therefore concluded that Google, despite being incorporated in the US, was subjected to the Data Protection Directive, also because it operated a subsidiary in Spain, which managed advertising on a Spanish-localised search engine. In fact, the GDPR has further expanded this state of affairs,[54] as Article 3(2) (entitled 'Territorial Scope') now foresees that

> This Regulation applies to the processing of personal data of data subjects who are in the Union by a controller or processor not established in the Union, where the processing activities are related to:
>
> (a) the offering of goods or services, irrespective of whether a payment of the data subject is required, to such data subjects in the Union; or
>
> (b) the monitoring of their behaviour as far as their behaviour takes place within the Union.

The extraterritorial reach of EU data protection law has led to important challenges – notably with regard to the right to be forgotten, as the ECJ has attempted to work out the circumstances when requests to remove online content are binding on businesses established overseas, and with worldwide effect. In particular, the matter was at the heart of two recent ECJ judgments concerning US companies Google and Facebook. In September 2019, in *Google v Commission Nationale de l'Informatique et des Libertés (CNIL)*,[55] the ECJ reviewed a sanction imposed on Google by the French data protection authority for failure to remove content worldwide from all its website domains, in pursuance of a right to be forgotten request.[56] Google had challenged the CNIL sanction, claiming that the removal of online content exclusively from the French version of its search engine sufficed. In its ruling, the ECJ – also taking note of the geo-blocking technology put in place by Google[57] – upheld the challenge.

The ECJ admitted that the GDPR objective is 'is to guarantee a high level of protection of personal data throughout the [EU]'[58] – and that 'a de-referencing carried out on all the versions of a search engine would meet that objective in full.'[59] However, the ECJ emphasised that 'numerous third States do not recognise

[53] *Google Spain* (n 37 above) at 53.

[54] See Paul de Hert and Michal Czerniawski, 'Expanding the European Data Protection Scope beyond Territory: Article 3 of the General Data Protection Regulation in Its Wider Context' (2016) 6 *International Data Privacy Law* 230.

[55] Case C-507/17, *Google v Commission Nationale de l'Informatique et des Libertés (CNIL)*, ECLI:EU:C:2019:772.

[56] See Quinn, Chapter 4 of this volume.

[57] *Google v CNIL* (n 55 above) at 42.

[58] Ibid, at 54.

[59] Ibid, at 55.

the right to de-referencing or have a different approach to that right',[60] and claimed that it was not apparent from the GDPR that the intent of the EU legislator was

> to confer a scope on the rights enshrined in those provisions which would go beyond the territory of the Member States and [...] to impose on an operator [...] like Google [...] a de-referencing obligation which also concerns the national versions of its search engine that do not correspond to the Member States.[61]

Hence, the ECJ concluded that

> where a search engine operator grants a request for de-referencing pursuant to those provisions, that operator is not required to carry out that de-referencing on all versions of its search engine, but on the versions of that search engine corresponding to all the Member States, using, where necessary, measures which, while meeting the legal requirements, effectively prevent or, at the very least, seriously discourage an internet user conducting a search from one of the Member States on the basis of a data subject's name from gaining access, via the list of results displayed following that search, to the links which are the subject of that request.[62]

Yet, if *Google v CNIL* seemed to draw a limit to the extraterritorial effects of the right to be forgotten, the ECJ decision in *Eva Glawischnig-Piesczek v Facebook* – delivered just a week later, in October 2019[63] – counter-balanced that. Although this case did not explicitly concern the right to be forgotten, it dealt with an analogous problem – namely the question whether a digital platform could be forced to remove worldwide content posted online which was regarded as defamatory. Mrs Eva Glawischnig-Piesczek, an Austrian politician, had obtained a court order to remove insulting language against her posted on Facebook, but the latter had only disabled access to the content in Austria, where it had initially been published, prompting the applicant to sue for breach of EU data protection law. In its judgment, the ECJ – after discussing the obligations of digital providers under the e-Commerce Directive[64] – examined whether EU law imposed 'any limitation, including a territorial limitation, on the scope of the measures which Member States are entitled to adopt' vis-à-vis information society services,[65] and ruled that EU law 'does not preclude those injunction measures from producing effects worldwide.'[66]

While the ECJ cautioned that 'in view of the global dimension of electronic commerce, the EU legislature considered it necessary to ensure that EU rules in that area are consistent with the rules applicable at international level'[67] – and that therefore '[i]t is up to Member States to ensure that the measures which they

[60] Ibid, at 59.
[61] Ibid, at 62.
[62] Ibid, at 73.
[63] Case C-18/18, *Eva Glawischnig-Piesczek v Facebook*, ECLI:EU:C:2019:821.
[64] Directive 2000/31/EC, OJ 2000 L 178/1.
[65] *Eva Glawischnig-Piesczek* (n 63 above), at 49.
[66] Ibid, at 50.
[67] Ibid, at 51.

adopt and which produce effects worldwide take due account of those rules'[68] – the consequence of the ECJ judgment was to open the door for Austrian courts to impose on Facebook obligations 'to remove information covered by the injunction or to block access to that information worldwide within the framework of the relevant international law.'[69]

VI. The Challenges of Extraterritoriality in Comparative Perspective

The problem of extraterritorial application of domestic laws in the digital realm is not exclusive of the EU. In fact, as Jennifer Daskal has pointed out, there are now an increasing number of cases adjudicated by courts worldwide which have raised 'critically important questions about the appropriate scope of global injunctions, the future of free speech on the internet and the prospect for harmonization (or not) of rules regulating online content across borders.'[70] In particular, other recent disputes involving US technology companies and decided in the jurisdictions of Canada and Australia have vividly exposed the challenges of an extraterritorial effect of data protection law.

In 2017, in the *Google Inc v Equustek Solutions Inc* case, the Canadian Supreme Court ordered Google to remove worldwide from its search engine the links to a company's website violating intellectual property rights.[71] Equustek, a Canadian IT company, had sued Google claiming that the search engine had failed to delist from its browser the websites of a competitor that had breached Equustek's intellectual property rights by misappropriating its trademarks. In June 2017 the Canadian Supreme Court, deciding an appeal on the matter, ruled in favour of Equustek and granted it the sought injunction, ordering Google to delist from its browser worldwide all the websites that harmed Equustek. According to the Canadian Supreme Court, a global enforcement of the delisting request was necessary to prevent harm to the plaintiff.[72] However, Google subsequently sought an injunction before the US District Court for Northern California to prevent enforcement in the US of the Canadian Supreme Court order on the ground, among others, of incompatibility with the US First Amendment guaranteeing freedom of speech and with principles of international comity. In November 2017, the US District Court granted Google the injunction sought, effectively nullifying the effects in the US of the Canadian Supreme Court ruling.[73] However, despite the favourable ruling of the Californian

[68] Ibid, at 52.

[69] Ibid, at 53.

[70] Jennifer Daskal, 'Google Inc. v. Equustek Solutions Inc.' (2018) 112 *American Journal of International Law* 727.

[71] *Google Inc v Equustek Solutions Inc*, 2017 SCC 34, [2017] 1 SCR 824.

[72] See Jeff Berryman. 'Equity in the Age of the Internet: Google Inc. v. Equustek Solutions Inc.' (2019) 31 *Intellectual Property Journal* 311.

[73] *Google Inc v Equustek Solutions Inc*, Case No 5:17-cv-04207-EJD (ND Cal Dec 14, 2017).

court, in April 2018, Google was eventually unsuccessful in its claims to vary or lift the injunction before the Supreme Court of British Columbia, a Canadian province. The Canadian court was adamant in its refusal to consider Google's demand to limit the scope of its delisting order.[74]

Similarly, also in 2017, in the case *X v Twitter*, the Supreme Court of New South Wales in Australia ordered the Californian company and its Irish subsidiary to remove at global level a raft of confidential information posted by a troll.[75] The applicant, X, lamented the publication of confidential financial information leaked on Twitter by an anonymous troll from various accounts, including one that used the name of X's CEO. Twitter was initially reluctant to suspend the incriminated accounts, but was eventually ordered by the Australian Court to provide the identity of the troll and to remove all illegal contents published online. In contrast to the Canadian Supreme Court in the *Google Inc v Equustek Solutions Inc* case, the Australian Court did not consider principles of international comity, nor did it carry out a comparative analysis of foreign law on breach of confidence.[76] Yet, in this case too, the Supreme Court of New South Wales did not hesitate to grant an extraterritorial injunction to remedy the detrimental situation of the domestic applicant.

Similarly to the Canadian and Australian courts, both the recent ECJ cases *Google v CNIL* and *Glawischnig-Piesczek v Facebook* at first sight leave the door open to a worldwide application of EU law. In *Glawischnig-Piesczek v Facebook*, such a global effect represented the primary solution proposed by the ECJ, only subject to the respect of international law.[77] In *Google v CNIL*, as seen in the previous section, the ECJ affirmed that an EU-only form of delisting would suffice. However, espousing the nuanced approach proposed by Advocate General Szpunar,[78] the ECJ also clarified that nothing would prevent Member States from allowing for global de-referencing, if the protection of individual privacy and personal data outweighed the safeguarding of other competing rights.[79]

From an EU perspective, such an extraterritorial application of EU law can be explained by the need to ensure effective protection of fundamental rights and limit the risk of circumvention.[80] The enforcement of the right to be forgotten is exemplary. We now live in a global digital society, which overtakes national boundaries. One's right to data protection may be violated even where a search

[74] *Equustek Solutions Inc v Jack*, 2018 BCSC 610.

[75] *X v Twitter* [2017] NSWSC 1300.

[76] See Michael Douglas, 'Extraterritorial Injunctions Affecting the Internet' (2018) 12 *Journal of Equity* 34.

[77] Ibid, at 52.

[78] See Case C-507/17 *Google v CNIL* Opinion of Advocate General Szpunar, ECLI:EU:C:2019:15, at 62.

[79] *Google v CNIL* (n 55 above) at 72.

[80] See Article 29 Working Party, 'Guidelines on the implementation of the Court of Justice of the European Union judgment on "Google Spain and Inc. v. Agencia Española de Protección de Datos (AEPD) and Mario Costeja González" – C-131/12' (2014) WP225 at 9.

engine shows a specific result in a country which is not that of residence of the data subject concerned. In principle, enforcing that right exclusively within the territory of the EU would not make any sense, given the ease with which data can be accessed worldwide. A violation of such right would occur if an individual, for example residing in France, having lawfully requested the delisting of specific search results, discovered that those links were still referenced not only in France, but also – say – in Germany or in the US, with no difference. And this consideration implies that – as much as uniform standards of data protection should apply *within* the EU – EU data protection rights should also have extraterritorial effects *outside* the EU.

Nevertheless, the extraterritorial application of EU data protection law poses a series of challenges – akin to those vividly exposed in the *Google Inc v Equustek Solutions Inc* case. Asserting domestic data protection standards outside a jurisdiction's borders may clash with duties of international comity and the need to respect diversity of legal systems. In fact, the balance between the right to be forgotten, freedom of information and free speech is struck differently in jurisdictions around the world – including states that share the same belief in democracy, the rule of law and human rights. Moreover, as the recent judgments of the Canadian and US courts point out, the enforcement of data protection standards outside a jurisdiction's borders may ultimately be nullified by opposing claims. In the Canadian Google litigation, in particular, the US federal district court blocked the application of the Canadian Supreme Court ruling – de facto limiting the application of the Canadian injunction in the US jurisdiction.

In light of these risks, the recent judgments of the ECJ in *Google v CNIL* and *Glawischnig-Piesczek v Facebook* can be seen as a pragmatic solution, trying to navigate between the Scylla of data protection imperialism and the Charybdis of digital sovereignty.[81] In fact, it is clear that tensions between these opposing trends are only likely to increase. While criticisms have been raised at the 'imperialist' attitude of EU data protection law,[82] other recent developments, including efforts by countries around the world to claim sovereign control over data, expose the risk of a fragmentation of the digital world. Different claims to digital sovereignty are emerging not only in the US[83] and the EU[84] – but also in illiberal regimes

[81] See further Edoardo Celeste, Chapter 13 of this volume.

[82] See Dan Svantesson, 'The Google Spain Case: Part of a Harmful Trend of Jurisdictional Overreach' (2015) EUI Working Papers, cadmus.eui.eu//handle/1814/36317, accessed 15 January 2020; Ravi Shankar Prasad, 'India Views Its Privacy Seriously, Data Imperialism Not Acceptable', *The Economic Times*, 6, November 2019: economictimes.indiatimes.com/tech/ites/india-views-its-privacy-seriously-data-imperialism-not-acceptable-ravi-shankar-prasad/articleshow/71937835.cms?from=mdr.

[83] See Clarifying Lawful Overseas Use of Data (CLOUD) Act, PL 115–141. The statute was purposefully adopted as a response to a case in which Microsoft contested a search warrant aiming to gather data stored on its Irish servers: see Dan Svantesson and Felicity Gerry, 'Access to Extraterritorial Evidence: The Microsoft Cloud Case and Beyond' (2015) 31 *Computer Law & Security Review* 478.

[84] See European Commission, 'European Cloud Initiative – Building a Competitive Data and Knowledge Economy in Europe', 19 April 2016, COM(2016) 178 final.

around the world,[85] potentially generating a progressive erosion of fundamental rights online. In this context, the development of transnational legal frameworks – at least among democratic regimes – seems to be the necessary path to preserve data protection rights beyond borders.

VII. Conclusion

The EU is at the forefront of data protection worldwide. The GDPR represents the most comprehensive and advanced regulatory framework for data privacy to date – and the ECJ has developed a progressive case law to protect human rights in the digital age, including outlining a right to be forgotten. In fact, the EU data protection law framework has proved so resilient that it has resisted even the outbreak of Covid-19, the largest pandemic the world has experienced since 1918: despite the effort to develop new digital technology to map and track infections, data privacy concerns have shaped the process, and ultimately avoided solutions which would have traded privacy in favour of health rights.

Nevertheless, despite its inherent strength, EU data protection law generally – and the right to be forgotten specifically – are increasingly facing a question of jurisdictional boundaries. From an EU perspective, the extraterritorial enforcement of EU fundamental rights is regarded as a way to guarantee full and effective protection and prevent the risk of circumvention. However, the reach of EU data protection law beyond the EU's borders also raises a series of challenges, clashing with the principles of international comity and respect for global diversity.

The issue of extraterritorial application of EU data protection law was at the heart of two recent judgments decided by the ECJ: in *Google v CNIL* and *Glawischnig-Piesczek v Facebook*, the ECJ dealt with the question of whether the right to be forgotten and the obligation to remove defamatory content applied worldwide or not. In the first case, the ECJ ruled that the removal was restricted to EU Member States only, while in the second it allowed a worldwide injunction. In both cases, however, the ECJ showed awareness for the cross-border implications of its decisions and for the need to recognise transnational diversity and international comity, thus finding pragmatic solutions to modulate the effects of EU data protection law beyond the EU borders.

As this chapter has shown, the challenges that the ECJ was facing are not unique to Europe. Other jurisdictions such as Australia and Canada have also been confronted with the dilemma of how to protect digital rights across borders. Theoretically, contemporary digital society, being global, would require worldwide

[85] In 2017, China passed a new National Intelligence Law obliging companies to collaborate with Chinese intelligence agencies. The Act de facto requires companies incorporated in China to disclose to Chinese authorities data that may have been collected and stored abroad: see See Yi-Zheng Lian (n 10 above). In the context of the trade war with the US, the legislation produced strong criticism, the US lamenting that a similar obligation could put in danger their national security.

rules. However, the extraterritorial application of data protection standards also raises significant challenges. In fact, the protection of privacy in the digital age increasingly exposes a tension between efforts by legal systems to impose their high standards of data protection outside their borders – and thus potentially regarded as a form of 'imperialism' – and sovereigntist claims by other legal systems to assert their own power over data.

In this context, states should seek to develop common international law frameworks, which promote transnational standards of data protection. Admittedly, this will not be an easy task. However, this is something that should be explored, particularly among liberal democracies, and at least in the transatlantic context.[86] Despite differences, jurisdictions such as the EU, Canada and Australia – as well as the US[87] – share a similar concern for the need to protect privacy, which puts them at odds with developments in other countries, such as China or Russia. Developing transnational rules for the protection of digital privacy, including outlining mutually acceptable claims to the right to be forgotten, represents therefore the best road forward to make sure that privacy remains a protected right, even in the digital era.

[86] See David Cole, Federico Fabbrini and Stephen J Schulhofer (eds), *Surveillance, Privacy, and Transatlantic Relations* (Hart Publishing, 2017).

[87] See Fischer, Chapter 3 of this volume.

3

The Challenges and Opportunities for a US Federal Privacy Law

JORDAN L FISCHER

I. Introduction

In 2016, the European Union (EU) made headlines with the passage of the General Data Protection Regulation (GDPR),[1] which created a uniform approach to data privacy across Europe. Since then, several countries around the world have followed suit[2] and adopted data protection regulations which pull directly from the language of the EU regulation. This 'GDPR Effect' is dominating and fuelling the global privacy conversation.

At the same time, these changes to data protection laws are addressing a period of massive data collection. Data has become a driver of economies and currency; data is 'the oil of the digital era'.[3] And that data collection can be shocking: 'The extent to which an individual's personal information is on display is startling: an average American's information can be found in anywhere between twenty-five and one hundred commercial databases'.[4] These massive 'data dossiers' established on individuals facilitate potential privacy violations that we can only barely begin to imagine.[5] The threats to the integrity of the data continue to evolve at a rapid pace.

[1] Regulation (EU) 2016/679 of the European Parliament and of the Council of 27 April 2016 on the protection of natural persons with regard to the processing of personal data and on the free movement of such data, and repealing Directive 95/46/EC.

[2] See, eg, Brazil's Lei Geral de Proteçao de Dados (LGPD), Law No 13,709, of 14 August 2018, amending Law No 12,965, of 23 April 2014, lgpd.akarion.app/en; Japan's Act on the Protection of Personal Information, Act No 57 of 2003, as amended in 2016, www.ppc.go.jp/files/pdf/Act_on_the_Protection_of_Personal_Information.pdf; see also Michael L Rustad and Thomas H Koenig, 'Towards a Global Privacy Standard' (2019) 71 *Florida Law Review* 365, 431–48 (discussing the impact of the GDPR across numerous regions on the world).

[3] *The Economist*, 'The world's most valuable resource is no longer oil, but data', 6 May 2017, www.economist.com/leaders/2017/05/06/the-worlds-most-valuable-resource-is-no-longer-oil-but-data.

[4] Ryan Moshell. 'And Then There Was One: The Outlook for a Self-Regulatory United States Amidst a Global Trend Toward Comprehensive Data Protection' (2005) 37 *Texas Tech Law Review* 357, 362.

[5] Erdem Büyüksagis, 'Towards a Transatlantic Concept of Data Privacy' (2019) 30 *Fordham Intellectual Property, Media & Entertainment Law Journal* 139, 156 ('Through data matching, data mining, and de-anonymization, technology leads to the creation of potentially massive "digital dossiers"').

Although the GDPR appears to be at the forefront of data privacy, some of the most influential technology companies, including Google, Facebook, Microsoft, and Twitter, all reside primarily in the United States (US), giving the US government jurisdiction over these entities. Given the critical roles of these technology companies within the global economy, it is fair to say that a global approach to privacy cannot be established without some input from the US.

This chapter will explore how the US can implement data privacy regulations that address this challenge and at the same time preserve the uniqueness of the American legal system and approach to privacy. Exploring the existing privacy infrastructure in the US, this chapter will provide a framework for discussing how the US can create a federal approach to privacy that meets the needs of current and future generations. The goal is to provide a framework to drive the privacy conversation within the US, ensuring that the correct questions are considered when developing a workable solution to balancing privacy, security, and the global economy. The US needs to define its data privacy goals and construct a privacy system that leverages the positive attributes of the US legal system to support those objectives. While some of these goals should incorporate components of the GDPR, the mechanisms of enforcing data privacy by the legislature, judiciary, and individuals will ultimately derive from concepts that are uniquely American.

This chapter is structured as follows. First, it will outline the fragmented approach to data privacy within the US legal system. Second, this chapter will explore the challenges and opportunities that exist within the US legal infrastructure to promote a federal privacy law. Ultimately, this chapter argues that any solutions to privacy protections within the US will need to balance the need to protect individuals while encouraging and promoting business and innovation.

II. Data Privacy in the US: The Fragmented States of America

The current approach to privacy in the US can be summed up nicely in one word: fragmented. The limited and disjointed framework derives from the historical evolution of privacy within the US and results in gaps in protections for Americans.[6] The US Constitution does not explicitly mention the term 'privacy' or 'data protection.'[7] In fact, there is no express individual right to privacy in the US, nor is there any general privacy protecting legislation to date.[8]

[6] Rustad and Koenig (n 2 above), at 381; see also Matthew Humerick, 'The Tortoise and the Hare of International Data Privacy: Can the United States Catch Up to Rising Global Standards?' (2018) 27 *Catholic University Journal of Law & Technology* 77, 81–82 (stating that US privacy protections support an 'antiquated, ineffective approach').

[7] *Roe v Wade*, 410 US 113 (1973); Moshell (n 4 above), at 373.

[8] Humerick (n 6 above), at 80.

The US derives its patchwork of current privacy protections from multiple sources. These include the First Amendment, Fourth Amendment, Fifth Amendment, and the Fourteenth Amendment to the Constitution. From an American perspective, the greatest historical threat to privacy was not private companies, but the government or state.[9] As a result, the US focused primarily on privacy from the government and the idea that individuals have a right to privacy in the home under the Fourth Amendment.[10] There has long been a distinct lack of focus on the collection of information by non-governmental actors.[11]

The Supreme Court of the United States first recognised a 'right to privacy' in *Griswold v Connecticut*,[12] where the Court held that 'the First Amendment has a penumbra where privacy is protected from governmental intrusion.'[13] In subsequent cases, the Supreme Court continued its protection of privacy, forming 'zones of privacy' that rely more on the Fourteenth Amendment than the First Amendment for support.[14] The Supreme Court again articulated a right to privacy in its recent decision in *Carpenter v US*,[15] holding that

> [w]hen an individual seeks to preserve something as private, and his expectation of privacy is one that society is prepared to recognize as reasonable, we have held that official intrusion into that private sphere generally qualifies as a search and requires a warrant supported by probable cause.[16]

These Supreme Court decisions reiterate that most US jurisprudence related to privacy involves protections against the state, and not in the private sector.

The current approach to privacy in the private sector is fragmented and complex, often relying on industries to self-regulate.[17] In self-regulation, absent a privacy standard defined in regulation, companies and industrial bodies establish codes, standards, and self-policing mechanisms to govern an industry and how it addresses privacy.[18] Moshell observes that 'The U.S. government […] traditionally relies upon the ability of industry to regulate itself, viewing a "complex legal or

[9] James Q Whitman, 'The Two Western Cultures of Privacy: Dignity versus Liberty' (2004) 113 *Yale Law Journal* 1151, 1211–12 ('Suspicion of the state has always stood at the foundation of American privacy thinking, and American scholarly writing and court doctrine continue to take it for granted that the state is the prime enemy of our privacy.').

[10] The history and evolution of Fourth Amendment protections is beyond the scope of this chapter. However, it is important to recognise that the US approach is strongest when dealing with the collection of information by the government, and already recognises protections, both in case law and in legislation. (See eg, the Privacy Act of 1974, as amended, 5 USC § 552a).

[11] Moshell (n 4 above), at 373.

[12] *Griswold v Connecticut*, 381 US 479 (1965).

[13] Ibid, at 483.

[14] Ibid, at 484; *Eisenstadt v Baird*, 405 US 438 (1972) (extending the right to privacy of a married couple to individuals); *Roe v Wade*, 410 US 113 (1973) (extending the right to privacy to a woman to have an abortion); *Lawrence v Texas*, 539 US 558 (2003) (extending the right to privacy to same-sex couples).

[15] *Carpenter v US*, 138 S Ct 2206 (2018).

[16] Ibid, at 2213 (citation omitted).

[17] Moshell (n 4 above), at 359, 372.

[18] Ibid, at 367.

regulatory infrastructure as an undue restriction on the market.'"[19] This approach is embraced by companies who fear the potential costs and burdens of robust privacy legislation in the US.[20]

Even within the self-regulatory environment prevalent throughout the US, there still exist some legal protections for privacy. US privacy governance can be grouped into four main sources: (i) federal regulations (enforced by federal agencies); (ii) State regulations (enforced primarily by State Attorneys General); (iii) the judiciary; and (iv) contracts and/or agreements between private actors.[21] Varying interpretations of these sources across different judiciaries and legislatures exacerbate the fragmented data privacy landscape in the US and create limited privacy protections in specific industries and related to certain types of data.[22] The following subsections discuss each of these sources individually to provide a clearer picture of US privacy governance.

A. Federal Regulations and Federal Agencies

There are a number of different federal laws, and as such, a number of different federal agencies, that play a role in regulating and enforcing privacy in the US. The federal efforts can be divided into three main categories: (1) regulation of the government's collection of private information; (2) regulation of the disclosure of personal information to the government from private entities; and (3) regulation of certain private-sector data practices.

Initially, government regulations focused on the collection of data by the government, drawing support from the Fourth Amendment. Two key federal regulations support these protections. First, the Freedom of Information Act (FOIA) of 1966[23] provides individuals with a right to access data collected about themselves by the government. Second, the Privacy Act of 1974[24] limits the ability of the government to collect and retain personal information, only allowing collection that is 'relevant and necessary to accomplish a purpose of the agency required to be accomplished by statute or by executive order of the President.'[25] Further, the Act places proactive requirements on federal government agencies to establish information security procedures,[26] which are overseen and administered by the Office of Management and Budget.[27]

[19] Ibid, at 374 (citation omitted).
[20] Humerick (n 6 above), at 91.
[21] Büyüksagis (n 5 above), at 158.
[22] Humerick (n 6 above), 83.
[23] 5 USC § 552 (1966).
[24] 5 USC § 552a, as amended.
[25] 5 USC § 552a(e)(1).
[26] 5 USC § 552a(e)(9)–(10); see also Lior Jacob Strahilevitz, 'Reunifying Privacy Law' (2010) 98 *California Law Review* 2007, 2024 (stating that '[t]he federal Privacy Act is in some ways the most ambitious piece of federal legislation in the domain of information privacy.')
[27] Office of Management and Budget, Privacy, www.whitehouse.gov/omb/information-regulatory-affairs/privacy/.

After several decades focusing on the collection of personal information by the government, lawmakers began to consider the disclosure to the government of information collected by private entities. The dramatic increase in data collection by companies made the private sector a valuable partner to provide information on individuals to the government. To provide privacy protections around the public-private sharing of information, the government created restrictions on the flow of information from the private sector to the public sector.[28]

Starting in the 1990s, legislative initiatives slowly focused on regulating private entities and their collection of personal information. These regulations have focused primarily on electronic communications,[29] the financial sector,[30] and healthcare data.[31] In some aspects, there is an advantage to this more sectoral approach to privacy laws because it allows for context-specific legislation, rather than a one-size-fits-all approach. Industry-specific legislation accounts for necessary deviations and differences when approaching data privacy.[32] However, this approach is increasingly used to the advantage of companies who receive the financial benefit of data at the expense of individuals, and is generally creating a less workable approach to promoting privacy protections.

Because there are numerous federal laws that impact privacy, either directly or indirectly, it is obvious that no single federal agency is charged with enforcing data protection.[33] The main federal agencies that play a role in shaping federal privacy include, but are not limited to, the Federal Trade Commission (FTC), the Federal Communications Commission (FCC), the Department of Health and Human Services (DHH), the Federal Reserve, the Department of Homeland Security (DHS), the Office of Management and Budget (OMB), the Department of Education (ED), and the Securities and Exchange Commission (SEC).

The FTC maintains the most prominent role in enforcing federal data privacy regulations. However, the FTC faces numerous challenges in this role, including limitations that stem from its overall mandate and jurisdiction. Primarily, the FTC is charged with overseeing the entirety of US commerce; therefore, data privacy enforcement must 'compete' for time and resources in the context of the FTC's overarching mandate and wide range of priorities.[34]

Further, the authority of the FTC to regulate privacy is limited to 'unfair or deceptive trade practices.'[35] This results in limited practical authority to enforce

[28] See, eg, Financial Privacy Act of 1978 (restricting government access to financial institution records without certain requirements being met).

[29] See, eg, the Electronic Communications Privacy Act of 1986 (ECPA), 18 USC §§ 2510 ff.

[30] See, eg the Gramm–Leach–Bliley Act (GLBA), also known as the Financial Services Modernization Act of 1999 (Pub L 106–102, 113 Stat 1338, enacted 12 November 1999).

[31] See, eg the Health Insurance Portability and Accountability Act of 1996 (HIPAA) and the Health Information Technology for Economic and Clinical Health Act (HITECH Act).

[32] Rustad and Koenig (n 2 above), 381.

[33] Moshell (n 4 above), 381.

[34] Ibid, 381.

[35] Federal Trade Commission Act, 15 USC §§ 41–58, as amended.

effective privacy practices across the private sector.[36] As such, the FTC must wait until a company is either unfair or deceptive in its interactions with a consumer before enforcing any privacy restrictions. The agency does not have the authority to direct that companies provide privacy in their data collection practices; instead, it can only enforce transparency of the data collection activities that companies choose to conduct.

Additionally, the FTC investigative process faces numerous hurdles because, in many cases, it first issues a settlement or consent decree requiring certain changes to privacy practices with annual reporting requirements. Typically, this allows the company to be monitored for a period of time during which fines are issued if the company violates that settlement or consent decree.[37]

The FTC itself has recognised these limitations in its authority. In 2000, the FTC submitted a report to Congress asking that Congress codify the Fair Information Privacy Principles[38] to provide a more comprehensive approach to privacy.[39] Ultimately, this initial recommendation was not adopted. However, the FTC renewed its request for comprehensive privacy legislation in its May 2014 report,[40] calling for Congress to consider adopting legislation, specifically in the data broker context.[41] The FTC's request was not pursued by Congress and the fragmented approach to data privacy at the federal level remains the status quo.

(i) State Regulations and Attorneys General

With a lack of guidance from the federal level, individual States are grappling with how to provide consumer privacy protections. A common approach in the US to privacy is State data breach notification laws. As of 2019, all 50 States have enacted data breach notification laws[42] to address situations in which a breach involves personally identifiable information (PII), a legally defined term in most States.[43]

[36] Humerick (n 6 above), 87 ('While the FTC can prescribe interpretive rules and general standards, it has minimal practical authority to make binding rules.').

[37] Humerick (n 6 above), at 90.

[38] The Fair Information Privacy Principles (FIPPs) were developed in the 1970s and provide a set of principles outlining certain data rights for individuals.

[39] Federal Trade Commission, 'Privacy Online: Fair Information Practices in the Electronic Marketplace, A Report to Congress' (May 2000), www.ftc.gov/sites/default/files/documents/reports/privacy-online-fair-information-practices-electronic-marketplace-federal-trade-commission-report/privacy2000text.pdf, accessed 23 February 2020.

[40] Federal Trade Commission, 'Data Brokers: A Call for Transparency and Accountability' (May 2014), available at: www.ftc.gov/system/files/documents/reports/data-brokers-call-transparency-accountability-report-federal-trade-commission-may-2014/140527databrokerreport.pdf.

[41] Federal Trade Commission, 'Data Brokers: A Call for Transparency and Accountability', at ix (May 2014), available at: www.ftc.gov/system/files/documents/reports/data-brokers-call-transparency-accountability-report-federal-trade-commission-may-2014/140527databrokerreport.pdf.

[42] National Conference of State Legislatures, 'Security Breach Notification Laws' (8 March 2020), www.ncsl.org/research/telecommunications-and-information-technology/security-breach-notification-laws.aspx, accessed 22 March 2020.

[43] In the US, data breach notification laws often define the term 'personally identifiable information' as a certain 'magical' combination of data. For example, in Pennsylvania, the data breach notification

However, these notification requirements are reactive and only penalise companies *after* a breach of security has already occurred. Fundamentally, these laws are often not tied to the concept of privacy; rather, they focus on unauthorised access to PII.

Further, certain States, such as California, expressly provide for a right to privacy in their constitutions.[44] Recognising a right to privacy creates a strong foundation for States to comprehensively regulate in the privacy space. However, US States are beginning to regulate approaches to protecting consumer privacy beyond any constitutionally provided protections. One of the most influential to date is the California Consumer Privacy Act of 2018[45] (CCPA), which went into effect on 1 January 2020. The CCPA focuses on providing consumers with increased transparency and communication around the collection and processing of their personal information. For instance, the CCPA provides consumers with rights to access, rectify, and delete personal information.[46] Uniquely to the CCPA, and driven by the more economic approach to data protection in the US generally, consumers are given the ability to restrict the 'sale' of their personal information through an opt-out provision.[47]

A wave of States in the US[48] are either following the CCPA model, by adopting or proposing CCPA-like legislation (the 'California Effect'[49]) or developing their own method to give more control to consumers in the collection and use of personal information.[50] However, States are oftentimes inexperienced in this realm and lack the appropriate resources to develop and enforce effective data privacy laws. States have limited jurisdiction when it comes to enforcing any privacy protection legislation, especially with larger companies that may interact with a State's citizens but are physically located outside of the State. Enforcement is often charged to Attorneys General who, like the FTC, have a long list of existing priorities; allocating limited resources across their wide range of responsibilities can be challenging.

law defines 'personally identifiable information' as 'An individual's first name or first initial and last name in combination with and linked to any one or more of the following data elements when the data elements are not encrypted or redacted: (i) Social Security number. (ii) Driver's license number or a State identification card number issued in lieu of a driver's license. (iii) Financial account number, credit or debit card number, in combination with any required security code, access code or password that would permit access to an individual's financial account.' Breach of Personal Information Notification Act (73 Pa Stat §§ 2301 ff).

[44] As of 2018, 11 states explicitly provide a right to privacy within their constitutions. National Conference of State Legislatures (NCSL), 'Privacy Protections in State Constitutions' (7 November 2018), www.ncsl.org/research/telecommunications-and-information-technology/privacy-protections-in-state-constitutions.aspx, accessed 23 February 2020; see also Humerick (n 6 above), 83.

[45] Cal Civ Code §§ 1798.100, ff.

[46] See Cal Civ Code §§ 1798.100, 1798.105, 1798.110, 1798.115.

[47] Cal Civ Code § 1798.120.

[48] Büyüksagis (n 5 above), at 178 ('The adoption of the CCPA constitutes a non-negligible shift in the nation's data privacy regime.').

[49] Rustad and Koenig (n 2 above), at 405.

[50] See, eg, New York's Stop Hacks and Improve Electronic Data Security Act (SHIELD Act) (requiring businesses to implement administrative, physical, and technical safeguards for personal information); Ohio Senate Bill 220 (providing a safe harbor for businesses from certain data breach tort claims).

With each State approaching the concept of privacy from a different perspective, a fragmented landscape of privacy protection across the US is created, heightening the burden of privacy compliance. The US is quickly heading towards having over 50 different data protection laws.[51] The result is confusion and complexity that increases costs – either real or perceived – for companies to create compliant privacy processes. Instead of trying to develop and implement a workable solution, many companies either look to insurance to cover any non-compliance risks, or turn a blind eye to privacy concerns altogether.

(ii) Judiciary

In the US common law tradition, the judiciary plays a strong role in defining and enforcing the laws enacted by the legislature.[52] Relying on various constitutional provisions,[53] the federal courts have been impactful in developing a loose right to privacy in the US.[54] The US Supreme Court concept of privacy focuses heavily on privacy against the government, with a standard developed around a 'reasonable expectation of privacy'.[55] Collectively, the Supreme Court's decisions establish a strong concept of privacy and robust protection around the Fourth Amendment when government collection of personal data is concerned, but do not provide support for a more general concept of information privacy. This results in a clear gap in privacy protections in the private sector.

Numerous challenges exist for individuals to bring lawsuits based on data breach or privacy concerns in the private sector, hindering a more general right to privacy in the US.[56] There exists a developing tension between freedom of speech rights afforded by the First Amendment and an individual's ability to protect her privacy. The courts have provided some guidance in the private sector when balancing these rights against an individual's privacy, typically upholding freedom of speech over any privacy concerns.[57]

[51] These challenges at the state level mirror criticisms of the EU's Directive 95/46/EC on the protection of individuals with regard to the processing of personal data and on the free movement of such data (the Directive) that was replaced by the GDPR. See Moshell (n 4 above), at 271; see also Humerick (n 6 above), at 101.

[52] William Tetley, 'Mixed Jurisdictions: common law vs civil law (codified and uncodified) (Part I)' (1990) 4 *Uniform Law Review* 591, 597.

[53] Fred H Cate and Beth E Cate, 'The Supreme Court and Information Privacy' (2012) 2(4) *International Data Privacy Law* 256, academic.oup.com/idpl/article/2/4/255/676934, accessed 21 March 2020.

[54] Strahilevitz (n 26 above), at 2016.

[55] Above, n 53 at 256; see also *Griswold v Connecticut* (n 12 above), 381 US 479 (1965) (finding a constitutional right to privacy, when the Supreme Court found a Connecticut birth control statute unconstitutional for prohibiting the use of contraceptives by married couples); *Whalen v Roe*, 429 US 589 (1977) (finding that a New York statute requiring the collection and storage of a patient's identifying information did not violate a citizen's constitutional right to privacy).

[56] Cate (n 53 above), at 258.

[57] Cate (n 53 above), at 259–61.

To date, one of the biggest hurdles for a plaintiff is overcoming a lack of standing, required under Article III of the US Constitution.[58] Standing is a constitutional doctrine in the US that relates to a party's ability to bring a suit in a court of law. The Supreme Court[59] articulated the *Lujan* test, which provides three criteria required to demonstrate that a party has standing: (1) the plaintiff has suffered an 'injury in fact', meaning the injury is either concrete and particularised, or actual or imminent; (2) there is a causal connection between the injury and the conduct before the court; and (3) the court can make a decision that will actually redress the injury, ie redressability.[60] For data breaches, the challenge in demonstrating standing originates in the first prong of the *Lujan* test: the ability to show 'actual harm' rather than potential future harm.[61]

Standing remains a large barrier to the individual enforcement of privacy within the US. Unless and until courts provide a workable solution that balances privacy against the fear of a flood of litigation, individuals will struggle to find opportunities to bring lawsuits to enforce privacy within the US. Alternatively, legislation can address this need by expressly including a private right of action within any data protection laws. This would circumvent the standing issue because a violation of the law alone would create an actionable harm.

(iii) Contracts/Agreements between Private Actors

The US has a strong tradition of promoting free market principles, and allowing markets – and contracts within those markets – to dictate the rules and responsibilities between parties.[62] In fact, one of the largest criticisms of the GDPR is the perceived impact of dictating the contractual relationships between businesses and individuals regarding the use of their data, creating additional costs within the digital market, and limiting innovation in technology.[63] To date, with its more limited and fragmented approach to privacy, the US appears to embrace the argument that any privacy regulations will hinder these same efforts.

As such, many areas of privacy within the US are addressed through contractual agreements between the data collector and the individual. The presumption is that these parties freely enter into these agreements around the collection and use

[58] Humerick (n 6 above), at 96.

[59] *Lujan v Defenders of Wildlife*, 504 US 555 (1992).

[60] *Lujan* (n 59 above), at 560–61.

[61] Büyüksagis (n 5 above), 208–9.

[62] Eline Chivot and Daniel Castro, 'What the Evidence Shows About the Impact of the GDPR After One Year', Center for Data Innovation, 17 June 2019, www2.datainnovation.org/2019-gdpr-one-year.pdf, accessed 4 March 2020; see also Rustad and Koenig (n 2 above), 387.

[63] Rustad and Koenig (n 2 above), 388, quoting Natasha Tiku, 'Europe's New Privacy Law Will Change the Web, and More', *WIRED* (19 March 2018): ('European data protection is criticized for driving up the price tag of goods and services through unwarranted regulations. Critics dismiss the GDPR as another example of "more protectionism from the E.U., which has challenged American tech platforms on antitrust and privacy grounds with expensive consequences."').

of personal information. An inherent concept of a contract in the US is that both parties have equal bargaining power and neither faces coercion from the other.[64] Provided that a company is not 'deceptive' or 'unfair', it can establish an agreement with a customer related to privacy. However, this current approach does not adequately capture the reality of the extreme information disparity and bargaining power that currently exists between corporations and consumers. Consumers are often provided with a 'take it or leave it' scenario with little say in how their privacy is addressed.

Further, many companies employ 'dark patterns'[65] and avoid providing consumers with an accurate and complete picture of how personal data is collected and used. By allowing these companies to set their own rules for privacy, the US cedes considerable power to corporations to dictate the scope of individuals' digital footprints. Exacerbating these dark pattern trends is the fact that many organisations, often downstream from those companies employing the dark patterns, struggle to keep pace with rapidly evolving complex technology and often have no concept of (i) what data they are collecting and (ii) how that data is being used.

From a pure economic perspective, the individual is expected to determine whether the service or good received is worth the corresponding forfeit of privacy, in addition to any monetary fees and costs. With no clarity around how their information will be used – or *could* be used – it is challenging to see how *any* consumer could be deemed to have entered into a contract with equal bargaining power and sufficient information to make an informed privacy decision.[66] The primary concern is that the rules of information exchange are dictated through contract and agreement, rather than privacy regulations. This regime disadvantages individual consumers and places control squarely in the hands of those companies collecting the data.

III. Challenges and Opportunities for a US Federal Privacy Law

The US faces unique challenges to develop a more comprehensive and nationwide privacy regime. But, there are some unique opportunities as well, including the ability, involving likely political capital, to create a data protection authority as

[64] Daniel D Barnhizera, 'Inequality of Bargaining Power' (2004) 76 *University of Colorado Law Review* 139, 194 (recognising that the doctrine of inequality of bargaining power derived from 'the late 19th Century social and economic reactions to the perceived abuses of laissez-faire economic regulation and Lochner-era freedom of contract doctrine').

[65] Subtle ploys of interface design used by websites and apps to force users to do things online (in this case the sharing of personal information) that they had not intended and would not otherwise do.

[66] See, eg, *United States Navigation Co v Cunard SS Co*, 284 US 474, 479–80 (1932). Barnhizera (n 64 above), at 194.

well as the use of its judiciary system to support and promote privacy across a wide variety of jurisdictions and industries.

A. The Challenge of an Economic Approach to Privacy

As discussed above, the US places a strong emphasis on the economic approach to data and privacy. Focusing on privacy from an economic perspective presents a glaring challenge to the creation of an effective right to privacy. Companies use agreements and contracts to shape the role of privacy with customers, placing the burden[67] on the consumer, who often does not have equal bargaining power with these companies, to attempt to create a workable and fair approach to the collection of the consumer's personal information.

One solution to balancing privacy with an economic approach is to create an actual 'market' for data which allows the consumer to share in the wealth generated from the collection of information. California Governor, Gavin Newsom, called for this approach in his 2019 State of the State Address:

> I applaud this legislature for passing the first-in-the-nation digital privacy law last year. But California's consumers should also be able to share in the wealth that is created from their data. And so I've asked my team to develop a proposal for a new Data Dividend for Californians, because we recognize that your data has value and it belongs to you.[68]

While this idea has not gained traction from a legislative stand-point, there is precedent in the US for creating programmes to diminish economic inequalities between citizens and private entities. The Alaska Permanent Fund pays dividends to Alaskans with revenues from the oil and gas industry to benefit current and future citizens.[69] The idea of using similar dividends grounded in 'data' provides a unique opportunity to diminish the inequalities in data collection and technology, and to provide consumers with some control within the privacy context.

The economic approach within the US is perhaps the most influential aspect of US privacy law, causing friction with the EU. Whitman observes that 'Europeans have aggressively condemned traffic in consumer data: It is, European lawyers believe, a serious potential violation of the privacy rights of the consumer if marketers can purchase data about his or her preferences, and regulation is thus imperative.'[70] There is an inherent distrust of the free market and data protection in Europe. Ultimately, the economic approach to privacy in the US, combined with

[67] Büyüksagis (n 5 above), at 156 ('Given these developments, fairness seems more clearly than ever to dictate against placing the burden of privacy protection solely on the data subject.').

[68] Office of the Governor, 'Governor Gavin Newsom, State of the State Address, February 12, 2019', www.gov.ca.gov/2019/02/12/state-of-the-state-address/, accessed 28 February 2020.

[69] Alaska Department of Revenue, 'Permanent Fund Dividend Division', pfd.alaska.gov/, accessed 28 February 2020.

[70] Whitman (n 9 above), at 1192.

the lack of transparency and true bargaining power for consumers, will likely allow the continued benefit of the market over the individual.

B. The Challenge of Moving Beyond Privacy Self-Regulation

Under the US self-regulatory model of privacy protection, advocates argue that self-regulation provides flexibility within marketplaces and allows innovation to flourish. This promotes the market-based approach to privacy,[71] with a strong presumption that government non-regulation will stimulate growth and business development. This 'cost-benefit' analysis in privacy protections often weighs against individual privacy concerns in the collection of personal information.[72] Putting aside whether that argument has merits, the general trend of self-regulation within the US has real implications for whether a federal privacy law will be successful.

Often, industries are left adrift in the privacy abyss and end up creating their own privacy rules, which results in industry interests winning out over individual privacy. This puts the private sector in the driving seat when it comes to technological decisions that have real privacy impacts.[73] Further, self-policing provides a host of opportunities for companies to disregard privacy requirements altogether, or to comply with only the bare minimum requirements, to produce the perception that they took their responsibility seriously.

Individual consumers are reliant on private industry to take proactive measures to create self-regulatory regimes that take into account the individual, which may come at the cost and detriment of the business who itself is drafting those standards: a lofty request for businesses that are typically set up to seek profits above all else. This approach is in direct conflict with the EU, where consumers are given the power to control the collection and use of their personal information during the entire data life cycle.[74]

These concerns tie into a common US approach to drafting privacy legislation that provides numerous carve outs and exceptions.[75] One of the broadest is the 'legitimate business activity/purpose' exception,[76] which allows for the widespread

[71] Büyüksagis (n 5 above), 146–47.

[72] Humerick (n 6 above), 94–95.

[73] Paul Timmers, Challenged by Digital Sovereignty (2019) 26(6) *Journal of Internet Law* 1, 13.

[74] Humerick (n 6 above), at 99–100.

[75] Moshell (n 4 above), at 377 ('Plaguing such legislative efforts, however, is the consistent inclusion of exceptions and exclusions that undercut the effectiveness of the measures.').

[76] See, eg, CCPA, Cal Civ Code § 1798.105(d)(1) (providing an exception for the right to delete information under the CCPA if 'reasonably anticipated within the context of a business' ongoing business relationship with the consumer'); GLBA, 15 US Code § 6802(b)(2) (providing an exception to notifications by financial institutions the information is used to 'perform services for or functions on behalf of the financial institution, including marketing of the financial institution's own products or services, or financial products or services offered pursuant to joint agreements between two or more financial institutions').

sharing of personal information under the guise of 'legitimate business purposes'.[77] Further, these exceptions afford businesses the opportunity to creatively side-step privacy in ways that can be very damaging and harmful to the individual. For example, marketers can often rely on their legitimate business purposes to personalise services for users. As such, even if a user does not consent to the collection of information (via cookie consents or other such mechanisms), the website could *still* use that information to personalise services under this exception.

Eliminating self-regulation in the privacy realm aligns with the US trend towards more comprehensive data breach notification laws. While there are still many limitations in the existing legal protections for individuals after a security breach occurs, the primary one being a lack of private right of action for individuals impacted by a breach, there is a general requirement across most of the US that companies must notify the public of a data breach within a reasonable time period.

Any federal regulation should include a balance between the interests of businesses and the rights of data subjects. For example, this balance is already seen in elements of the GDPR[78] and the CCPA.[79] Both provide businesses some flexibility when complying with the right to be forgotten and the right to erasure; requests to delete information may be denied in certain circumstances. A US federal privacy law should take the lessons learned from the GDPR and the CCPA to strike a stronger balance between the interests of businesses and individuals, ideally finding an approach which aligns with both parties and provides robust privacy protections.

C. The Challenge of Preemption and Federalism

There are clear limitations and restrictions to the power of the US federal government. Under the US Constitution, the federal government is limited to exercising only those powers enumerated in the Constitution, with all other authority reserved to the States.[80] However, the ability of the federal government to regulate the flow of data, and therefore create a federal privacy law, is already established by the Supreme Court. In the 2000 decision in *Reno v Condon*,[81] the US Supreme Court held that the Driver's Privacy Protection Act (DPPA), which 'regulates the

[77] Rustad and Koenig (n 2 above), at 416–17.

[78] GDPR, Recital 65 ('the further retention of the personal data should be lawful where it is necessary, for exercising the right of freedom of expression and information, for compliance with a legal obligation, for the performance of a task carried out in the public interest or in the exercise of official authority vested in the controller, on the grounds of public interest in the area of public health, for archiving purposes in the public interest, scientific or historical research purposes or statistical purposes, or for the establishment, exercise or defence of legal claims.').

[79] Cal Civ Code § 1798.105(d) (outlining nine exemptions to the right to delete personal information).

[80] US Constitution, Tenth Amendment.

[81] *Reno v Condon*, 528 US 141 (2000).

disclosure of personal information contained in the records of state motor vehicle departments',[82] fell under Congress's authority to regulate inter-State commerce under the Commerce Clause.[83] The Court explained that:

> the personal, identifying information that the DPPA regulates is a 'thin[g] in interstate commerce,' and that the sale or release of that information in interstate commerce is therefore a proper subject of congressional regulation.[84]

The ability of the federal government to regulate in this area is not absolute for two reasons: firstly, federalism restrictions, and secondly, state sovereignty. Under the GDPR, each Member State may rely on a local data protection authority (DPA) to create a cohesive approach to privacy within that state. A similar approach would be difficult to enact in the US because, under federalism restrictions, 'Congress cannot compel the States to enact or enforce a federal regulatory program.'[85] As such, any federal privacy regulation would necessarily require some agency (or agencies) at the federal level to oversee and enforce its provisions.

Further, when federal law is appropriately enacted, it is considered the 'supreme law of the land' and will preempt any State law.[86] In order to preserve the benefits of a comprehensive privacy regime, a federal law would need to expressly preempt State laws.[87] However, in the absence of federal law, or even if a federal law exists, a State can provide protections above and beyond what is provided for under a federal law. Often, States ruthlessly guard their authority to provide protections to their citizens that they feel are appropriate.[88]

In the privacy context, this creates a situation where companies may still be confronted with differing State obligations that go *above* the requirements of a federal privacy regulation. The worst outcome of allowing States to provide heightened protections would be if all 50 States opted to do so. This could easily result in preserving the status quo, where companies find 50 different State laws *too* burdensome and therefore decide to take the riskier approach of disregarding privacy requirements all together. Therefore, it is worth considering whether the federal privacy regulation should explicitly limit the ability for States to provide additional or heightened protections.

[82] *Reno* (n 81 above), at 143.

[83] *Reno* (n 81 above), at 148. The Commerce Clause provides the federal government with the enumerated power '[t]o regulate Commerce with foreign Nations, and among the several States, and with the Indian Tribes.' US Constitution, Article I, Section 8, Clause 3.

[84] *Reno* (n 81 above), at 148.

[85] *Reno* (n 81 above), at 149 (citing *Printz v United States*, 521 US 898).

[86] US Constitution, Article VI (the Supremacy Clause).

[87] The doctrine of preemption is based on the Supremacy Clause of the US Constitution. US Constitution, Amendment VI.

[88] The California Attorney General, in a letter to members of the US Congress on 25 February 2020, reiterated this point, stating: 'I am optimistic Congress will be able to craft a proposal that guarantees new privacy rights for consumers, includes a meaningful enforcement regime, and respects the good work undertaken by states across the country, looking to state law as providing a floor for privacy protections, rather than a ceiling.' Letter to the US Congress on the California Consumer Privacy Act and Federal Privacy Legislations, 25 February 2020, oag.ca.gov/system/files/attachments/press-docs/Letter%20to%20Congress%20on%20CCPA%20preemption.pdf, accessed 28 February 2020.

While a federal law may provide fewer privacy protections than certain States would find adequate, it would likely be more successful in enforcing a baseline of privacy compliance across all industries. Further, companies may be more willing to embrace privacy as there would be one comprehensive standard to meet, creating fewer operational burdens.

D. The Opportunity to Create a Single Federal Data Protection Authority

A core component of a comprehensive privacy regime is to create an entity whose sole mission is to oversee and enforce privacy. Currently, this role does not exist within the US.[89] Addressing this gap is key to creating any lasting and impactful federal privacy framework within the US, and would help to align the US with the approaches taken internationally in the enforcement of privacy protections.[90]

The use of data protection authorities under the GDPR provides an example of more streamlined privacy enforcement.[91] Creating one group that focuses on protecting and enforcing privacy across all industries and the entire US has similar merit. First, such an agency would be better positioned to develop a comprehensive perspective on privacy challenges. Further, the agency would be able to focus on establishing deep expertise in technology, privacy, and security. These skill sets would enable the agency to strike an appropriate balance between privacy imperatives and realistic technological limitations.

The proposed agency would require the authority to thoroughly and comprehensively enforce privacy across the country. The FTC has become the de facto 'beleaguered leader in advocating data privacy advances'.[92] One short-term solution is to expand the authority of the FTC to better enable it to make real and effective change in privacy across all industries and the country.[93]

However, to effect more sustainable changes, privacy should receive its own agency that can coordinate a cohesive federal mandate. Ideally, this agency would operate with sufficient independence from both the executive and legislative branches, to ensure that privacy is upheld beyond the commercial context. Further, with one federal agency governing the universe of data privacy, it could

[89] However, in February 2020, Senator Kirsten Gillibrand (D-NY) introduced a bill in the US Senate that would create an independent federal Data Protection Authority to oversee federal privacy laws. Gillibrand, Kristen, 'Confronting A Data Privacy Crisis, Gillibrand Announces Landmark Legislation To Create A Data Protection Agency', www.gillibrand.senate.gov/news/press/release/confronting-a-data-privacy-crisis-gillibrand-announces-landmark-legislation-to-create-a-data-protection-agency#:~:text=Washington%2C%20DC%20%E2%80%93%20U.S.%20Senator%20Kirsten,practices%20are%20fair%20and%20transparent.

[90] See, eg, GDPR, Chapter VI.

[91] GDPR, Chapter VI.

[92] Moshell (n 4 above), 381.

[93] Humerick (n 6 above), 112.

devote all of its resources to investigating companies, while also actively enforcing privacy protections. Enforcement is a key driver of compliance; without strong mechanisms backed by a strong enforcement arm, a privacy regime is set up to fall short of ensuring real privacy.

The creation of a federal data protection authority would not necessarily eliminate the role and authority of existing agencies charged with promoting privacy under the various existing regulations. It is not likely that agencies such as the Consumer Fraud Protection Bureau (CFPB) or the Department of Health Services will willingly give up their authority over certain realms of privacy. Consequently, it will take careful understanding of the value of these agencies, and the privacy protections they oversee, to craft a federal data protection authority that works seamlessly with this existing federal infrastructure.

E. The Opportunity for the Judiciary to Promote Privacy

The necessary mechanisms to enforce the protection of individuals' privacy already exist within the US court framework. Court opinions can define key concepts under the law and set precedent for generations, effectively expanding privacy rights and protections. However, the very real barrier of standing, discussed previously, must be addressed to allow for the judiciary to fully embrace this role.

The judiciary can play a strong role in the use of class action lawsuits and defining harm in the privacy context. There have already been attempts to use class action lawsuits as a mechanism to enforce privacy. For example, in *Adkins v Facebook, Inc*,[94] the Northern District of California certified a class action lawsuit to determine whether Facebook was liable for privacy violations but declined to certify a damages class. By failing to certify the class for damages, the District Court effectively limited the ability of all class recipients to seek a higher damage amount that would materially impact the finances of the company. Adjudicating injuries on an individual basis does not typically represent any real threat to a company; not all individuals will opt to participate and the aggregate financial impact could remain small. However, hundreds, thousands, or even millions of plaintiffs banding together in a class action lawsuit represent greater power to hold a company accountable. While these class certifications are not uniformly applied, or allowed, across the US, they can be used proactively to ensure effective compliance with any privacy law.

Further, the concept of monetary damage when harm is caused by one party to another is a well-defined concept within US jurisprudence.[95] The US allows for wealth-based damages that can more directly reflect a true 'punishment' for any

[94] *Adkins v Facebook, Inc*, No 3:18-cv-05982, 2019 WL 7212315 (ND Cal, 26 November 2019).

[95] In fact, it could be argued that the GDPR borrowed from this US tradition by providing for a private right of action and damages under the GDPR. See GDPR, Art 82; see also Rustad and Koenig (n 2 above), 420–21.

non-complying company.[96] By already providing robust jurisprudence to assess damages, US courts are well positioned to enforce privacy through damages and sanctions.

However, without corresponding regulations that provide causes of action, privacy and security claims will likely continue to fail at early stages of litigation. Courts tend to focus on the 'reasonable expectation of privacy' as the basis for adjudicating whether that expectation has been violated. However, the idea of a 'reasonable expectation of privacy' does not fit squarely within the exchange of information within the digital economy. Justice Sotomayor highlighted the challenge succinctly in her concurring opinion in *United States v Jones*:

> the premise that an individual has no reasonable expectation of privacy in information voluntarily disclosed to third parties ... is ill suited to the digital age, in which people reveal a great deal of information about themselves to third parties in the course of carrying out mundane tasks.[97]

The concept of a reasonable expectation of privacy needs to be re-visited to take account of the necessity for individuals to exchange information in many facets of everyday life. This updated concept can be harnessed to protect individuals. Would a reasonable person expect information to be accessed by additional parties beyond those whom the person gave the information to? This standard can actually provide the capability for real protections by focusing on the view of individuals instead of the perspective of companies.

Federal regulation should provide a pathway to enforce privacy within the judiciary, while ensuring that the floodgates do not open to drown businesses in privacy litigation. When provided with the tools under a federal regulation, the courts can play a pivotal role in helping to strike that balance.

IV. Conclusion

Ultimately, any US federal privacy law will need to take into account the US privacy journey and the many stakeholders involved. The 'GDPR Effect', while likely strong in creating a need for a federal dialogue in the US on privacy, will not necessarily convert into a GDPR-like federal law in the US.

However, with the inherent global nature of technology and the digital economy, the US must enact some form of privacy protections in order to continue to participate in the global marketplace and remain a source of legal influence. As Chief Justice Roberts recognised, 'the fact that technology now allows an individual to carry such information in his hand does not make the information any less worthy of the protection for which the Founders fought.'[98]

[96] Rustad and Koenig (n 2 above), 429.
[97] *United States v Jones* 132 S Ct 945, 957 (2012).
[98] *Riley v California*, 573 US 373, 403 (2014).

As differences between the US and EU approaches to data protection widen[99] and exacerbate current frictions, technology will continue to plough forward and evolve with the hope that a workable solution will appear. Some harmony must be found between the US data protection approach and the EU's GDPR.[100] Otherwise, the US risks moving into a marginalised role when it comes to its influence on the global digital economy.

Tensions are rising between individuals, businesses and the government agencies enforcing privacy. These tensions highlight the need for proactive privacy measures to be expressly addressed at the federal level, which balance individual protections with encouraging companies to innovate around privacy. With increasing emphasis on data localisation,[101] the global economy risks the segmentation of data and markets, potentially creating borders to networks, data, and technology. This result would completely negate the value and purpose of the internet in the first place. While the US is falling behind the rest of the international community in terms of its approach to comprehensive privacy regulation, it is not too late to turn the ship around. Capitalising on the opportunities to leverage the judiciary to promote privacy and create a single federal agency to enforce a federal privacy regulation are the most effective paths towards ensuring the protection of individuals' data privacy.

[99] Humerick (n 6 above), 106 ('The GDPR's implementation has further increased the data privacy gap that existed between the United States and the European Union.').

[100] Moshell (n 4 above), 361 (stating that there is a 'requirement of international cooperation that must be met in order to reach harmonious coexistence of different data protection regimes.')

[101] See Celeste, Chapter 13 in this book.

PART II

Tensions

4

Google v CNIL: Circumscribing the Extraterritorial Effect of EU Data Protection Law

JOHN QUINN

I. Introduction

The internet provides us with a vast abundance of information. The ease of access to this information, made possible by search engines and the personal PC/smart phone, has offered countless benefits. However, like any major transformative innovation, the benefits have come with costs. One of the costs is that incorrect, out of date, damaging or embarrassing information about identifiable individuals is available simply by entering their name into a search engine. The ease of access to this online information – or personal data – may harm the person to which it refers, distorting or ruining their reputation, especially when it appears in the top results of a search.[1] Even if the data is not obviously defamatory or damaging, the individual may not want to be permanently associated with it and may wish for it to be erased or 'forgotten'. However, the ease of access to personal data in the internet age has made moving on from the past an almost impossible task.[2]

The free availability of potentially damaging information was a problematic issue long before the internet era, particularly in connection to mass media publications.[3] However, the internet age, with the digitisation of press archives and the free availability of personal data through search engines, has meant the issue has grown to unprecedented levels. An important question for the internet era was how the ever-expanding amount of freely available personal data was going to interact with privacy rights: in particular, from the EU perspective, the right

[1] Miguel Peguera, 'The Right to be Forgotten in the European Union' in Giancarlo Frosio (ed), *The Oxford Handbook of Online Intermediary Liability* (OUP, 2019), 1.

[2] Michael L Rustad and Sanna Kulevska, 'Reconceptualizing The Right to Be Forgotten to Enable Transatlantic Data Flow' (2015) 28 *Harvard Journal of Law and Technology* 349, 352.

[3] See Alessandro Mantelero, 'The EU Proposal for a General Data Protection Regulation and the Roots of the "Right to Be Forgotten"' (2013) 29 *Computer Law and Security Review* 229.

to privacy in the European Convention of Human Rights[4] and the right to the protection of personal data in the Charter of Fundamental Rights of the European Union.[5] As an important element of these rights, EU law has long recognised the need for certain data to be erased.[6] The 1995 Data Protection Directive granted an express right of erasure so that data subjects may obtain, as appropriate, 'the rectification, erasure or blocking of data the processing of which does not comply with the provisions of this Directive, in particular because of the incomplete or inaccurate nature of the data'.[7] The General Data Protection Regulation (GDPR),[8] which replaced the 1995 Directive, retains the right to erasure in Article 17, the title of which includes the expression 'right to be forgotten'. However, it was not clear how the right to erasure would be given practical effect. Given the global nature of the internet and the potentially infinite number of distinct, separately hosted web pages, it is practically impossible to completely guarantee that personal data is permanently erased across the entirety of the internet.

The Court of Justice of the European Union's (CJEU) decision in *Google Spain*[9] offered some insight into how the right to erasure under the 1995 Data Protection Directive would be practically implemented. The judgment held that internet search engines were obliged to dereference results from a search of a data subject's name which directed users to personal data deemed to be 'inadequate, irrelevant or no longer relevant, or excessive'.[10] The decision in *Google Spain* was the subject of much criticism, particularly from across the Atlantic.[11] This was, at least in part, because the judgment left many important questions unanswered. One such question was the territorial scope of a successful dereferencing request. *Google Spain* did not address whether a search engine operator must dereference the relevant data on the search engine's website in the country where the search was made (eg, google.ie in the case of Ireland) or must dereference the data on all EU domains, or whether the data must be dereferenced from all versions of the search engine. The latter interpretation would include, in Google's case, Google.com and would mean that the data would become unavailable no matter where the search was carried out or what domain of the search engine was used. This question has significant importance to the issue of the extraterritorial reach of the GDPR and

[4] Article 8 of the European Convention of Human Rights.

[5] Article 8 of the Charter of Fundamental Rights of the European Union.

[6] See Chapter 2 in this volume by Fabbrini and Celeste.

[7] Directive 95/46/EC of the European Parliament and of the Council of 24 October 1995 on the protection of individuals with regard to the processing of personal data and on the free movement of such data [1995] OJ L 281/31, Art 12(b).

[8] See Regulation 2016/679/EU of 27 April 2016 on the protection of natural persons with regard to the processing of personal data and on the free movement of such data, and repealing Directive 95/46/EC [2016] OJ L 119/1 (GDPR).

[9] C-131/12 *Google Spain SL v Agencia Española de Protección de Datos*, ECLI:EU:C:2014:317.

[10] Ibid [94].

[11] See Ann Cavoukian and Christopher Wolf, 'Sorry, but there's no online "Right to be Forgotten"', *National Post* (25 June 2014); The Washington Post, 'Ungoogled: The Disastrous Results of The Right to Be Forgotten', *The Washington Post* (12 July 2014).

the extent to which the CJEU's interpretation of the GDPR could affect people outside the EU. If the default position was that every dereferencing request was to be applied globally then EU law would be restricting the ease of access to information of internet users across the globe. This would inevitably raise questions about EU law exceeding its territorial jurisdiction, particularly when many countries outside the EU do not recognise a right to erasure/right to be forgotten. From an international perspective, it may appear that the EU was greatly exceeding its legal jurisdiction. However, from an EU perspective, the global nature of the internet and the many search engine domains may necessitate an extraterritorial effect to adequately give effect to the privacy rights of EU citizens.

This chapter examines the 2019 CJEU decision in *Google v CNIL*, which directly addressed these questions.[12] The judgment held that the default position of EU law was that search engines, following a successful dereference request, must dereference the relevant information on its EU domains only and not across all versions of its search engine. Therefore, the case limited the territorial scope of a successful dereferencing request to within the EU. Geoblocking technology played a central role in the case's outcome. The technology can be used to prevent users geographically located within the EU from gaining access to dereferenced material, regardless of the domain name used. The technology meant that the right to erasure could be practically implemented within the EU without dereferencing information across all versions of Google. The right to be forgotten is not absolute and must be balanced against other competing rights, most notably, the right of access to information. As Advocate General Szpunar noted, the EU institutions lack the capacity to engage in a balancing of rights on a global scale, especially when many countries do not recognise a right to be forgotten.[13] Given the complexity of attempting to balance rights globally and the existence of geoblocking technology, this chapter argues that *Google v CNIL* was a proportionate decision. However, *Google v CNIL* allowed scope for a global dereferencing order should the circumstances require it. The CJEU in other contexts, has been willing to allow global orders to remove online content, most recently in *Eva Glawischnig-Piesczek v Facebook*[14] which dealt with whether and the E-Commerce Directive[15] prevented a national court from issuing an injunction to remove defamatory content globally. Therefore, *Google v CNIL* has not entirely ended the potential for a global dereferencing order and some questions remain unanswered.

This chapter uses *Google v CNIL* as a lens through which to examine: 1) the right to erasure/right to be forgotten; 2) the inherent issues of extraterritoriality in matters of online privacy and data protection; and 3) the complex issue of

[12] Case C-507/17 *Google LLC v Commission Nationale de l'Informatique et des Libertés (CNIL)*, ECLI:EU:C:2019:772.

[13] Case 507/17 *Google Inc. v CNIL*, Opinion of AG Szpunar, ECLI EU:C:2019:15.

[14] Case C-18/18, *Eva Glawischnig-Piesczek v Facebook*, judgment of 3 October 2019, ECLI:EU:C:2019:821.

[15] Directive 2000/31/EC OJ 2000 L 178/1.

balancing competing rights on a global scale. Section II illustrates the inherent territorial difficulties in this area of law by examining the broader context of the right to erasure/right to be forgotten, *Google Spain* and Google's response to that judgment. Section III outlines the specific issues in *Google v CNIL*, the decision of the CJEU, the importance of geoblocking technology in the case's outcome. Finally, section IV provides analysis of the case, examines the question of proportionality and the tensions between the EU's aim of giving practical effect to the right to erasure/right to be forgotten and the difficulties of EU law determining what information is accessible at the global level. Section V concludes.

II. The Extraterritorial Nature of the Right to Erasure

It is important to define what exactly is meant by a data subject's right to erasure/right to be forgotten. As numerous authors have pointed out, it is impossible, given the nature of the internet, for defined personal data to be completely erased or forgotten.[16] Personal data can be stored on thousands of separate web pages hosted across the world. It is, in practice, impossible to ensure that every one of these web pages is erased. Further, if the law required the direct erasure of web pages from the internet it would raise significant questions of undue interference with the right to access information.[17] This is especially true as the data, while it may be viewed as damaging or irrelevant by the data subject, may be true and legally acquired and published. However, given that most internet users navigate the internet through search engines, usually Google, limiting the results provided to users through Google can be an effective means to functionally limit the ease of access to web pages – and therefore the relevant data – without directly deleting information. Given this context, *Google Spain*[18] was an important development in the practical implementation of the right to be forgotten/right to erasure. The facts of *Google Spain* are well known. In brief, it dealt with a complaint by Mr Mario Costeja González about two newspaper articles which appeared on a Google search of his name. The articles described the repossession and auction of his home because of unpaid social security debts. Mr González wanted the information removed by deleting the articles or altering their content on the original website and for Google Spain to remove or conceal the information from the results of any future search of his name.

[16] Selen Uncular, 'The Right to removal in the time of post-Google Spain: Myth or reality under General data protection Regulation?' (2019) 33(3) *International Review of Law, Computers and Technology* 309, 311; A Bunn, 'The Curious case of the right to be forgotten' (2015) 31(3) *Computer Law and Security Review* 336; David Hoffmann, Paula Bruening and Sophia Carter, 'The Right to Obscurity: How Can We Implement the Google Spain Decision' (2016) 17(3) *North Carolina Journal of Law and Technology* 437.

[17] Article 11 of the Charter of Fundamental Rights of the European Union.

[18] C-131/12 *Google Spain SL v Agencia Española de Protección de Datos*, ECLI:EU:C:2014:317.

The first question the Court had to answer was whether the Data Protection Directive was applicable to the company Google Spain. Article 4(1)(a) of the Data Protection Directive stated that the Directive will apply where 'processing is carried out in the context of the activities of an establishment of the controller on the territory of the Member State'. The issue was that Google Spain was a marketing subsidiary which only sold advertising and was not itself directly involved in personal data processing. Instead, the data processing was carried out by the parent company Google Inc. Firstly, the CJEU held that Google Spain was a subsidiary of Google Inc on Spanish territory and, therefore, an 'establishment' within the meaning of the Directive. Secondly, the CJEU held that for the Directive to apply there was no requirement that the data be processed by the subsidiary itself but only that the processing is carried out 'in the context of the activities' of the subsidiary. The Court went on to hold that the processing of personal data by a search engine operated by a non-EU company with a subsidiary within the EU is carried out 'in the context of the activities' when the subsidiary is incorporated to promote and sell advertising space in that Member State. The decision extended the scope of EU data protection law to include non-EU companies that have a subsidiary in an EU Member State that collects data in its business activities in the EU. The effect of the ruling was that non-EU companies would come within the scope of EU law because they had subsidiaries in the EU.[19]

Concluding that Google Spain, as a subsidiary of Google Inc., fell within the meaning of the 1995 Data Protection Directive was not a straightforward legal determination.[20] To make this determination the CJEU was required to adopt a particularly broad interpretation of the meaning of Article 4(1) of the Directive. However, as De Hert and Papakonstantinou note, this was justified and necessary, given Google's legal scheme of subsidiaries, which was quite clearly aimed at circumventing EU data protection law.[21] The Court was dealing with a piece of legislation which was outdated in the internet age and a broad interpretation of the language used in the Directive was necessary to achieve the primary purpose of the Directive. The CJEU explicitly stated that achieving the purpose of the Directive required a broad interpretation of the language:

> in the light of the objective of Directive 95/46 of ensuring effective and complete protection of the fundamental rights and freedoms of natural persons, and in particular their right to privacy, with respect to the processing of personal data, those words cannot be interpreted restrictively.[22]

[19] Christopher Wolf, 'The Impact of the CJEU's Right to be Forgotten' (2014) 21(3) *Maastricht Journal of European and Comparative Law* 547.

[20] See Brendan van Alsenoy and Marieke Koekkoek, 'Internet and Jurisdiction after Google Spain: The Extraterritorial Reach of the "right to be delisted"' (2015) 5 *Internet Data Privacy Law* 109.

[21] Paul De Hert and Vagelis Papakonstantinou, 'Google Spain: Addressing Critiques and Misunderstandings One Year Later' (2015) 22(4) *Maastricht Journal of European and Comparative Law* 624, 628.

[22] C-131/12 *Google Spain SL v Agencia Española de Protección de Datos*, ECLI:EU:C:2014:317, [53].

In terms of expanding the territorial scope of the Directive to companies registered outside the EU, the CJEU said the Directive was intended to have a broad territorial scope:

> it is clear in particular from recitals 18 to 20 in the preamble to Directive 95/46 and Article 4 thereof that the European Union legislature sought to prevent individuals from being deprived of the protection guaranteed by the directive and that protection from being circumvented, by prescribing a particularly broad territorial scope.[23]

The view taken by the CJEU in *Google Spain* that EU data protection law should carry a broad territorial scope was subsequently codified in the GDPR. Article 3(1) states that the Regulation applies to the processing of personal data 'regardless of whether the processing takes place in the Union or not.' Further, Article 3(2) states that the Regulation applies to processing of personal data of data subjects within the EU by a controller or processor not established in the EU where the processing activities are related to:

> (a) the offering of goods or services, irrespective of whether a payment of the data subject is required, to such data subjects in the Union; or
> (b) the monitoring of their behaviour as far as their behaviour takes place within the Union.

Therefore, the GDPR continued the trend, first made explicit in *Google Spain*, of expanding the territorial scope of EU data protection law to have effects beyond the borders of the EU.

The next important part of *Google Spain* was that the CJEU determined that a search engine could be categorised as a data controller, despite not altering the content of the data. The CJEU held that a search engine processes data with objectives that are distinct from those of the original content providers and so may be defined as a controller of that data. This finding placed a requirement on search engine operators to observe the responsibilities of data controllers relating to the processing of personal data under EU law. These responsibilities included complying with the right to erasure expressed in the 1995 Data Protection Directive. As part of that right to erasure, the CJEU held that search engines were obliged to remove results of searches for a data subject's name which directed users to personal data deemed 'inadequate, irrelevant or no longer relevant, or excessive'.[24] This requirement included results which contain truthful and accurate data but which nevertheless violate an individual's right to privacy.[25]

Importantly, the CJEU stated that the right to a dereferencing was to be balanced against the legitimate interest of internet users' ability to access information but that, as a general rule, data subjects' rights take priority over the rights of

[23] Ibid, [54].
[24] Ibid, [94].
[25] The Court relied on Articles 7 and 8 of the Charter of Fundamental Rights of European Union, [2000] OJ C 326/02.

internet users, although it would depend on the specific context.[26] The information about Mr González was found to be no longer relevant, as the issue had been resolved for over a decade. The Court ordered Google to dereference the articles from a search for González's name. However, the Court did not order the original articles to be changed or web pages to be taken down. Therefore, *Google Spain* is not about erasing personal data or personal data being forgotten; rather it is about erasing links to personal data, thereby reducing the ease of access to information through search engines.[27] The right to erasure/to be forgotten expressed in Article 17 of the GDPR is practically implemented by requiring search engines to dereference web pages from their search results.

After the judgment in *Google Spain*, Google immediately began dereferencing websites from its search engines. Between May 2014 and May 2019, Google received 811,029 dereference requests, and according to its own data, it dereferenced 44.6 per cent of the requests and rejected the remaining 55.4 per cent.[28] However, *Google Spain* did not specify the geographical extent of the dereferencing necessary to comply with EU law. While Google began dereferencing, it was doing so only on its European domains. This meant that a data subject in Germany could make a dereference request, have it approved by Google who would then dereference the material on all EU domains, but the references would still be available on American and other non-European Google domains. Importantly, internet users within the EU's territory could use Google.com to access dereferenced data.

Certain Data Protection Authorities and the Article 29 Working Party (now the European Data Protection Board) had a different interpretation of the territorial scope of a successful dereferencing request. The Article 29 Working Party guidelines on implementing *Google Spain*[29] stated that successful dereference requests 'must be implemented in a way that guarantees the effective and complete protection' of the data subject's rights such that EU law cannot be 'easily circumvented'.[30] Further, the guidelines provide that data subjects must be 'effectively protected against the impact of the universal dissemination and accessibility of personal information'.[31] Therefore, according to the guidelines, limiting dereferencing to EU domains 'cannot be considered a sufficient means to satisfactorily guarantee

[26] C-131/12 *Google Spain SL v Agencia Española de Protección de Datos*, ECLI:EU:C:2014:317, [81]. The Court specifically referred to the public role played by the data subject in public life as something which was an important factor in balancing the different interests.

[27] Paul De Hert and Vagelis Papakonstantinou, 'Google Spain: Addressing Critiques and Misunderstandings One Year Later' (2015) 22(4) *Maastricht Journal of European and Comparative Law* 624, 637.

[28] Googles Transparency Report (2019) available at: https://transparencyreport.google.com.

[29] Art 29 Working Party (WP29), 'Guidelines on the implementation of the Court of Justice of the European Union judgment on "Google Spain and Inc v. Agencia Española de Protección de Datos (AEPD) and Mario Costeja González" C-131/12' (26 November 2014) 14/EN WP 225, ec.europa.eu/justice/article-29/documentation/opinionrecommendation/files/2014/wp225_en.pdf.

[30] Ibid, [20].

[31] Ibid.

the rights of data subjects' and in practice, a successful dereferencing request should be applied to 'all relevant domains, including.com'.[32] The guidelines use the words 'relevant domains' and so stop short of stating that the dereferencing should be applied on all versions of a search engine across the globe. However, the guidelines expressly include.com, which indicates that the dereferencing should apply to domains which go beyond the territorial scope of the EU.[33] The message of the guidelines was clear: the Article 29 Group wanted a successful dereference to mean global application so that EU law could not be 'easily circumvented'.[34]

Google ignored the Working Party's guidelines and continued to only carry out dereferencing on its EU domains. In direct response to the Working Party's guidelines, Google's Global Privacy Counsel, Peter Fleischer stated that 'we do not read the decision by the CJEU in *Google Spain* as global in reach – it was an application of European law that applies to services offered to Europeans'.[35] The Advisory Council to Google on the right to be forgotten pointed out that even when a European types 'google.com' as a domain, they are automatically redirected to the regional website and that over 95 per cent of searches originating in Europe are on regional versions of the search engine.[36] Assuming this figure is accurate, dereferencing on EU domains would cover the vast majority of searches. If the CJEU's interpretation of the right to erasure was about ease of access to information, then dereferencing the information on regional Google domains would seriously limit the ease of access to information.

III. *Google v CNIL*

The opposing interpretation of the territorial scope of the right to dereferencing was to be resolved in a judgment delivered by the CJEU in September 2019. In June 2015, the Commission Nationale de l'Informatique et des Libertés (CNIL), France's Data Protection Authority, put Google on notice that it must begin dereferencing approved requests on all domains of its search engines.[37] Google declined to comply with CNIL's notice and instead filed an informal appeal, asking

[32] Ibid.

[33] Miguel Peguera, 'The Right to be Forgotten in the European Union' in Giancarlo Frosio (ed), *The Oxford Handbook of Online Intermediary Liability* (OUP, 2019), 10.

[34] Dan Svantesson, 'Limitless Borderless Forgetfulness? Limiting the Geographical Reach of the Right to be Forgotten' (2015) 2 *Oslo Law Review* 116, 120.

[35] Peter Fleischer, 'Response to the Questionnaire addressed to Search Engines by the Article 29 Working Party regarding the implementation of the CJEU judgment on the "right to be forgotten"', 31 July 2014 available at: docs.google.com/file/d/0B8syaai6SSfiT0EwRUFyOENqR3M/view?pli=1&sle=true.

[36] Report of the Advisory Council to Google on the Right to be Forgotten (6 February 2015), 19. Available at: static.googleusercontent.com/media/archive.google.com/en//advisorycouncil/advisement/advisory-report.pdf.

[37] CNIL Orders Google to Apply Delisting on All Domain Names of the Search Engine, CNIL (12 June 2015), see www.cnil.fr/fr/node/15790.

CNIL to withdraw its public notice.[38] Their appeal argued that dereferencing across all its domains would impede the public's access to information and would amount to a form of censorship and that no one jurisdiction should be able to control what other jurisdictions can view through their search engine. In other words, Google viewed CNIL's request as exceeding its legal jurisdiction. Google further claimed that it would be disproportionate and unnecessary to apply the dereferencing on all versions of its search engine as 97 per cent of French citizens use a European version of Google, namely Google.fr. CNIL refused the request to withdraw its public notice and ordered Google to remove thousands of links from non-European domains.

In response, Google offered to use geoblocking technology which would redirect users undertaking a search from an IP address inside the EU toward the respective national Google domain. The result would be that, regardless of the domain name used, any search carried out from an IP address inside the EU could not access dereferenced data. Users of Google.com geographically located within the EU would not be able to access the dereferenced data but users of Google.com located outside the EU would still have access to it. CNIL refused Google's offer, noting that it is possible to circumvent geoblocking and that dereferenced data could still be accessible within the EU through technical means of using a non-European IP address and a non-European domain.[39] CNIL seemed to follow the Article 29 Working Party's view that a successful dereference request must be implemented in such a way that could not allow EU law to be circumvented. Therefore, in their view, to adequately give effect to the right to erasure it must be impossible to access the dereferenced information through search engines.

While it may indeed be possible to circumvent geoblocking technology, it still provides an additional hurdle to accessing dereferenced information and would prevent access to the information in the overwhelming majority of cases.[40]

CNIL ultimately issued a €100,000 fine against Google for violating the order to dereference across all versions of the search engine. Google requested the Conseil d'État, France's supreme administrative court, to annul CNIL's decision to issue the fine. The Conseil d'État referred the matter to the CJEU asking essentially three questions: 1) Did EU law require search engine operators to dereference globally, across all versions of their search engine?; 2) if not, must a search engine dereference on the national version of the search engine where the search was made or must it dereference on all EU versions of the search engine; 3) to what extent were additional restrictions, such as geoblocking, required to be implemented by search engine operators as part of a successful deference request? In short, was the cope of a successful dereference request limited to the single Member State where the request was made, the EU territory or the whole world?

[38] 'Right to Delisting: Google Informal Appeal Rejected', CNIL (21 September 2015), see www.cnil.fr/english/news-and-events/news/article/right-to-delisting-google-informal-appealrejected/.

[39] Case 507/17 *Google Inc v CNIL*, ECLI:EU:C:2019:772.

[40] For a further discussion of this point see, Dan Svantesson, *Solving the Internet Jurisdiction Puzzle* (Oxford University Press, 2017) 205–6.

Advocate General Szpunar delivered his Opinion on 10 January 2019.[41] He stated that the rights of a data subject must be balanced against other fundamental rights, particularly the right of access to information. He noted that if there was an obligation on search engines to dereference globally, EU authorities would not have the ability to define a right of access to information in a global context, let alone engage in a complex balancing of rights, which will vary from jurisdiction to jurisdiction.[42] He recommended limiting the dereferencing to searches carried out within the EU. He stated that EU law required an 'effective and complete' protection of data subjects' rights and therefore the dereferencing should extend to all searches carried out within the EU. He concluded that the search engine operator should employ all means at its disposal to ensure that the dereferencing is 'effective and complete', including geoblocking techniques.[43] Finally, he noted that there may be circumstances which *did* call for a global dereferencing, but that such circumstances were not present in the case.

The CJEU began its analysis in *Google v CNIL*[44] by emphasising that internet users' access – including by those outside the EU – to information relating to an individual based in the EU is likely to have an immediate and substantial effect on that person. Therefore, the Court stated that a global dereferencing would meet the objective of the protections of personal data referred to in EU law.[45] However, it accepted that the right to dereferencing was not a global right and that numerous states outside the EU did not recognise such a right.[46] The Court also emphasised, as it did in *Google Spain*, that the right to the protection of personal data is not absolute, and that it must be balanced against other fundamental rights, in accordance with the principle of proportionality.[47] In combining the two points, the Court pointed out that the balancing necessary between the right to privacy and the protection of personal data versus the freedom of information of internet users is likely to vary significantly around the world.[48]

The CJEU decided that the scope of the right to dereferencing does not usually extend beyond the territory of the EU.[49] As a result, EU law could not impose a dereferencing obligation on search engines that did not correspond to the Member States. The Court concluded that there was no obligation under EU law for a successful dereference request to be carried out on all the versions of its search engine worldwide but clarified that EU law *does* require that successful dereference requests are dereferenced on all *EU* versions of the search engine.[50] The Court

[41] Case 507/17 *Google Inc v CNIL*, Opinion of AG Szpunar, ECLI EU:C:2019:15.
[42] Ibid, [60].
[43] Ibid, [78].
[44] Case C-507/17 *Google LLC v Commission Nationale de l'Informatique et des Libertés (CNIL)*, ECLI:EU:C:2019:772.
[45] Ibid, [55].
[46] Ibid, [59].
[47] Ibid, [60].
[48] Ibid.
[49] Ibid, [62].
[50] Ibid, [65].

went further and stated that a search engine must take sufficiently effective measures to ensure the effective protection of the data subject's fundamental rights. Therefore, the Court stated that, if necessary, a dereferencing must be accompanied by further measures which effectively prevent or, at the very least, seriously discourage an internet user within the EU from gaining access to dereferenced data through a version of the search engine with a domain from outside the EU.[51] This stance seemed to endorse search engine operators using geoblocking technology to limit the access to dereferenced data from any search within the EU.

Importantly, the Court pointed out that EU law does not *prohibit* a global dereferencing on all versions of a search engine.[52] Indeed, as noted above, the CJEU stated that a global dereferencing on all versions of a search engine would serve the objective of the protections of personal data referred to in EU law. The Court stated that there was potential for such a global dereferencing order to be made in the future, and stated that the authorities of the Member States remained competent to order a search engine to carry out a global dereferencing across all versions of its search engine.[53] However, such an order should only be made after the authority had engaged in a balancing between a data subject's rights to privacy and the protection of personal data on one hand and the right to freedom of information on the other.[54] Therefore, an order for a global dereferencing is still possible, but will only be made on a case-by-case basis after the relevant authority has engaged in a balancing of rights. This was despite Advocate General Szpunar's concerns about the competencies of EU competencies to effectively carry out such a balancing. Therefore, the judgment in *Google v CNIL* does not entirely resolve the different interpretations of the territorial scope of *Google Spain* and there is potential for further disputes on the geographical scope of dereferencing. What *Google v CNIL does* make clear is that the general rule is that a standard dereferencing request is limited to the EU domains of the search engine, plus necessary additional techniques such as geoblocking. A global dereferencing is still *possible* but only as an exception where the relevant EU authority believes that the threat to the data subject's rights to privacy outweighs concerns for access to information. The grounds for such a determination remain unclear and may well be the subject of a future case. However, looking to other related contexts where the CJEU has allowed for a global order, may provide a useful insight.

IV. Circumscribing the Right to Erasure

The decision in *Google v CNIL* has circumscribed the extraterritorial effects of EU data protection law. Prior to the judgment there was a clear trend, among both the

[51] Ibid, [70].
[52] Ibid, [72].
[53] Ibid.
[54] Ibid.

judiciary and legislature, to expand the geographical scope of the right to erasure/right to be forgotten. In *Google Spain* the CJEU made a series of determinations expanding the territorial application of EU data protection law: first, by classifying Google Spain as an 'establishment' within the meaning of the 1995 Data Protection Directive; second by classifying a search engine as a data controller; and third by determining that processing of personal data by a search engine operated by a non-EU company with a subsidiary within the EU is carried out 'in the context of the activities', bringing companies registered outside the EU within the scope of EU law. These interpretations of EU law and their extraterritorial effect were endorsed and codified in Article 3 of the GDPR. Given this previous trajectory, it is worth analysing why the CJEU circumscribed the territorial expansion of the right to erasure/right be forgotten.

In other contexts, the CJEU has provided for and allowed orders with global effect,[55] most recently in *Eva Glawischnig-Piesczek v Facebook.*[56] The fact that the CJEU allowed a global removal of content in *Eva Glawischnig-Piesczek v Facebook* appears to fit with the direction of EU jurisprudence on the right to be forgotten prior to *Google v CNIL*, but runs directly contrary to *Google v CNIL*. However, the differing contexts can explain the different directions of the two decisions. Additionally, the different context in *Eva Glawischnig-Piesczek v Facebook* may provide a limited insight as to what grounds may be necessary for the CJEU to consider a global order in the context of the right to dereferencing.

Eva Glawischnig-Piesczek is an Austrian politician who was a member of the National Council, the upper house of Austria's Parliament, and chair of the Austrian Green Party. A Facebook user shared a magazine article about her and posted a comment of an insulting nature. Facebook Ireland, following a request from Eva Glawischnig-Piesczek, failed to withdraw the comments. Eva Glawischnig-Piesczek then took a case to the Handelsgericht Wien (Austrian Commercial Court, Vienna) which found the comments to be harmful to her reputation, insulting and defamatory, and issued an injunction against Facebook Ireland to remove the insulting language. Facebook Ireland disabled access to the content in Austria alone. On appeal, the Oberster Gerichtshof (Austrian Supreme Court) referred the matter to the CJEU, asking for a clarification of Article 15(1) of the E-Commerce Directive[57] on whether it prevented the Austrian courts from issuing an injunction requiring Facebook to remove the content worldwide. The CJEU examined whether EU law imposed 'any limitation, including a territorial limitation, on the scope of the measures which Member States are entitled to adopt'.[58]

[55] For example, in the context of intellectual property. See *Nintendo Co Ltd v BigBen Interactive GmbH* and *BigBen Interactive SA*, Joined Cases C-24/16 and C-25/16, judgment of 27 September 2017, ECLI:EU:C:2017:724.

[56] Case C-18/18, *Eva Glawischnig-Piesczek v Facebook*, judgment of 3 October 2019, ECLI:EU:C:2019:821.

[57] Directive 2000/31/EC OJ 2000 L 178/1.

[58] Case C-18/18 *Eva Glawischnig-Piesczek v. Facebook*, judgment of 3 October 2019, ECLI:EU:C:2019:821, [49].

The Court decided that EU law 'does not preclude those injunction measures from producing effects worldwide'.[59] The consequence of the decision was to allow the Austrian courts to oblige Facebook 'to remove information covered by the injunction or to block access to that information worldwide'[60] provided the measures taken were within the framework of relevant international law.[61]

While *Eva Glawischnig-Piesczek v Facebook* is similar to *Google v CNIL* in the sense that both cases deal with limiting access to online material, they are different in important ways. *Eva Glawischnig-Piesczek v Facebook* dealt with a national court's power to order removal of online content it has previously declared to be illegal, rather than the CJEU itself issuing a global order against a search engine to dereference links to personal data. Essentially, in *Eva Glawischnig-Piesczek v Facebook* the CJEU interpreted the E-Commerce Directive in such a way that it did not prohibit a national court from issuing an injunction against an online platform to remove content globally, provided the measures were within the relevant framework of international law. Therefore, the case has a very different legal background and caution must be used in drawing comparisons between the areas of law. What can be said is that the relevant content in *Eva Glawischnig-Piesczek v Facebook* was found to be defamatory, insulting and illegal, a classification which is quite a different and more serious to the criteria necessary for a dereferencing request of 'inadequate, irrelevant or no longer relevant, or excessive'. In the future, when considering the possibility for a global dereferencing order, the relevant content may need to be close to that in *Eva Glawischnig-Piesczek v Facebook*. In other words, after *Google v CNIL*, any content that may warrant a global dereferencing order is likely to be much more serious that standard set out in *Google Spain* of 'inadequate, irrelevant or no longer relevant, or excessive'[62] and instead may need to be highly damaging to the person's reputation in a global context.

Advocate General Szpunar, in delivering his Opinion in *Google v CNIL*, made it very clear that he was against requiring search engines to dereference globally. If the right to erasure/right to be forgotten is not absolute, which it is certainly not, then it is necessary to balance it against other competing rights the nature of which will vary across the globe. Szpunar believed that EU national authorities did not have the ability to engage in such a complex balancing exercise on a global scale. In making this point, Szpunar had grave concerns about the broader impact of an obligation to dereference globally.[63] He warned that limiting the access to information of persons in jurisdictions outside the EU could prompt other countries to similarly limit the access to information based on their own laws and values, which could slowly erode the competing rights of freedom of expression and access to information.[64]

[59] Ibid, [50].
[60] Ibid, [53].
[61] Ibid.
[62] C-131/12 *Google Spain SL v Agencia Española de Protección de Datos*, ECLI:EU:C:2014:317, [94].
[63] Case 507/17 *Google Inc. v CNIL* Opinion of AG Szpunar, ECLI EU:C:2019:15, [60].
[64] Ibid, [61].

Christopher Wolf has expressed similar, albeit distinct, concerns in the wake of *Google Spain*.[65] Wolf argued that privately-run companies – rather than non-EU states – would excessively limit access to information. He believed that companies, facing potentially large fines and reputational damage, would err on the side of caution and engage in mass dereferencing. Such widespread dereferencing could have serious consequences for free expression and access to information and that Google, a privately-run corporation, would be serving as judge and jury as to what information was supressed and what information would be freely available.[66] Wolf's argument is made more powerful given that *Google Spain* and *Google v CNIL* provided little detail as to what information qualified as 'inadequate, irrelevant or no longer relevant, or excessive'. Ultimately Google, a privately-run company, is left to interpret the meaning of that legal standard in practice, albeit under the supervision of national data protection authorities. Wolf was ultimately concerned about the global application of a system of dereferencing overseen by privately-run companies, and believed that 'the application of privacy rights in such a vague, shotgun manner threatens free expression on the internet'.[67]

Szpunar's and Wolf's slightly different points both relate to a general concern about the unintended consequences of the widespread application of the right to erasure/right to be forgotten. They are worried about the normalisation of suppression of information, which could lead to national governments outside the EU and privately-run companies limiting access to information in a damaging or self-serving way in a manner that was never intended by the EU. Such unintended consequences could mean that the EU, by aiming to protect EU citizen's privacy, could undermine, at a global level, one the most fundamental rights it seeks to protect: the freedom of access to information.[68] In other words, their fear is that the right to erasure/right to be forgotten will not be adequately balanced against other rights, particularly if it is applied on a worldwide level where competing rights vary.

However, these concerns, while important, must not be overstated. At every step of the evolution of the right to dereferencing, the CJEU emphasised that the right to erasure/right to be forgotten is not absolute and that there is a need for a balancing of rights and proportionality.[69] The judgment in *Google v CNIL* demonstrates this commitment to the principles of balancing and proportionality. Despite stating clearly that a requirement of global dereferencing would achieve the objectives of EU law, the CJEU decided that only a dereferencing within the EU was

[65] Christopher Wolf, 'The Impact of the CJEU's Right to be Forgotten' (2014) 21(3) *Maastricht Journal of European and Comparative Law* 547.

[66] Ibid, 553.

[67] Ann Cavoukian and Christopher Wolf, 'Sorry, but there's no Online "Right to be Forgotten"', *National Post* (25 June 2014).

[68] Article 11 of the Charter of Fundamental Rights of the European Union.

[69] See C-131/12 *Google Spain SL v Agencia Española de Protección de Datos*, ECLI:EU:C:2014:317, [74] and Case C-507/17 *Google LLC v Commission Nationale de l'Informatique et des Libertés (CNIL)*, ECLI:EU:C:2019:772, [60].

required from search engines. Therefore, the default position is that no balancing of rights is needed on a global scale and Google within the EU will continue to be monitored by the relevant data protection authorities.

When considering the issue of proportionality and balancing of rights, it is important to reiterate the precise nature of the right to dereferencing. *Google Spain* and *Google v CNIL* fundamentally deal with ease of access to information about identifiable individuals made possible by the internet and search engines. Dereferencing has never meant erasing information. Instead, the right to erasure/right to be forgotten is given practical effect in the internet age by a right to have personal data removed from the results of a search of a person's name on a search engine. Search engines were defined in *Google Spain* as providers 'of content which consists in finding information published or placed on the internet by third parties'.[70] This definition, coupled with the decision in *Google Spain* to not remove the original news articles, places important limits on the right to dereferencing. News websites, online newspapers, blogs do not fit within the definition of a search engine, and cannot be obliged to take down any published material due to a dereferencing request. As Paul De Hert and Vagelis Papakonstantinou point out, freedom of journalism and freedom of expression are not relevant issues when it comes to dereferencing as it currently stands under EU law.[71]

The right to dereferencing does impact on the right to access information, but only in a narrow way. As stated above, dereferencing does not prevent publishing of information and personal data online and it does not prevent persons from accessing that published information. While Article 17 of the GDPR includes a right to erasure/right to be forgotten, in practice this is given effect through a right to dereferencing (originally in *Google Spain*) which does not provide for information to be erased outright. Dereferencing is about making information that is 'inadequate, irrelevant or no longer relevant, or excessive' harder to access. When balancing the right to dereferencing against the right of access to information it is important to remember that dereferencing is about ease of access to information. The right of access to information does not guarantee a right of immediate information at one's fingertips, and persons who wish to gain information that is 'inadequate, irrelevant or no longer relevant, or excessive', according to De Hert and Papakonstantinou, should 'have to do some research and make some effort to access it'.[72] Nevertheless, the relatively limited impact on the freedom to access information intended by EU law does not offer an absolute guard against the concerns of Szpunar and Wolf. There remains a potential issue that if it was to be applied globally, the delicate balance between these two rights would become misaligned and the right to be forgotten/right to erasure could potentially have a

[70] C-131/12 *Google Spain SL v Agencia Española de Protección de Datos*, ECLI:EU:C:2014:317, [21].

[71] Paul De Hert and Vagelis Papakonstantinou, 'Google Spain: Addressing Critiques and Misunderstandings One Year Later' (2015) 22(4) *Maastricht Journal or European and Comparative Law* 624, 631.

[72] Ibid, 632.

far greater impact on freedom of expression when applied outside the EU, particularly when the EU institutions lose the ability to keep it aligned with its original purpose and ensure its balance with the right of access to information.

V. Conclusion

Google v CNIL clarified how the right to erasure/right to be forgotten expressed in Article 17 of the GDPR was to be practically implemented in the internet era. Given the global nature of the internet and the potentially infinite number of distinct web pages, it is practically impossible to completely guarantee that personal data is permanently erased. Further, permanently deleting legally published information would have a great impact on other fundamental rights of freedom of expression and freedom of access to information. Instead of erasing information, the right to erasure/right to be forgotten is given practical effect by requiring search engines to dereference certain web pages from the results of a search of a data subject's name. Dereferencing limits the ease of access to information through search engines, which serves to protect the personal data of EU data subjects without excessively impacting freedom of access to information. The significance of *Google v CNIL* is that it limits what had previously been interpreted as an expansionary vision of dereferencing: in its ruling, the CJEU clarified that the right to be forgotten is limited to within the geographical boundaries of the EU in line with the balancing of rights and proportionality. However, the CJEU left open the possibility to make such a global dereferencing order in the future. The big question which is left unanswered is what set of facts are necessary for the CJEU to make a global dereferencing order. If a data protection authority encounters a set of facts upon which it views the threat to a data subject's privacy rights as sufficiently serious to request a search engine to dereference the information globally, many of these arguments will need to be revisited.

5

Digital Sovereignty and Multilevel Constitutionalism: Whose Standards for the Right to be Forgotten?

DANA BURCHARDT

I. Introduction

Who regulates what? In the digital sphere, delimiting regulatory competences presents a major challenge. Classical territorial boundaries for legal regulation are difficult to uphold as various state and non-state actors compete for control over the digital sphere. The term 'digital sovereignty' reflects this competition. Applied to governing bodies, this term attempts to translate classical regulatory competences of states or the EU to the digital sphere, aiming to avoid regulatory overlaps. However, 'digital sovereignty' is a claim rather than a reality. So far, regulatory competences are not clearly distinguished.[1] Thus, when two regulatory regimes are competing in a certain case, the question arises whose standards are applicable.

For the right to be forgotten, this question is crucial. In Europe, both the EU and its Member States claim regulatory competence on the matter. On the one hand, the applicability of the EU General Data Protection Regulation brings cases involving the right to be forgotten into the realm of EU fundamental rights protection. On the other hand, domestic constitutional law also includes relevant protections for the right to be forgotten. So, whose fundamental rights standard should govern the right to be forgotten and how far should the regulatory effect of these standards reach? Delimiting regulatory competences for the right to be forgotten is challenging in various ways. Here, two issues coexist: the territorial delimitation of regulatory competences in the digital sphere and the delimitation of competences in the context of multilevel constitutionalism. In the multilevel structure of the EU, it is not clear-cut in every case whether EU or domestic

[1] For example, the recent decision of the CJEU in *Schrems II* addresses such competing regulatory claims: CJEU,Case C-311/18, *Data Protection Commissioner v Facebook Ireland Ltd, Maximillian Schrems and others*, judgment of 16 July 2020, ECLI:EU:C:2020:559.

fundamental rights constitute the standard for the right to be forgotten. This also creates the risk of diverging standards within the EU on this subject, potentially leading to a fragmented protection of the right to be forgotten.

In two recent landmark decisions, the German Federal Constitutional Court (CC) has taken a new stance on this matter. This jurisprudence – which also impacts multilevel constitutionalism in general[2] – demonstrates that distinguishing regulatory competences between the EU and its Member States is particularly challenging for the right to be forgotten. Furthermore, this jurisprudence highlights that the claim for 'digital sovereignty' that several states seem to make more and more vigorously in recent years is in line with a tendency of some legal orders and their constitutional courts to reclaim more control over constitutional matters vis-à-vis the EU.

The twin decisions delivered on 7 November 2019 (1 BvR 276/17 and 1 BvR 16/13) overturned the previous jurisprudence on the relationship between the domestic fundamental rights protection and the fundamental rights protection provided by EU law. The CC now goes beyond its previous approach to clearly distinguish between the applicability of EU law and domestic law. It establishes a novel framework of 'parallel applicability' in which the room for applying EU fundamental rights seems to be reduced. This new framework is based on a distinction between subject matters that are fully harmonised by EU law and subject matters in which Member States have leeway. Moreover, the CC has adopted, for the first time, EU fundamental rights as a standard of review – which allows the CC to influence how the right to be forgotten under EU law is interpreted and applied within the German legal order. Both elements of this jurisprudence broaden the regulatory reach of domestic actors. For the right to be forgotten, this approach would support a claim by Member States to 'digital sovereignty'.

In this chapter, I engage with this jurisprudence and the CC's approach on dealing with competing standards for the right to be forgotten. I first give a brief overview of the decisions that the CC takes on the complainant's right to be forgotten (section II). Second, I outline the new legal framework developed by the CC, which determines for the German legal order how to distinguish between the applicability of domestic and EU fundamental rights. I argue that this framework not only gives considerable room to domestic law but also has the potential to

[2] See on these decisions and their relevance for multilevel constitutionalism eg, Karsten Schneider, 'The Constitutional Status of Karlsruhe's Novel "Jurisdiction" in EU Fundamental Rights Matters: Self-inflicted Institutional Vulnerabilities' (2020) 21 *German Law Journal* 19–26; Matej Avbelj, 'The Federal Constitutional Court Rules for a Bright Future of Constitutional Pluralism' (2020) 21 *German Law Journal* 27–30; Ana Bobić, 'Developments in The EU-German Judicial Love Story: The Right To Be Forgotten II' (2020) 21 *German Law Journal* 31–39; Dana Burchardt, 'Backlash against the Court of Justice of the EU? The Recent Jurisprudence of the German Constitutional Court on EU Fundamental Rights as a Standard of Review' (2020) 21 *German Law Journal* 1–18; Matthias Wendel, 'Das Bundesverfassungsgericht als Garant der Unionsgrundrechte' (2020) 75 *JuristenZeitung* 157–68; Jörn Axel Kämmerer and Markus Kotzur, 'Vollendung des Grundrechtsverbunds oder Heimholung des Grundrechtsschutzes?', *Neue Zeitschrift fur Verwaltungsrecht (NVwZ)* 2020, 177.

broaden the control by the CC on distinguishing between the respective regulatory regimes (section III). Third, I illustrate the specific implications of the new framework for the right to be forgotten. Here, I focus on the risk of fragmented protection of this right under EU law as well as the risk of inconsistencies due to diverging domestic and EU law standards (section IV).

II. The Right to be Forgotten before the German Constitutional Court

The twin judgments of the CC from November 2019 address the right to be forgotten in two constellations: as a claim against the content provider; and as a claim against the search engine operator. In the first constellation, the CC assesses the right to be forgotten based on domestic fundamental rights; and in the second constellation, based on European fundamental rights.

In the first case (*Right to be forgotten I*, 1 BvR 16/13), the complainant sued the German weekly news magazine *Der Spiegel*. In 1982 and 1983, the magazine had published two articles about the complainant's criminal trial, in which he had been convicted of murder. These articles had been available in the online archive of the magazine since 1999. A search for the complainant's name via an online search engine showed these articles among the top results. The complainant argued that given the time that had passed since the events, his general right of personality pursuant to Articles 2(1) and 1(1) of the German Basic Law gave him the right to request that these articles should be deleted from the online archive or that they should at least not appear as results of a simple name-based online search anymore. The CC assessed this case based on German constitutional law. It reviewed the balancing of the personality right of the claimant and the freedom of opinion and the freedom of press of the magazine. Even though the CC considered that there was still an interest of the public in having access to these journal articles via the online archive of the magazine, the CC emphasised that the element of time was of particular importance in this case, giving the right to be forgotten considerable weight.[3] Accordingly, the CC decided that, although there was no obligation for the magazine to delete the articles from its archive, the magazine could have an obligation to ensure through technical measures that these articles were not included in the top results of a simple name-based search by general online search engines. The CC ruling thus establishes that, in addition to a 'notice-and take down' approach vis-à-vis the content provider, a less far-reaching 'notice-and-react' approach should be considered, depending on the facts of the case.[4]

[3] The CC considered the content and societal implications of 'self-determination in time', BVerfG, Nov. 7, 2019 *Right to be forgotten I*, docket number 1 BvR 16/13, para 108.

[4] On these appraoches Nadine Klass, 'Das Recht auf Vergessen(-werden) und die Zeitlichkeit der Freiheit', *Zeitschrift für Urheber- und Medienrecht* 2020, 265, 273.

The second case (*Right to be forgotten II*, 1 BvR 276/17) evolved around a TV broadcast that was uploaded to an online archive in 2010. In the broadcast entitled 'Dismissal: the dirty practices of employers', the complainant was identified by name and accused of unfair treatment of an employee, who was dismissed by her company. A search for the complainant's name on Google displayed the link to this broadcast among the top results – a situation that the complainant sought to change. In contrast to the above case, the complainant did not take legal action against the broadcaster but against the search engine operator, who refused to remove the broadcast from the search results. Here, the CC based its reasoning on EU fundamental rights as enshrined in the Charter. The CC emphasised that in this situation, three sets of rights need to be balanced: the complainant's right to private and family life and to the protection of personal data, pursuant to Articles 7 and 8 of the Charter; Google's freedom to conduct a business pursuant to Article 16 of the Charter; and the freedom of expression of the broadcasting corporation pursuant to Article 11 of the Charter as a directly affected fundamental right of a third party (see, on this aspect, section IV below). Based on the specific circumstances of the case, in particular the relatively short time that had passed since the broadcast was first published and the fact that the complainant had voluntarily contributed to it by agreeing to be interviewed, the CC concluded that the complainant's right did not have precedence over the other rights concerned.

Both cases are governed by EU legislation on data protection, currently the General Data Protection Regulation (GDPR). The cases differ with regard to the applicable EU law in one aspect: in the case *Right to be forgotten I*, the so-called media privilege applies. According to Article 85 of the GDPR, Member States shall reconcile the right to the protection of personal data with the right to freedom of expression and information, including processing of data for journalistic purposes. The CC said that where this provision is applicable – as in the case *Right to be forgotten I* – Member States are given leeway in how to reconcile the rights mentioned in Article 85 GDPR. In contrast, where this provision does not apply – as in the case *Right to be forgotten II* – the Member States do not have any leeway, ie the subject matter is fully harmonised by EU law. This distinction is crucial because, as I discuss in the following section of this chapter, the court creates different frameworks for the applicability of EU fundamental rights depending on whether the subject matter in the case is fully harmonised by EU law or not.

III. Distinguishing the Applicability of Domestic and EU Regulatory Regimes

Understanding why the CC has applied domestic fundamental rights to one of the cases on the right to be forgotten and European fundamental rights to the other requires a closer look at the new framework that the CC has established for the relationship between domestic and EU fundamental rights protection. This new framework has two components: EU fundamental rights as a standard of review; and the 'parallel' applicability of EU and domestic fundamental rights. I present both pillars of this jurisprudence below.[5]

Both pillars of this jurisprudence affect how German courts will in future distinguish between the applicability of the domestic and EU regulatory regimes. They have the potential to broaden the control by German courts, in particular by the CC, of how to manage this distinction. They also give more room to domestic law in the case of 'parallel applicability'. When applied to the right to be forgotten, this framework fosters a claim by Member States to 'digital sovereignty'.

A. EU Fundamental Rights as the Standard of Review

The first major innovation of this jurisprudence relates to the standard used by the CC in the context of its constitutional review. For the first time, the CC used the rights enshrined in the EU Fundamental Rights Charter as a standard for review. Previously, the CC had considered itself competent only to review whether domestic constitutional rights have been violated in a given case brought before it by way of a constitutional complaint. So far, the CC had repeatedly stated that

> it is inadmissible to challenge the violation of European Community law. Rights under Community law are not among the fundamental rights, or rights that are equivalent to fundamental rights, the violation of which can be challenged under Article 93.1 no. 4a of the Basic Law ...[6]

The Court now takes a different approach. In *Right to be forgotten II*, it reasons that based on its 'responsibility with regard to EU integration', the Court shall ensure that EU fundamental rights are guaranteed.[7] The notion of 'responsibility with regard to EU integration' is an established concept of German constitutional jurisprudence that the CC deduces from Article 23 of the Basic Law, a norm that addresses matters of Germany's participation in the EU. The CC reasons that, in light of this concept, German constitutional law has provided it with the mandate to engage in a review of EU fundamental rights because these rights are a part

[5] The remarks in this section (III.) are based on: Dana Burchardt, 'Backlash against the Court of Justice of the EU? The Recent Jurisprudence of the German Constitutional Court on EU Fundamental Rights as a Standard of Review' (2020) 21 *German Law Journal* 1–18, section B.

[6] BVerfG, 28 March 2006, docket number 1 BvR 1054/01, para 77. This decision has been rendered by the Second Senate of the CC, while the decision *Right to be forgotten II* is a decision of the First Senate. To avoid the perception of a conflict between the two senates (which also would have had procedural implications), the First Senate has gone to great length arguing that both approaches are in fact compatible (paras 87–93). The First Senate said: 'The treatment of corresponding constitutional complaints as inadmissible [by the Second Senate] was not based on an independent statement by this case law that fundamental Union rights were not applicable, but was merely a reflection of the inapplicability of the Basic Law' (para 89). It remains to be seen how the Second Senate will respond to this argumentation.

[7] BVerfG, 7 November 2019, *Right to be forgotten II*, docket number 1 BvR 276/17, paras 53, 67.

of European integration. The contention thus is that German constitutional law requires the CC to ensure the protection of *both* domestic and EU fundamental rights. In addition, the CC states that without using the Charter as review standard, the court would be less and less able to exercise its judicial function with regard to fundamental rights protection.[8] This is due to an increasing density of EU law in many subject matters and thus to a broadening applicability of EU fundamental rights.[9]

By adopting this new approach, the CC joins a number of other constitutional courts in the EU that have recently started to apply the EU Fundamental Rights Charter as a standard of review.[10] In contrast to these other courts, the German CC, however, takes a more restrictive approach, establishing a rather complex system of applicable review standards. The CC does not simply accept EU fundamental rights as a standard of review in situations in which EU fundamental rights are *applicable according to EU law*. Instead, the CC creates its own criteria for determining when EU fundamental rights are to be applied. The CC thus has taken control of how to manage the respective scopes of application. Furthermore, it reduces to a minimum the cases in which it uses EU fundamental rights as the standard of review and thus limits the applicability of the EU regulatory regime on the matter. In order to do so, the CC establishes a distinction between subject matters that are fully harmonised by EU law and subject matters in which Member States have leeway.

Concerning fully harmonised subject matters, the CC exclusively applies EU fundamental rights as the standard of review. As before, domestic fundamental rights have in general no role to play here (save for the existing jurisprudence on ultra vires and constitutional identity).[11] Using EU fundamental rights as the standard of review enables the CC to exercise jurisdiction in a field in which, at least in principle, it has not adjudicated since the *Solange II* decision of 1986.[12] However, in contrast to the pre-*Solange II* era, the CC will now use EU fundamental rights rather than domestic fundamental rights as the standard of review. This approach allows the CC to exercise some control on the interpretation of EU fundamental rights standards within the German legal order. Section III below illustrates this point further.

To determine whether, in a particular case, EU fundamental rights are used as the standard of review for the right to be forgotten, the CC refers to the GDPR as the determining factor. The CC uses EU fundamental rights to assess cases in which

[8] Ibid.

[9] CC, decision of 7 November 2019 (*Right to be forgotten II*), 1 BvR 276/17, para 60.

[10] Austrian Constitutional Court, 14 March 2012, docket number U 466/11-18, U 1836/11-13; Conseil constitutionnel, 26 July 2018, decision No 2018-768DC; Corte Costituzionale, 23 January 2019, docket number 20/2019. See also Conseil d'Etat [Belgium], 15 March 2018, docket number 29/2018.

[11] Eg BVerfG, 21 June 2016, *OMT*, docket number 2 BvR 2728/13; 15 December 2015, *Solange III/ European Arrest Warrant II*, docket number 2 BvR 2735/14.

[12] BVerfG, 22 October 1986, *Solange II*, docket number 2 BvR 197/83, para 132.

the GDPR provides for a full harmonisation of the subject matter. In practice, this means that in all cases in which the media privilege according to Article 85 of the GDPR is not applicable, the CC refers to Articles 7 and 8 of the Charter to adjudicate on the right to be forgotten. The specific consequences that follow from this approach for the protection of the right to be forgotten are addressed in section III below.

For subject matters beyond full harmonisation, the novel framework created by the CC is more multilayered. As I outline in the next section, EU fundamental rights can potentially be a standard of review in these cases – but their role is very limited. The CC gives as much space as possible to domestic fundamental rights.

B. 'Parallel' Applicability of EU and Domestic Fundamental Rights

The second novelty of the twin decisions is that the CC abandons its concept of an exclusive relationship between EU and domestic fundamental rights for situations beyond full harmonisation. Here, the CC's approach to distinguishing between the applicability of regulatory regimes has changed. While thus far the CC has considered that *either* EU *or* domestic fundamental rights are applicable to a case at hand,[13] it has now turned to recognising a parallel applicability of both sets of fundamental rights. However, this parallel applicability only relates to subject matters that are not fully harmonised by EU law. As highlighted above, the CC exclusively uses EU fundamental rights as the standard of review in situations of full harmonisation. In this regard, the exclusiveness approach of the CC with its clear-cut distinction between regulatory competences in fundamental rights matters is still alive. *Only beyond full harmonisation* has the CC changed its opinion on this issue. Both EU and domestic fundamental rights are now considered (at least prima facie) as standards of review by the CC.

In so far as the CC has turned to parallel applicability, the approach corresponds – at its basis – to the approach taken by the CJEU on the matter. In *Åkerberg Fransson*, the CJEU has accepted that in a 'situation where action of the Member States is not entirely determined by European Union law', EU and domestic fundamental rights standards can be applied at the same time.[14] The CC, however, does not simply adopt the jurisprudence of the CJEU on the matter. It creates its own framework on how the newly-recognised 'parallel applicability' should translate into practice. The CC thus takes control over the distinction between regulatory regimes.

Moreover, the new framework allows more room for the applicability of domestic law than of EU law, de facto strengthening the domestic regulatory competence.

[13] This approach has been prominent in the decision BVerfG, 24 April 2013, *Antiterrorism Legislation*, docket number 1 BvR 1215/07.

[14] CJEU, Case C-617/10, *Åklagaren v Hans Åkerberg Fransson*, ECLI:EU:C:2013:105, para 29.

Despite its label, the new 'parallel applicability' framework for situations beyond full harmonisation does not amount to the CC using in an equal and/or simultaneous manner EU and domestic fundamental rights as standards of review. Rather, in *Right to be forgotten I*, the CC establishes *domestic law as the primary standard of review*: in general, the CC will use domestic fundamental rights as the standard of review – and only exceptionally will it use EU fundamental rights.

This concept follows from a two-step argumentation. The starting point of this rationale is a novel presumption that the CC presents for the first time. This presumption has two elements. The first element serves as a justification for parallel applicability beyond full harmonisation. According to the CC, whenever EU law leaves leeway to the Member States for implementing the EU law provisions in question, it can be presumed that this leeway for implementation includes discretion with regard to fundamental rights protection.[15] That means that beyond full harmonisation, it is for the Member States to decide how and to what extent they protect fundamental rights. In this argumentation, the limits to parallel applicability as called for by the CJEU, ie primacy, unity and effectiveness of European Union law,[16] do not play a role. For the CC, wherever there is no full harmonisation, there is in principle room for domestic fundamental rights standards.

The second element of the presumption relates to the substantive level of fundamental rights protection. The CC claims that it can be presumed that domestic fundamental rights guarantee a level of protection equivalent to that required by the EU Charter of Fundamental Rights.[17] The reasoning is that even if domestic fundamental rights are used as the standard of review, their application also ensures – in substance – the Charter rights. Therefore, the CC states, domestic fundamental rights can be used as a primary standard of review. Their application does not undermine the level of protection required by the Charter.

For the right to be forgotten, this presumption means that whenever the media privilege according to Article 85 of the GDPR applies, there is leeway for Member States and thus domestic fundamental rights are the primary standard of review.

The presumption for domestic fundamental rights as the primary standard of review is rebuttable. If it is rebutted, the CC will use EU fundamental rights as the standard of review even in situations beyond full harmonisation.[18] However, the Court sets the bar for rebutting the presumption very high. Only 'in exceptional circumstances' will the CC in fact apply EU fundamental rights.[19] Two scenarios are possible for such a rebuttal: when there are 'specific and sufficient indications' that either (1) the ordinary EU legislation in the case contains stricter fundamental

[15] BVerfG, 7 November 2019, *Right to be forgotten I*, docket number 1 BvR 16/13, para 50.
[16] CJEU, Case C-617/10, *Åklagaren v Hans Åkerberg Fransson*, ECLI:EU:C:2013:105, para 29.
[17] BVerfG, 7 November 2019, *Right to be forgotten I*, docket number 1 BvR 16/13, para 55.
[18] BVerfG, 7 November 2019, *Right to be forgotten I*, docket number 1 BvR 16/13, paras 63, 72.
[19] Ibid at paras 63, 65, 67, 68, 72 (original '*ausnahmsweise*' – 'exceptionally').

rights requirements than if Member States were allowed to apply their domestic fundamental rights standards; or (2) the specific level of protection required by the Charter exceptionally does not correspond to domestic constitutional law. In order to establish the first scenario, the CC requires that the provisions of ordinary EU legislation determine a specific fundamental rights standard, explicitly expressing the wish of the EU legislator that this specific standard be applied by Member States as a harmonised standard. Notably, the Court clarifies that it does *not* consider it to be a sufficient indication when the EU legislator merely refers to certain provisions of the Charter in the recitals to a legal act.[20] This clarification shows that the CC is likely to be rather reluctant in recognising that the presumption for domestic law as a primary standard of review is rebutted. A similarly high bar seems to apply to the second scenario. Here, the CC considers the presumption – that domestic fundamental rights standards correspond to those required by the Charter – to be rebutted when it is evident from the jurisprudence of the CJEU that the CJEU regards certain Charter provisions as requiring specific standards that are not guaranteed by domestic fundamental rights law. For the CC, this is the case when the Charter contains guarantees that are not part of the domestic fundamental rights law.[21]

This overview shows that in situations beyond full harmonisation, the parallel applicability of EU and domestic fundamental rights amounts to a superior position for domestic fundamental rights in this area. They are the primary standard of review based on a presumption that can only be rebutted in very limited circumstances. In practice, the parallel applicability is thus likely to remain largely rhetorical.

For the right to be forgotten, situations in which the media privilege is applicable will continue to be governed by domestic fundamental rights as long as the presumption is not rebutted. The presumption could, for example, be rebutted if the EU legislator amended the GDPR in a way that it would contain specific requirements for the balancing of fundamental rights in the case of the media privilege, thereby expressing the wish of the EU legislator that the Member States apply a harmonised fundamental rights standard.

The CC's new framework for the applicability of domestic and European fundamental rights protection gives rise to various general concerns as to the relationship between domestic and EU law as well as to the relationship between the CJEU and the CC. I have addressed these issues elsewhere.[22] In the remainder of this chapter, I turn to the particular implications that the new framework has for the right to be forgotten.

[20] Ibid at para 68.

[21] Ibid at para 69.

[22] Dana Burchardt, 'Backlash against the Court of Justice of the EU? The Recent Jurisprudence of the German Constitutional Court on EU Fundamental Rights as a Standard of Review' (2020) 21 *German Law Journal* 1–18.

IV. The Implications of the New Framework for the Right to be Forgotten

The way in which the CC applies EU fundamental rights as a basis for the right to be forgotten and distinguishes the applicability of EU and domestic standards has two specific effects on the right to be forgotten. First, the CC shapes the right to be forgotten under EU law in a manner that risks diverging from the jurisprudence of the CJEU. The CC takes some control over the interpretation of the right to be forgotten *under EU law*, an approach that would support claims of 'digital sovereignty' of the Member States. So doing, the CC creates the risk of territorial fragmentation among Member States as to the protection of the right to be forgotten *under EU law*. Second, the CC's framework for distinguishing the applicability of EU and domestic fundamental rights can generate inconsistencies in how cases that are comparable in substance are treated. In this regard, the protection of the right to be forgotten might become incoherent. I outline both these aspects in turn.

A. Risk of Territorial Fragmentation of EU Fundamental Rights Standards

The way in which the CC applies EU fundamental rights as basis for the right to be forgotten can lead to diverging interpretations of this right as compared to the interpretation provided by the CJEU. If the CC takes a unilateral approach in developing the right to be forgotten without engaging in judicial dialogue with the CJEU, this can contribute to diverging standards on the matter *within EU law*. The previous judicial practice of the CC as well as the reasoning in the twin decisions of November 2019 show that the CC has in fact a tendency to decide unilaterally on matters related to EU law without involving the CJEU via preliminary reference.[23]

This adds to the risk of territorial fragmentation inherent in the regulation of the right to be forgotten. As discussed by other contributions in this volume, the intended territorial scope of remedies that implement the right to be forgotten can vary, for example if certain personal content is made unavailable for internet users in one state or group of states but not in others.[24] As a result of domestic jurisprudence such as the recent twin decisions by the CC, there is thus a dual risk of fragmentation: concerning the reach of the remedy; and concerning the substantive standards to be applied to a case.

The decision in *Right to Be Forgotten II* illustrates the risk of diverging standards. One of the key issues discussed in the proceedings was whether, according to the

[23] For rare examples of preliminary references by the CC see BVerfG, Order of the Second Senate of 14 January 2014–2 BvR 2728/13; BVerfG, Order of the Second Senate of 18 July 2017–2 BvR 859/15.

[24] On the territorial scope of remedies: CJEU, *Google Inc v Commission nationale de l'informatique et des libertés (CNIL)*, C-507/17, judgment of 24 September 2019, ECLI:EU:C:2019:772.

CJEU decision in *Google Spain*, the right to be forgotten generally prevails over other interests concerned. This discussion refers to the CJEU's statement that

> inasmuch as the removal of links from the list of results could, depending on the information at issue, have effects upon the legitimate interest of internet users potentially interested in having access to that information, in situations such as that at issue in the main proceedings a fair balance should be sought in particular between that interest and the data subject's fundamental rights under Articles 7 and 8 of the Charter. Whilst it is true that the data subject's rights protected by those articles also *override, as a general rule*, that interest of internet users, that balance may however depend, in specific cases, on the nature of the information in question and its sensitivity for the data subject's private life and on the interest of the public in having that information, an interest which may vary, in particular, according to the role played by the data subject in public life (emphasis added).[25]

The German government, who participated in the proceedings before the CC, argued that *Google Spain v AEPD* established a general prevalence of the right to be forgotten; Google, as the respondent, contested that view. This disagreement reflects a general debate about the substance of this jurisprudence. Legal scholars have broadly discussed the implications of this formulation by the CJEU.[26] The CJEU has repeated this formulation in its decision *GC et al v CNIL*[27] and similarly in *Google Inc v CNIL*.[28]

The German CC, however, did not consider these diverging readings as a sufficient reason to involve the CJEU via a preliminary reference procedure in order to give the Court an opportunity to clarify its jurisprudence on the matter. Rather, the CC proclaimed its own reading of *Google Spain*, presenting it as necessary result of the general jurisprudence of the CJEU on fundamental rights matters. The CC stated that:

> in the present case, it cannot be presumed that protecting the right of personality takes precedence; rather the conflicting fundamental rights must be balanced on an equal basis […]

[25] CJEU, *Google Spain v Agencia Espanola de Proteccion de Datos (AEPD)*, C-131/12, judgment of 13 May 2014, EU:C:2014:317, para 81.

[26] See eg Emmanouil Bougiakiotis, 'The enforcement of the Google Spain Ruling' (2016) 24 *International Journal of Law and Information Technology* 311, 314–15; Herke Kranenborg, 'Google and the Right to Be Forgotten'(2015) (1) *European Data Protection Law Review* 70, 78; Stefan Kulk and Frederik Zuiderveen Borgesius, 'Freedom of Expression and 'Right to Be Forgotten' Cases in the Netherlands After Google Spain, EDPL' (2015) (2) *European Data Protection Law Review* 113, 116–17; Mistale Taylor, 'Google Spain Revisited: The Misunderstood Implementation of a Landmark Decision and How Public International Law Could Offer Guidance' (2017) 3(2) *European Data Protection Law Review* 195, 197; Eleni Frantziou, 'Further Developments in the Right to Be Forgotten: The European Court of Justice's Judgment in Case C-131/12, *Google Spain, SL, Google Inc v Agencia Espanola de Proteccion de Datos*' (2014) 14 *Human Rights Law Review* 761, 766; Gerald Spindler, 'Durchbruch für ein Recht auf Vergessen(werden)?' (2014) *JuristenZeitung* 981, 986.

[27] CJEU, *GC et al v CNIL*, C-136/17, judgment of 24 September 2019, ECLI:EU:C:2019:773, para 53.

[28] CJEU, *Google Inc v CNIL*, C-507/17, judgment of 24 September 2019, ECLI:EU:C:2019:772, para 45.

> It was not necessary to request a preliminary ruling from the CJEU regarding the aspect that, in the present constellation – in contrast to those decisions (see CJEU, judgment of 13 May 2014, *Google Spain*, C-131/12, EU:C:2014:317, para. 81; judgment of 24 September 2019, *GC et al*, C-136/17, EU:C:2019:773, paras. 53 and 66) – it cannot be presumed that protecting the right of personality takes precedence. This presumption was also determined by the specific constellation of those proceedings. In *Google Spain*, the freedom of expression of the content providers concerned was not to be taken into account because it was an announcement of a public authority (see ECJ, judgment of 13 May 2014, C-131/12, EU:C:2014:317, paras. 14, 16) […] In contrast, there is no indication either in the Charter of Fundamental Rights itself or in the jurisprudence of the Court of Justice of the European Union suggesting that, when balancing the right of personality and the freedom of expression, both rights are not on an equal basis. On the contrary, it can be inferred from the jurisprudence of the Court of Justice of the European Union that the court incorporates the freedom of expression, where relevant, into the assessment and that it does not consider this freedom to have a lower rank than other fundamental rights.[29]

The fact that the CC chose to decide without involving the CJEU on a controversial matter shows that, despite its own rhetoric, the CC is reluctant to engage in judicial dialogue in order to realise the CJEU's monopoly on interpretation of EU law.[30] This bears the risk that the CC, while deciding on the right to be forgotten under EU law, develops its own particular standard for this concept. Such a development would lead to the CC taking some degree of control over the interpretation of the right to be forgotten under EU law. In such a case, domestic regulatory competence on the matter (by domestic courts) would be strengthened.

A further aspect of the decision in *Right to Be Forgotten II* corroborates the impression that the CC adopts its own interpretation of the right to be forgotten under EU law. This aspect relates to the fact that the CJEU balances the right to be forgotten against other *interests* such as the 'economic interest' of the search engine and the 'interest of internet users potentially interested in having access to that information'.[31] The CC takes a different approach. It balances the right to be forgotten against other 'rights' rather than against mere 'interests'.[32] These rights not only include the right of the search engine operator to conduct a business, under Article 16 of the Charter, but also the right to freedom of expression, under Article 11 of the Charter as a directly affected fundamental right of a third party.

[29] BVerfG, 7 November 2019, *Right to be forgotten II*, docket number 1 BvR 276/17, paras 121, 141 – author's informal translation.

[30] On the rhetoric of the CC, see BVerfG, 7 November 2019, *Right to be forgotten II*, docket number 1 BvR 276/17, para 70.

[31] CJEU, *Google Spain v AEPD*, C-131/12, judgment of 13 May 2014, EU:C:2014:317, para 81.

[32] Critical about the use of the term interest rather than rights in the jurisprudence of the CJEU, are Eleni Frantziou, 'Further Developments in the Right to Be Forgotten: The European Court of Justice's Judgment in Case C-131/12, *Google Spain, SL, Google Inc v Agencia Espanola de Proteccion de Datos*' (2014) 14 *Human Rights Law Review* 761, 768–69; Stefan Kulk and Frederik Zuiderveen Borgesius, 'Freedom of Expression and "Right to Be Forgotten" Cases in the Netherlands After Google Spain' (2015) *European Data Protection Law Review* 113, 116.

This is an important difference between the approach of the CJEU and the CC. The CC explicitly highlights this difference. It states that

> the fundamental rights of the content providers whose publication is at stake must also be taken into account when balancing the rights of the affected person and the rights of search engine operators [...]
>
> The balancing must take into account the freedom of expression on the part of the content provider as a directly affected fundamental right of third parties – and not merely as an interest to be considered – which would be negatively impacted by the prohibition sought by the complainant.[33]

The CC is aware that formally including the right to freedom of expression is a step that is not part of the jurisprudence of the CJEU on the right to be forgotten against search engines. While the CC extensively cites CJEU decisions to support other aspects (such as the inapplicability of the media privilege to search engines; and user interests being balanced against the right to be forgotten) in the paragraphs before and after the paragraph that mentions the rights of the content provider, it does *not* cite CJEU jurisprudence with regard to the relevance of the right to freedom of expression.[34] This demonstrates the diverging approaches as well as the fact that the CC unilaterally develops the EU law framework of the right to be forgotten, ie without including the CJEU in this process via preliminary reference. Here, the CC takes some control over the interpretation of the right to be forgotten under EU law, accepting that this might lead to a fragmented interpretation of EU law standards within the EU.

B. Risk of Inconsistencies between Domestic and European Standards

The second effect of this new jurisprudence results from the fact that diverging domestic and European standards are applied to what are, in substance, very similar cases. There is a risk of inconsistencies in how such cases are treated. Such an inconsistency follows for the right to be forgotten from the formalistic criterion that the CC uses to distinguish between the applicability of EU law and domestic law. The standard for the right to be forgotten differs merely because of a formal criterion (applicability of Article 85 of the GDPR). Substantively, this differentiation seems artificial – but the CC does not consider the structural implication of its differentiation. Depending on whether the claimant acts against the content provider (if the content provider is part of the media) or the search engine operator, domestic or European fundamental rights are applicable. This is the case – and

[33] BVerfG, 7 November 2019, *Right to be forgotten II*, docket number 1 BvR 276/17, paras 106, 121 – author's informal translation.

[34] BVerfG, 7 November 2019, *Right to be forgotten II*, docket number 1 BvR 276/17, paras 106–109.

here lies the issue – even though the relationship between the claimant and the content provider plays a direct role in the claim *against the search engine* as well. Both in a case against a content provider and against a search engine, the right to freedom of expression is balanced against the right to be forgotten (see above). Both situations are thus not substantively different in nature – instead, they overlap. Although the media privilege is not directly applicable in the scenario against the search engine, its underlying rationale – the protection of the freedom of expression – is relevant here as well. Using different standards for balancing the freedom of expression and the right to be forgotten therefore seems inconsistent.

This is even more so when, as in *Right to Be Forgotten I*, the remedy for a claim against the content provider is de facto the same as against the search engine. In *Right to Be Forgotten I*, the remedy considered by the CC was that the content provider could take technical steps so that the content on its website was not searchable via a general search engine anymore (while still being available by accessing the website directly).[35] This means that in this case, the remedy against the search engine and the remedy against the content provider could be functionally equivalent. In both cases, the remedy concerns the searchability of a result by general search engines. Considering such a potential equivalence of remedy and the substantive overlap regarding the rights concerned, it seems difficult to justify why the CC, as a result of its formalistic approach, applies different legal standards to these cases.

Admittedly, the CC refers with this distinction to a regulation by the EU legislator. The GDPR *does* give leeway to the Member States when legislating for the media context. In principle, there would thus be room for the application of domestic fundamental rights even according to the jurisprudence of the CJEU (see above). However, in contrast to the CC, the CJEU's approach takes into account the structural implications of applying domestic fundamental rights in a specific case (such as implications for primacy, unity and effectiveness of EU law). The CC's formalistic approach does not do so. It does not consider that by applying different fundamental rights standards in the specific case of the right to be forgotten, structural inconsistencies emerge. For the protection of the right to be forgotten, considering such structural implications would have been beneficial. What is more, some might even argue that the current inconsistencies run counter to the effectiveness of EU law in this context, thus requiring the general application of EU standards to the right to be forgotten.

But are the standards under EU and domestic law really different? When comparing the domestic and the European standards of fundamental rights protection that are relevant to determining the right to be forgotten, a preliminary glance at the relevant provisions *could* convey the impression that there is no considerable difference between these standards. In EU law, the right to be forgotten is an expression of the rights to private life and data protection, which

[35] BVerfG, 7 November 2019, *Right to be forgotten I*, docket number 1 BvR 16/13, paras 139, 153.

are enshrined in Articles 7 and 8 of the Charter. In the German legal order, the right to be forgotten is based on the general right of personality, which includes the rights to private life and data protection. Although the general right to personality is not explicitly phrased as such in the German Basic Law, it is established in the jurisprudence of the CC as being part of constitutionally protected rights. Both in the European and the domestic legal framework, the right to be forgotten has a constitutional backing.

However, the differences become apparent when these constitutional rights are applied in practice. Using domestic law as the standard for the right to be forgotten means that the whole systematisation of domestic fundamental rights jurisprudence (*Grundrechtsdogmatik*) is applicable as well. For example, the general right of personality which includes the right to be forgotten is, according to the CC, based on the protection of human dignity and the general freedom of action (Articles 1(1) and 2(1) of the German Basic Law). As a result of this link to human dignity, the CC recognises that the general right to personality, although not being an absolute right as such, has an absolute core which prevails over other conflicting rights. This is due to the predominant status that human dignity has in German constitutional law. It translates, according to the established jurisprudence of the CC, into a three-pronged model of the general right of personality. This right is composed of a protection of the 'social sphere' (*Sozialsphäre*), the 'private sphere' (*Privatsphäre*) and the 'personal sphere' (*Intimsphäre*). The level of protection differs according to the sphere concerned. The personal sphere enjoys the highest protection due to its high human dignity relevance. The German CC applies this specific systematisation of the spheres to the right to be forgotten.[36]

In contrast, the right to be forgotten under EU law does not have this direct and explicit formal link to human dignity. It is based on Articles 7 and 8 of the Charter which, although they relate to human dignity as an underlying value, are not formally referred to in combination with Article 1 of the Charter. The role for human dignity is thus not the same. As a result, EU law and domestic law provide diverging foundations for the right to be forgotten.

In addition to a specific understanding of the right(s) on which the right to be forgotten is founded, the general notions of fundamental rights jurisprudence can create differences between the domestic and the European standards of protection. For example, the CC has developed a specific approach to multipolar fundamental rights constellations which determines how to balance the rights of several right-bearers with opposing contents. For the situation in which the right to be forgotten is claimed against a search engine, this understanding of multipolar fundamental rights constellations is particularly relevant. As I have described above, the CC considers this situation to be of a multipolar nature, involving the rights of the claimant, the search engine operator and the content provider. Such multipolar

[36] BVerfG, 7 November 2019, *Right to be forgotten I*, docket number 1 BvR 16/13, para 121; BVerfG, 7 November 2019, *Right to be forgotten II*, docket number 1 BvR 276/17, para 128.

rights constellations require legal justification of a limitation of any of these rights. For example, a court would need to justify that, in a certain case, the content provider's right to freedom of expression is constrained when the court orders the search engine not to list the content provider's content anymore.[37] Such a formal justification would not be necessary if, in a claim against the search engine, one factors in the content provider's *interests* rather than their *rights*. Considering such constellations as multipolar rights constellations makes it conceptually more difficult for the right to be forgotten to prevail.

In addition to these conceptual differences, the fact that any case involving the right to be forgotten requires the court to *balance* rights opens the door for further divergences between domestic and EU standards. Depending on how the CJEU and domestic courts use balancing to shape this relationship between rights, various practical aspects of the protection of the right to be forgotten could potentially differ. This could, for example, concern the issue of whether and to what extent individuals enjoy a lower level of protection of their right to be forgotten if they have consented or contributed to the media report against which they later try to defend themselves. According to the CC, giving an interview, as the complainant has done in *Right to Be Forgotten II*, and criminal behaviour which triggers media coverage, as in *Right to Be Forgotten I*, are examples of such behaviour that diminished the level of protection. With regard to such practical aspects, future decisions will show whether the CJEU and the CC take similar or diverging approaches.

This shows that the formalistic way in which the CC distinguishes between the applicability of regulatory regimes can have repercussions on the substantive protection of fundamental rights. For the right to be forgotten, the new framework leads to conceptual inconsistencies. Using the criterion of full harmonisation by EU secondary law, which, for the right to be forgotten, translates into the criterion 'applicability of the media privilege', creates an artificial distinction between these two constellations of the right to be forgotten which does not reflect the similarities and overlaps between the constellations. These conceptual issues add to the general doubts as to the practicability of the CC's new framework.[38]

In sum, the applicability of EU law or domestic law to different constellations of the right to be forgotten can go in two directions. It could lead to increasingly diverging standards depending on whether, in a certain case, EU or domestic law is the basis for the right to be forgotten. It is questionable whether such differences between constellations are justified. Alternatively, EU and domestic standards could develop in a concurrent manner until they virtually meet in substance. While this would reduce inconsistencies between different constellations, the risk is that fragmentation will occur on the EU level. If a domestic court such as the CC interprets EU law unilaterally to create coherence with the domestic framework,

[37] BVerfG, 7 November 2019, *Right to be forgotten II*, docket number 1 BvR 276/17, para 107.

[38] Further doubts concern, for example, the question as to whether it will be always possible to clearly distinguish between fully harmonised and not fully harmonised subject matters, see Matthias Wendel, 'Das Bundesverfassungsgericht als Garant der Unionsgrundrechte' (2020) 75 *JuristenZeitung* 157, 164.

diverging understandings of the European standard of the right to be forgotten would emerge among various courts and the CJEU's monopoly on interpretation would be undermined. This shows that either way, the CC's new framework for the right to be forgotten raises both conceptual and practical concerns.

V. Conclusion

The jurisprudence discussed above on the right to be forgotten shows the far-reaching impact of determining 'who regulates what?'. When various governing bodies claim regulatory competence over a particular subject matter, the distinction between the respective regulatory regimes becomes much more than a legal technicality. This is particularly the case when the challenges of regulating the digital sphere are added to the challenges of a complex multi-level governance structure such as the EU. Here, the implications are manifold: they concern the control that domestic or EU courts have over shaping the right to be forgotten, the uniform application of EU law versus the risk of fragmentation of the protection of the right to be forgotten under EU law, and the questionable consistency of using diverging domestic and EU standards for similar cases. Against this backdrop, it remains to be seen how the CC will further translate its new framework into practice: whether it will do so in a way that would corroborate claims to 'digital sovereignty' or not.

6

Data Protection and Freedom of Expression Beyond EU Borders: EU Judicial Perspectives

ORESTE POLLICINO

I. Introduction

In the information society, European law has extended its influence to global dynamics.[1] The rights to privacy and data protection are paradigmatic examples of extending fundamental rights protection beyond EU borders. To fully understand this tendency, it is necessary to develop some premises regarding the dynamic force of the European fundamental rights to data protection and privacy in the digital world and the cleavage between the European vision and the US version of the right to privacy online and data protection.

Firstly, if it is true that the milestone in the reconstruction of the birth and evolution of the protection of privacy and personal data is its theorisation by Warren and Brandeis,[2] it is also certain that, compared to the US legal system, in Europe, the protection of personal data and digital privacy has acquired the status of a fundamental right.[3] This fundamental right assumes the nature of a 'super' fundamental right, which seems to not find any limits in the territorial dimension of the EU, following EU residents even in the data processing outside the EU territory, as well as in the balancing process between fundamental rights.[4]

[1] Anu Bradford, *The Brussels Effect: How the European Union Rules the World* (Oxford University Press, 2020).

[2] Samuel D Warren and Louis D Brandeis, 'The Right to Privacy' (1890) 4 *Harvard Law Review* 193.

[3] In the ECHR system, see: *S and Marper v United Kingdom*, Application nos 30562/04 and 30566/04, (2008) 48 EHRR 50. In the EU system, see: Joined cases C-92/09 and C-93/09 *Volker und Markus Schecke GbR v Land Hessen* and *Hartmut Eifert v Land Hessen* [2010] ECR I-11063.

[4] In the 'data privacy-oriented' case law of the European Court of Justice, the status of protection of data privacy as a 'super' fundamental right could be confirmed by the lack of any references to freedom of information in the reasoning of the Court, which does not even mention Article 11 (freedom of expression) in its judgments. A few more times it cited the economic freedoms, but even this balance has soon disappeared.

This evolution started in the second half of the twentieth century in the European Convention on Human Rights (ECHR) system, when the right to privacy was codified, looking at it as a sort of habeas corpus concerning one person's spatial and relational projections.[5] As in the US, in the European constitutional framework too, the recognition and codification of the right to privacy were originally made along 'negative' lines; that is the recognition of the right to have their own private life respected. Indeed, the right to privacy was conceived as a liberty against the interference of public actors in the individual's private life.

However, in the subsequent decades, this right underwent a deep transformation. Because of an acceleration of technology, a 'positive' dimension of the right to the protection of personal data has enriched the 'negative' dimension, typical of the right to privacy. This widening of the protection of personal data has marked the expansion of a right initially limited to the 'negative' dimension of such a liberty (ie the right to be left alone).[6] In this scenario, the role played by the European Court of Human Rights (ECtHR) has been relevant when facing some technological changes and the challenges of online data processing.[7]

Against this background, the institutions of the then European Community were slower to codify a right to data protection or digital privacy, due to their original economical inspiration. For a long time, in the legal system of the European Union, individual rights were recognised almost exclusively in order to ensure economic fundamental freedoms: as a consequence, in this context, it was difficult to make the protection of personal data a matter that could capture the attention of the European institutions for its direct impact on some fundamental right.

The breaking point was the adoption of Directive 95/46, the so-called Data Protection Directive, even if an economic dimension inspired it. This Directive was the first legal instrument in the EU legal system that promoted the harmonisation of privacy and data protection rules, and established both some general principles concerning the processing of personal data and special rules based on specific and particular processing.

In this scenario, the embryonic fundamental right to personal data protection and digital privacy started to acquire a concrete shape. Actually, the recognition and 'constitutionalisation' of this right was closely connected to the evolution of the European Union's identity. This has perhaps been an additional reason for

[5] The first document that at the European level incorporated the right to privacy was Article 8 of European Convention on Human Rights of 1950.

[6] The first step was the Convention on the Protection of Individuals with regard to Automatic Processing of Personal Data, the so-called Convention no 108/1981. Finally, in 1987, the European Court of Human Rights clarified that the collection and processing of personal data must be included within the scope of Article 8 ECHR (*Leander v Sweden*, Application no 9248/81, (1987) 9 EHRR 433). See also *Amann v Switzerland*, Application no 27798/95, (2000) 30 EHRR 843; *S and Marper v United Kingdom* (n 3 above); *MM v United Kingdom*, Application no 24029, [2012] ECHR 1906.

[7] In 2007, the web was formally included in the scope of application of Article 8 ECHR: *Copland v UK*, Application no 62617/00, (2007) 45 EHRR 37. See also, more recently: *Węgrzynowski and Smolczewski v Poland*, Application no 33846/07, [2013] ECHR 690 and *Bărbulescu v Romania*, Application no 61496/08, [2017] ECHR 742.

the creation and consolidation of this 'super' fundamental right. The right to the protection of personal data and digital privacy was finally codified in the Charter of Fundamental Rights of the European Union (EU Charter) and enshrined in Article 16 of the Treaty on the Functioning of the European Union (TFEU), which provides the legal basis for the adoption of a new regulatory framework for the processing of personal data. Specifically, the EU Charter devotes two provisions to the matter; namely, Article 7, concerning the respect for private life and family life, and Article 8, regarding the protection of personal data.[8]

Secondly, it is clear that the right to privacy, designated by Warren and Brandeis as the right to be left alone, experienced a process of migration from the US to Europe, progressively acquiring a dimension that does not exclusively protect the individual's expectation of privacy, but which sees in the definition of a system of principles and rules for data protection a further essential momentum to protect the individual personality. The European system created a *unicum*, an innovative and pervasive right to data protection that has transfigured the Internet environment and has deeply influenced other legal systems, generating a new migration of this right.[9] However, this migration was preceded by a very pervasive case law of the European Court of Justice (ECJ) oriented toward applying the European vision of the right to digital privacy on the Internet – or, better, on every hosting provider operating in Europe – and then was followed by European laws, above all the GDPR.[10] From this perspective, while the EU fundamental right to data protection and digital privacy was wrapping its tentacles around the Internet, guaranteeing to the EU citizens the protection of their European rights in the digital world, the US system was stuck in the quicksand of the definition of the right to privacy, granting a right to data protection only in some specific fields.[11] Additionally, it has to be stressed that, in the US, the main role in protecting users' data was played at the federal level by the Federal Trade Commission (FTC),[12] and not by the US Supreme Court.[13]

[8] Despite the attempt in the Explanatory Notes to the Charter to restrict the purpose of this provision to a mere reproduction of the existing *acquis* (see Explanations regarding Article 8 of the Charter), the contribution of Article 8 is quite significant. Not only has this provision supplied the right to data protection with constitutional status, but it also definitively emancipated the right from its connection to the economic dimension that characterised, at least at the outset, the Directive 95/46. See: *Volker und Markus Schecke* (n 3 above). For more details see section II of this chapter.

[9] Krystyna Kowalik-Bańczyk and Oreste Pollicino, 'Migration of European Judicial Ideas Concerning Jurisdiction Over Google on Withdrawal of Information' (2015) 17 *German Law Journal* 315.

[10] DJB Svantesson, 'European Union Claims of Jurisdiction over the Internet – An Analysis of Three Recent Key Developments' (2018) 9 *Journal of Intellectual Property, Information Technology and Electronic Commerce Law (JIPITEC)* 112.

[11] Francesca Bignami and Giorgio Resta, 'Transatlantic Privacy Regulation: Conflict and Cooperation' (2015) 8 *Law & Contemporary Problems* 231. On the 'third party doctrine' and the general idea of privacy in the US, see Daniel J Solove, 'Fourth Amendment Pragmatism' (2010) 51 *Boston College Law Review* 1511.

[12] Woodrow Hartzog and Daniel J Solove, 'The Scope and Potential of FTC Data Protection' (2015) 83 *George Washington Law Review* 2230.

[13] See, however, *Carpenter v United States*, No 16-402, 585 US (2018).

In this scenario, we witness a clash between the US and European perspectives. While the EU has adopted secondary legislation (mainly the General Data Protection Regulation) to protect this new fundamental right to privacy and data protection, and has accordingly regulated the Internet, the US system has not prepared a general regulation, consequently feeling the pressure of the European rules. Moreover, it has to be underlined how many of the Internet companies are based in the US and how they are deeply influenced by European rules, since the European market is one of the most important for Internet companies.[14] It is above all in relation to the US-based giants of the Web – in particular, Facebook and Google – that an extraterritorial scope of EU law takes shape.[15]

If it is true that this phenomenon does not concern only the US, it should be remembered that the three main actors in regulating the Web are the EU, the US and China.[16] While China is less connected with the other two systems in terms of cross-border data flow, the US system seems to be the most embroiled in the struggle for data protection online,[17] as also confirmed by the recent decision in *Schrems II*.[18] From this perspective, the issue of the 'Europeanisation' of data protection appears a very central topic that contains a challenge to the digital sovereignty of third countries.[19]

In the field of privacy, the two aforementioned elements – the new fundamental right to digital privacy and data protection in the EU and the difference in regulations (and balance of fundamental rights) between the EU and the US – have indeed generated the phenomenon called 'Europeanisation' of data protection online, which involves the potential application of EU law beyond the borders of the EU territory.

To analyse the issue of the extraterritorial scope of EU law in the data protection field and beyond, this chapter will focus on the case law of the ECJ. Indeed, the General Data Protection Regulation (GDPR) is the heir of a set of cases decided by the ECJ over the past few years, and the same Court seems to be the main actor in widening the scope of EU law. From this perspective, digital privacy is probably the best case study for analysing the European 'imperialism' on the Internet, but it is not the only one: the second part of this chapter will show how the EU approach

[14] Cf Daniel J Solove, *Understanding Privacy* (Harvard University Press, 2008), 2–6.

[15] Kimberly A Houser and W Gregory Voss, 'GDPR: The End of Google and Facebook Or a New Paradigm in Data Privacy' (2018) 25 *Richmond Journal of Law & Technology* 1.

[16] Nicholas F Palmieri III, 'Data Protection in an Increasingly Globalized World' (2019) 94 *Indiana Law Journal* 297. About the influence see also: Griffin Drake, 'Navigating the Atlantic: Understanding EU Data Privacy Compliance Amidst a Sea of Uncertainty' (2017) 91 *Southern California Law Review* 163, 175–76.

[17] Cf Paul M Schwartz, 'The EU-U.S. Privacy Collision: A Turn to Institutions and Procedures' (2013) 126 *Harvard Law Review* 1966.

[18] Case C-311/18 *Data Protection Commissioner v Facebook Ireland Limited and Maximillian Schrems*, ECLI:EU:C:2020:559.

[19] The expression has been used both to describe the internal phenomenon of harmonisation and centralisation of data protection (Orla Lynskey, 'The "Europeanisation" of Data Protection Law' (2017) 19 *Cambridge Yearbook of European Law Studies* 252). I will use this expression to underline the tendency to widen the territorial scope of the EU Law.

to digital privacy seems to be embraced by the ECJ also in the free speech field, inaugurating new trends in the conflict between different digital sovereignties on the Web.

Against this background, this chapter aims to investigate the extraterritorial effect of EU law by looking at the case law of the ECJ, and how the balancing process of rights developed by the Court is impacting on third countries' digital sovereignty. In order to develop these considerations, section II will analyse the legal framework of the extraterritorial effect of EU law in the ECJ's case law concerning privacy, while section III will explore the most recent trends in the jurisprudence of the Court, focusing on the decisions *Google v CNIL* and *Glawischnig-Piesczek v Facebook*, and trying to understand if in the framework of EU policies this last decision could herald a new field in which digital imperialism could take shape. Finally, the conclusion will recap some considerations about the ECJ's position concerning the extraterritorial effect of EU law and some possible new trends.

II. The ECJ's Case Law On Digital Privacy and Digital Sovereignty

First of all, to get a better understanding of the ECJ's approach when it comes to new technologies and extraterritoriality, it is worth focusing on the decision invalidating Directive 2006/24/EC (Data Retention Directive). Specifically, the *Digital Rights Ireland* case is a leading example showing the degree of protection that under the EU Charter is guaranteed to the right to respect private life and the protection of personal data.[20]

In this scenario, the European judges did not pass up the chance to invalidate, for the first time in the history of the European integration process, an act of secondary law as a result of its inconsistency with the EU Charter. The Data Retention Directive required national authorities to obtain very intrusive and delicate information about many aspects of the private life of users of telecommunications service providers.

There is no doubt that *Digital Rights Ireland* is about territorial use of data. Despite the alleged new 'digital' dimension of privacy, the physical 'atomic' infrastructure becomes, in the words of ECJ, a crucial criterion to assess the validity of the Data Retention Directive. In other words, there is a shift, which could sound

[20] Joined cases C-293/12 and C-594/12 *Digital Rights Ireland Ltd v Minister for Communications, Marine and Natural Resources and Others* (C-293/12) and *Kärntner Landesregierung and Others* (C-594/12), ECLI:EU:C:2014:238. On the retention of data, see also C-203/15 *Tele2 Sverige AB v Post- och telestyrelsen and Secretary of State for the Home Department v Tom Watson and Others*, ECLI:EU:C:2016:970; Joined Cases C-511/18, C-512/18 and C-520/18 *La Quadrature du Net and Others v Premier ministre and Others*, Opinion of AG Campos Sánchez-Bordona delivered 15 January 2020.

paradoxical in the digital arena, from law to geography. Territory and sovereignty still matter in the digital world. Even if *Digital Rights Ireland* involves a 'territorial use' of data, however, the decision sets up the legal basis of the centripetal force of the EU right to data protection. Indeed, what is really important to stress about this decision is the high standard of the EU system in protecting fundamental rights of privacy and data protection and the beginning of a reconstruction of the 'super' right to digital privacy. Additionally, the last innovative aspect of the decision is the use of the principle of proportionality. From this perspective, it could also be highlighted that by referring to the principle of proportionality as a 'separate' element of the balancing process, the Court had the opportunity both to find new 'infringements' of the 'super' right to privacy online and to limit that right in order not to infringe the digital sovereignty of third states.

The second decision to take into account is the famous *Google Spain* judgment.[21] In this case, the ECJ interpreted the relevant parameters, aiming, in particular, to give the widest possible protection to the rights to privacy and data protection. In this case, the applicant appealed for the removal from the Google search results of a piece of news published online by a legal bulletin relating to a proceeding implicating him which had happened many years before. Against this background, the US search engine rejected the request, pointing out that a US-based company was not subject to EU law.

This was the first clash between the US and European legal approaches to privacy and data protection. The point of view expressed by Google was deeply influenced by the US paradigm of fundamental rights. Indeed, according to the US-based search engine operator, an injunction like that proposed under Spanish law would have most likely restricted the freedom of expression of the website owners. This viewpoint was founded both on the idea that search engines enjoy an autonomous right to free speech and on the different approach to the protection of data in the US legal system.

The core of the case was – as stressed by Advocate General Jääskinen – the possible application of the individual's right to be forgotten against the Internet search engine services providers.[22] Taking into consideration the balancing process developed by the ECJ judges, it should be stressed that the Court claimed the existence of the right to be forgotten by providing it with some (maybe improper) legal bases. In the balancing process, the Court sacrificed the freedom of information, contradicting AG Jääskinen's Opinion that had ranked freedom of expression and information as 'primary rights'. In doing so, the ECJ denied the right to free speech of search engine operators or web owners,[23] but above all, considered that a US-based company is subject to EU law as long as it operates in the EU. In this

[21] Case C-131/12, *Google Spain SL, Google Inc v Agencia Española de Protección de Datos (AEPD) and Mario Costeja González*, ECLI:EU:C:2014:317.

[22] Opinion of Advocate General Jääskinen, delivered on 25 June 2013. *Google Spain SL and Google Inc v Agencia Española de Protección de Datos (AEPD) and Mario Costeja González*, ECLI:EU:C:2013:424.

[23] One of the most evident anomalies in the reasoning of the Court is the lack of mention of Article 11 and Article 16 of the Charter, which respectively protect freedom of expression and information and freedom to conduct business.

case, it is evident how the extreme degree of protection granted to personal data on the Internet under Articles 7 and 8 of the EU Charter involved the risk of an excess of 'Europeanisation' of Internet regulation.

In the *Google Spain* case, the ECJ considered EU law to be applicable when the data of EU residents are affected, regardless of the place where the servers on which the processing of personal data is carried out are located. This is due to the broad interpretation given to the expression 'context of the activities' of an establishment pursuant to the Data Protection Directive, which allows the ECJ to apply a criterion very similar to the current Article 3(2) GDPR ('Territorial scope'). In this way, the Court created an *ante litteram* extraterritorial protection of the European right to data protection on the Internet. *Google Spain* was the first complete attempt to build a fortress for the protection of personal data of individuals residing in the Old Continent. This fortress was founded on two pillars: European law and the EU 'territory'. The digital 'territory' seems to be the most critical point of this reconstruction: the transnational nature of the Internet appears to be irreconcilable with the attempts to regionalise the protection of data in the online environment.

The third important step in what one can view as a sort of EU 'imperialism' is the *Schrems* decision.[24] In this very famous case, the Court invalidated the so-called Safe Harbour agreement, consisting of the authorisation by the Commission to transfer personal data to the United States. This decision forced the EU and the US to renegotiate the conditions for effective protection of personal data. Looking at the decision of the Court, it can be underlined that, following the approach adopted in *Digital Rights Ireland* and *Google Spain*, the ECJ tried to extend the protection of personal data online up to hilt. The premise of this action is the nature of fundamental right of data protection and privacy. In this sense, the ECJ analysed and reviewed the consistency of the conditions of the Commission's Decision 2000/520 with the 'adequate' level of protection for personal data to be transferred to third countries required by Article 25 of the Data Protection Directive. Thus, the ECJ reviewed whether the US legal system and the Safe Harbour principles guaranteed 'an adequate level of protection' of personal data of European residents. In undertaking this review, the Court applied a fundamental rights-based assessment, looking at Articles 7 and 8 of the EU Charter. In this sense, the Court developed a sort of standard requiring equivalence in protecting personal data between the legal orders. As a consequence, the ECJ ended up extending the territorial coverage of the fundamental right to data protection by requiring a geographical extension of the guarantees provided for by EU law.[25]

This decision also constituted the basis for the aforementioned decision in *Schrems II* where the ECJ invalidated the Privacy Shield.[26] In its report on the

[24] C-362/14, *Maximillian Schrems v Irish Data Protection Commissioner (Schrems I)*, ECLI:EU:C:2015:650, para 38.

[25] Ibid, 73.

[26] C-311/18, *Data Protection Commissioner v Facebook Ireland Limited and Maximillian Schrems (Schrems II)*, ECLI:EU:C:2020:559.

annual joint reviews of Privacy Shield, the European Data Protection Board questioned in its reports the compliance with the data protection principles of necessity and proportionality in the application of US law.[27] As Churches and Zalnieriute wrote the same day on which the *Schrems II* decision was published, reading the judgment gives more than a simple 'déjà vu' feeling; it rather looks like a full-blown 'Groundhog Day'.[28] The shift (and manipulation) was easier in this case than it was first time around (*Schrems I*) because of recital 104 of the GDPR which states that 'The third country should offer guarantees ensuring an adequate level of protection essentially equivalent to that ensured within the Union, in particular where personal data are processed in one or several specific sectors'.[29] However, Article 45 still clarifies that such cases only involve an evaluation as to the adequacy of the level of protection, and not a comparison. It should not therefore have been any surprise when the ECJ asserted that

> The first sentence of Article 45(1) of the GDPR provides that a transfer of personal data to a third country may be authorised by a Commission decision to the effect that that third country, a territory or one or more specified sectors within that third country, ensures an adequate level of protection. In that regard, although not requiring a third country to ensure a level of protection identical to that guaranteed in the EU legal order, the term 'adequate level of protection' must, as confirmed by recital 104 of that regulation, be understood as requiring the third country in fact to ensure, by reason of its domestic law or its international commitments, a level of protection of fundamental rights and freedoms that is essentially equivalent to that guaranteed within the European Union by virtue of the regulation, read in the light of the Charter.[30]

Furthermore, in *Schrems II*, the ECJ underlined that the 'essentially equivalent' level of protection applies not only to adequacy decisions by the Commission but also the use of Standard Contractual Clauses (SCCs).[31] Specifically, by interpreting Article 46(1) and (2)(c) with Article 45(2), the transfers of personal data based on SCCs have to take into consideration any access by the public authorities of that third country to the personal data transferred, the relevant aspects of the legal system of that third country, in particular those set out in a non-exhaustive manner in Article 45(2). The ECJ did not invalidate the Commission Decision 2010/87/EU.

[27] See European Data Protection Board (EDPB), 'EU-U.S. Privacy Shield – Second Annual Joint Review report', www.edpb.europa.eu/our-work-tools/our-documents/other/eu-us-privacy-shield-second-annual-joint-review-report-22012019_en, accessed 29 July 2020; EDPB, 'EU-U.S. Privacy Shield – Third Annual Joint Review report' www.edpb.europa.eu/our-work-tools/our- documents/eu-us-privacy-shield-third-annual-joint-review-report-12112019_en, accessed 29 July 2020.

[28] Genna Chuches and Monika Zalnieriute, 'A Groundhog Day in Brussels. Schrems II and International Data Transfers', *Verfassungsblog.de* (16 July 2020), www.verfassungsblog.de/a-groundhog-day-in-bruessels/, accessed 29 July 2020.

[29] Oreste Pollicino, 'Diabolical Persistence. Thoughts on the Schrems II Decision', *Verfassungsblog.de* (25 July 2020), www.verfassungsblog.de/diabolical-persistence/, accessed 29 July 2020.

[30] C-311/18, *Data Protection Commissioner v Facebook* (n 18 above) 94.

[31] ibid, 104, 137.

Since SSCs 'are not capable of binding the authorities of that third country',[32] the controller established in the Union and the recipient of personal data have to verify, prior to any transfer, whether the level of protection required by EU law is respected in the third country concerned.[33] Furthermore, the supervisory authorities have the obligation to suspend or prohibit such a transfer if, in their view and in the light of all the circumstances of that transfer, those clauses are not or cannot be complied with in that third country and the protection of the data transferred that is required by EU law cannot be ensured by other means, where the controller or a processor has not itself suspended or put an end to the transfer.[34] On the one hand, the ECJ seems to underline the role of economic operators to assess the compliance of the SSCs. In a way, as observed by Daskal, companies can do even more, since

> they can ensure that all the data is encrypted in transit, applying the strongest encryption protocols possible – so that it cannot be deciphered if acquired as it crosses underseas cables. They can challenge – and demand individual reviews of – all intelligence community demands for EU citizen and resident data.[35]

However,

> there is no guarantee that the companies will win such challenges; they are, after all, ultimately bound by U.S. legal obligations to disclose. And even more importantly, there is absolutely nothing that companies can do to provide the kind of back-end judicial review that the Court demands.[36]

On the other hand, the ECJ underlined the primary role of the national competent authority in the context of third-country transfers of data.

This decision, as also welcomed by the EDPB,[37] can be considered another expression of the path of the ECJ towards digital privacy. Nonetheless, the consequences of this case are far from just an expression of digital sovereignty. As observed by Irion, '[t]he judgment is emblematic of the formal strength of the EU's fundamental rights approach to personal data protection but also its limits in the age of digital interdependency'.[38] The increasing digital connection in the flow

[32] ibid, 136.
[33] ibid, 135, 137, 142.
[34] ibid, 146.
[35] Jennifer Daskal, 'What Comes Next: The Aftermath of European Court's Blow to Transatlantic Data Transfers', *Just Security* (17 July 2020), www.justsecurity.org/71485/what-comes-next-the-aftermath-of-european-courts-blow-to-transatlantic-data-transfers/, accessed 29 July 2020.
[36] ibid.
[37] EDPB, 'Statement on the Court of Justice of the European Union Judgment in Case C-311/18 – *Data Protection Commissioner v Facebook Ireland and Maximillian Schrems*' (17 July 2020), www.edpb.europa.eu/sites/edpb/files/files/file1/edpb_statement_20200717_cjeujudgmentc-311_18_en.pdf, accessed 29 July 2020.
[38] Kristina Irion, 'Schrems II and Surveillance: Third Countries' National Security Powers in the Purview of EU Law', *EU Law Blog* (24 July 2020), www.europeanlawblog.eu/2020/07/24/schrems-ii-and-surveillance-third-countries-national-security-powers-in-the-purview-of-eu-law/, accessed 29 July 2020.

of personal data has clear consequences for the balance between security and the protection of fundamental rights online. Bignami stressed that

> the unstable geopolitics and the illiberal developments of the past couple of years highlight the many competing considerations – combating election interference based on the unlawful manipulation of personal data is one of the important activities of national security agencies, yet at the same time expansive surveillance laws threaten rights and, in the case of democratic-backsliding, can be used to consolidate authoritarian rules.[39]

As already underlined in *Google Spain*, the EU Charter, specifically Articles 7 and 8, becomes the trump card to strengthen the protection required by EU law and to extend the 'territorial scope' of EU law in the online environment. In the *Google Spain* case, this happens through a manipulation of EU law, ie, in this case, the concept of 'adequacy' of Article 25 of Directive 95/46. Additionally, the standard of adequacy should not be seen only from a geographical point of view, but also as requiring the Commission to assess such a standard over time.[40]

Thus, the *Schrems* cases constitute a further step toward the 'Europeanisation' of data protection online. Even if the Court has conceded that third countries can develop their own solutions to grant an 'adequate level of protection', this assumption did not lead the Court to take a self-restrained approach. Indeed, in reviewing whether an adequate protection is actually met by the US legal system, the ECJ analysed the actual and current legal tools in force in the US and their consistency with the EU law. In this perspective, as stressed in the introduction to this chapter, the absence of a fully recognised protection of the right to data protection in the US system probably influenced the approach of the Court.

III. The Recent Trends in The ECJ's Case Law

Two decisions seem to have recently reversed the polarity of the territorial scope of EU law: *Google v CNIL* and *Glawischnig-Piesczek v Facebook*.[41] The two judgments will be analysed together here because they seem to inaugurate a new trend in the approach to the territorial scope of EU law. If on the one hand, the first decision seems to have stopped the expansion of the territorial application of EU law in the field of digital privacy, on the other hand, the second one seems to have opened an eventual expansion of the EU balance between fundamental rights in the field of freedom of expression. It is no longer data protection to go beyond the

[39] Francesca Bignami, 'Schrems II: The Right to Privacy and the New Illiberalism' verfassungsblog.de (29 July 2020), www.verfassungsblog.de/schrems-ii-the-right-to-privacy-and-the-new-illiberalism/?fbclid=IwAR1wXiMQ1HL_KwaOTw3TzTIFOGRBtNzTaTMrd3mVMGovHyLonTjvNye-vMk, accessed 29 July 2020.

[40] Opinion of Advocate General Bobek, delivered on 14 November 2017. *Maximillian Schrems v Facebook Ireland Limited*, ECLI:EU:C:2017:863, paras 146–148.

[41] For a comment on both cases, see Giovanni De Gregorio, 'Google v. CNIL and Glawischnig-Piesczek v. Facebook: Content and Data in the Algorithmic Society' (2020) 4(1) *MediaLaws* 249.

EU territory, but it is also the right to freedom of expression to deal with global phenomena, in particular the moderation of content by social media platforms. This last field of action – even if this is not a harmonised matter under EU treaties – could be the new challenge for the coexistence of different digital sovereignties on the Internet.

In *Google v CNIL*,[42] the core of the decision is the nature of the right to be forgotten and its territorial scope: the single Member State, the EU territory or the whole world? From this point of view, two diametrically opposed solutions were proposed in the past. The Google advisory council opted for a limitation of the right to be forgotten to the EU territory only,[43] while the Article 29 Working Party proposed a global application of that right, without limiting it to European search domains (eg '.es', '.eu', etc).[44]

The Opinion of Advocate General Szpunar showed an approach of self-restraint. He claimed that neither EU legislation nor the ECJ case law faced the specific issue of the territoriality of the de-referencing in the protection of the rights under Articles 7 and 8 of the EU Charter.[45] Or, to be more precise, neither the EU rule-maker nor the EU judges had dealt with the issue of how to treat and consider searches made outside of the EU physical borders that infringe the right to be forgotten. As a consequence, the main question was:

> If the provisions of Directive 95/46 are thus intended to protect the fundamental rights, on the basis of Articles 7 and 8 of the Charter, of the person 'searched' and subsequently 'referenced', they are silent, however, on the question of the territoriality of the de-referencing. By way of example, neither those provisions nor the judgment in *Google Spain and Google* make clear whether a search request made from Singapore must be treated differently from a search request made from Paris or from Katowice.[46]

The core of the argument of the Advocate General focused on the main reason behind the 'digital imperialism' of the EU law and ECJ case law, ie the protection of fundamental rights online. From this point of view, admitting that in some fields it is possible for there to be an extraterritorial effect, the Advocate General excluded the possibility of an expansion of the territorial scope of fundamental rights beyond the EU borders, both rejecting the argument of the extraterritorial effects of the ECHR and excluding the idea that data privacy held the status of a

[42] Case C-507/17, *Google LLC, successor in law to Google Inc v Commission nationale de l'informatique et des libertés (CNIL)*, ECLI:EU:C:2019:772.

[43] 'The Advisory Council to Google on the Right to be Forgotten' (6 February 2015), static.googleusercontent.com/media/archive.google.com/it//advisorycouncil/advisement/advisory-report.pdf, accessed 26 April 2020.

[44] Working Party Article 29, 'Guidelines on the implementation of the Court of Justice of the European Union Judgment on "*Google Spain and Inc v. Agencia Española de Protección de Datos (AEPD) and Mario Costeja González*" C-131/12' (November 2014), ec.europa.eu/newsroom/article29/item-detail.cfm?item_id=667236, accessed 26 April 2020.

[45] Opinion of Advocate General Szpunar delivered on 10 January 2019. *Google LLC, successor in law to Google Inc v Commission nationale de l'informatique et des libertés (CNIL)*, ECLI:EU:C:2019:15.

[46] C-507/17, *Google v CNIL*, judgment of the CJEU (n 42 above).

'super' right not being subjected to any balancing process of the right to be forgotten. Above all, this second element appears relevant, since the balance between fundamental rights is a territorial-based constitutional issue:

> If worldwide de-referencing were admitted, the EU authorities would not be in a position to define and determine a right to receive information, still less to strike a balance between that right and the other fundamental rights to data protection and to private life, *a fortiori* because such a public interest in having access to information will necessarily vary, depending on its geographic location, from one third State to another.[47]

The point raised by the Advocate General concerns not only the problem of the 'invasion' of third countries' sovereignty in designating their own balance between fundamental rights, but also the increasing risk of triggering counteraction:

> If an authority within the European Union could order de-referencing on a worldwide scale, an inevitable signal would be sent to third countries, which could also order de-referencing under their own laws. Let us suppose that, for whatever reason, third countries interpret certain of their rights in such a way as to prevent persons located in a Member State of the European Union from having access to information which they sought. There would be a genuine risk of a race to the bottom, to the detriment of freedom of expression, on a European and worldwide scale.[48]
>
> In conclusion, the proposal of the Advocate General is that of applying 'geo-blocking' technology to the EU territory.[49]

Against this background, the ECJ, once it had reaffirmed the application of EU law to the activities of search engines and observed that the CNIL had refused the proposal of a 'geo-blocking' application as formulated by Google, analysed the questions proposed for a preliminary ruling: whether, according to Articles 12(b) and 14 of the Data Protection Directive and Article 17(1) of the GDPR, the de-referencing is due on all the versions of the search engine, only on the versions of that search engine corresponding to all the EU's Member States, or even only on the version corresponding to the particular Member State where the de-referencing has been required.

The nature of the Internet – a global network without borders – and the claims of the right to digital privacy and data protection seemed to open the door to a new chapter of the extraterritorial saga.[50] However, the Court – embracing the Advocate General's opinion – highlighted the different approach to the right to data protection and digital privacy in the different legal systems and the non-absolute nature of this right. Two of the pillars at the foundation of the extraterritorial effect seem to fall. On the one hand, the limited digital sovereignty of EU law – or better, the presence of different sovereignties even within the digital

[47] Opinion of AG Szpunar in *Google v CNIL* (n 45 above), para 60.
[48] Ibid, 61.
[49] ibid, para 100.
[50] See C-507/17, *Google v CNIL* (n 42 above) para 58.

world – is recognised, and, on the other hand, the trump card of the absolute right to data protection and privacy online seems to have been partially declined. As a consequence, even if the best solution for the ECJ would have been the global one, the Court opted for an action of self-restraint, limiting a potential European legal colonisation of privacy and data protection.

This decision seems more a tactical retreat than a surrender to the criticism against the Europeanisation of Internet regulation. It appears to be more of a restrained approach taken by the judicial power waiting for the decision of the political branches. The Court indeed affirmed:

> While the EU legislature has, in Article 17(3)(a) of Regulation 2016/679, struck a balance between that right and that freedom so far as the Union is concerned [...], it must be found that, by contrast, it has not, to date, struck such a balance as regards the scope of a de-referencing outside the Union.[51]

Beside these considerations, the obligation to remove content infringing the right to privacy seems to be restricted to the EU Member states.[52] A certain 'margin of appreciation' is left to national authorities to demand a global removal in a particular case. Nonetheless, like in *Google Spain*, this decision has a clear effect even on the right to freedom of expression. Before moving to the second relevant decision of the ECJ in this field, it is worth observing how the ECJ indirectly also addressed the limits of freedom of expression in the European Union. By recognising that EU law does not require a search engine operator to delist links on a global scale, the ECJ is also influencing the right to inform by expanding its boundaries on a global scale. Even if this decision also leaves national authorities free to decide the territorial extension of a domestic order, nonetheless, this mitigates that asymmetry between, on the one hand, privacy and data protection, and, on the other hand, freedom of expression.

The second decision, *Glawischnig-Piesczek v Facebook*,[53] deals with content removal and freedom of expression, which, unlike data protection, is not a harmonised field of EU law.[54] Still it is quite relevant for the extension of the territorial scope of EU law. From this perspective, it is worth recalling that the EU has made considerable inroads into the free speech field,[55] even if that matter is not a fully harmonised one, and different balancing processes exist in the Member States concerning the limits of freedom of expression. The willingness of the EU

[51] ibid, para 61.

[52] ibid, para 66.

[53] Case C-18/18, *Glawischnig-Piesczek v Facebook Ireland Ltd*, ECLI:EU:C:2019:821.

[54] See the Opinion of Advocate General Szpunar delivered on 4 June 2019. *Eva Glawischnig-Piesczek v Facebook Ireland Ltd*, ECLI:EU:C:2019:458, para 79.

[55] See for instance, Directive 2011/93/EU on combating the sexual abuse and sexual exploitation of children and child pornography; Directive (EU) 2017/541 on combating terrorism; Commission Recommendation (EU) 2018/334 on measures to effectively tackle illegal content online C/2018/1177; Proposal for a Regulation of The European Parliament and of the Council on preventing the dissemination of terrorist content online, COM/2018/640 final.

institutions to create a *droit acquis communautaire* in the free speech field could derive from various factors, including helping the political integration of the EU, answering to the populist challenge, facing the crisis of European values and the rise of far-right parties and illiberal democracies, and fighting the foreign propaganda and influences. In this sense, the EU action in the free speech field consists of two soft-law tools: the Code of Conduct on countering illegal hate speech online,[56] aimed at censuring hate speech on the Internet platforms, and the Code of Practice on disinformation,[57] which enshrined the first attempt to regulate the giants of the Web in the field of disinformation and misinformation. Both the initiatives follow a broad range of expert groups, European Parliament resolutions, and even Member States' laws.

In this framework, it should be stressed that the European balance of fundamental rights to privacy and free speech is quite different from the US one.[58] As a consequence, another clash of digital sovereignties could deflagrate on the Internet, feeding the conflict on the territorial scope of protection of fundamental rights. In this sense, it should be stressed that, in contrast to digital privacy, in the field of free speech, there is a lack of one of the two elements that characterise the digital privacy issue, ie the presence of a 'super' fundamental right, or better, an undisputed balance of fundamental rights in the matter of free speech. However, looking closer at the EU policies it is possible to highlight that, in founding their legal basis on the ECHR case law, the Code of Conduct and the Code of Practice are working on this. These two tools are proposing a very clear idea of what the limits of freedom of speech should be, even if they are only little outlined in Article 11 of the EU Charter or in the ECJ case law.[59]

In this scenario, the decision *Glawischnig-Piesczek v Facebook* deals with the removal of defamatory content from Facebook. The two main issues of the decision are the type of content that can be removed and the scope of application of EU law. In this chapter the issue of the removal of identical allegations and/or 'equivalent content' will not be explored under the key of the privatisation of censorship,

[56] 'The EU Code of Conduct on countering illegal hate speech online' (2016), available at www.ec.europa.eu/info/policies/justice-and-fundamental-rights/combatting-discrimination/racism-and-xenophobia/eu-code-conduct-countering-illegal-hate-speech-online_en, accessed 26 April 2020.

[57] 'Code of Practice on Disinformation' (2018), available at www.ec.europa.eu/digital-single-market/en/news/code-practice-disinformation, accessed 26 April 2020.

[58] While, in the US legal system, the doctrine of the marketplace of ideas would consider the state's intervention in the public discourse as inconsistent with the First Amendment, the European scenario in the ECHR's case law has embraced a different balancing process of the limits of free speech. Under Article 10 of the ECHR and Article 11 of the Charter of Nice not all forms of speech enjoy the same regime of protection, and this is particularly evident in the fields of hate speech and 'fake news'. See Frederick Schaurer, 'Freedom of expression adjudication in Europe and America: A case study in comparative constitutional architecture' in Georg Nolte (ed), *European and US Constitutionalism* (Cambridge University Press, 2005), 49; and Oreste Pollicino and Elettra Bietti, 'Truth and Deception Across the Atlantic: A Roadmap of Disinformation in the US and Europe' (2019) 11 *Italian Journal of Public Law* 43, 57.

[59] In this section, the issue of the legitimacy of this EU action, which could be disputed since this is not a harmonised or EU competence field, will not be analysed.

confining the analysis to the matter of the territorial application of EU law and on the similarities to the other decisions in terms of territorial scope.

Briefly analysing the first issue, the Court chose not to limit the removal to identical content but to allow the removal of equivalent content, widening the content-based control over the information spread. This seems to be the first problematic profile linked to the decision. Allowing the removal of more content considered equivalent in its nature to the banned content could increase the chances that a different balance of rights would have been assumed in a third country concerning the expression not covered by free speech clauses.

Again, as in *Google v CNIL*, the Opinion of the Advocate General is oriented towards a geographically limited application of the national law even in the digital world. First of all, the problems of other states' digital sovereignty as linked to a general application of a national law are underlined:

> [A]s regards defamatory infringements, the imposition in one Member State of an obligation consisting in removing certain information worldwide, for all users of an electronic platform, because of the illegality of that information established under an applicable law, would have the consequence that the finding of its illegality would have effects in other States. In other words, the finding of the illegal nature of the information in question would extend to the territories of those other States. However, it is not precluded that, according to the laws designated as applicable under those States' national conflict rules, that information might be considered legal.[60]

Highlighting the non-harmonised nature of defamation law and how no European provisions preclude an order for removal on a global scale, the Advocate General stated:

> [I]n the interest of international comity [...] that court should, as far as possible, limit the extraterritorial effects of its junctions concerning harm to private life and personality rights. The implementation of a removal obligation should not go beyond what is necessary to achieve the protection of the injured person. Thus, instead of removing the content, that court might, in an appropriate case, order that access to that information be disabled with the help of geo-blocking.[61]

Given the above, the ECJ, as in *Google v CNIL*, affirmed that no EU provisions impose a territorial limitation in that field. However, the Court ruled:

> [I]t is apparent from recitals 58 and 60 of that directive that, in view of the global dimension of electronic commerce, the EU legislature considered it necessary to ensure that EU rules in that area are consistent with the rules applicable at international level.[62]

The decision of the Court can be read as a green light for national courts to impose a global scope in their decisions regarding the free speech issue.[63] Thus, the ECJ in

[60] Opinion of AG Szpunar (n 54 above), para 80.
[61] ibid, para 100.
[62] *Glawischnig-Piesczek v Facebook* (n 53 above), para 51.
[63] As stressed by Thomas Hughes, Executive Director of ARTICLE 19: 'CJEU judgment in Facebook Ireland case is threat to online free speech' available at www.article19.org/resources/cjeu-judgment-in-facebook-ireland-case-is-threat-to-online-free-speech/, accessed 26 April 2020.

Glawischnig-Piesczek v Facebook did not stop the possibility of an extraterritorial effect of the EU Member States' laws.

Given the growing convergence of the principles regulating content moderation and data protection,[64] it is perhaps possible to read this decision as part of a broader trend: the 'Europeanisation' of Internet regulation, regardless of its consequence for third countries' sovereignty. Additionally, it has to be stressed that a Sword of Damocles is hanging over this apparent self-restrained approach of the ECJ: the Court seems to leave room for the political powers to decide on the territorial scope of EU law.

IV. Conclusions

The 'digital' dimension has distorted some categories of constitutional law. The global nature of the Internet has allowed – in some circumstances – the extension of the sovereignty of a legal order beyond its own territory. The ECJ, sometimes going beyond the limits of interpretation, on the one hand, has created a sort of super fundamental right to privacy online and, on the other hand, has widened the territorial scope of the aforementioned right.

By creating a continental fortress around the right to privacy and data protection online, the ECJ has sometimes lowered drawbridges allowing extraterritorial effectiveness of the European rules in relation to the protection of digital privacy. Indeed, if the Court with its case law makes of the EU a fortress for personal data, it seems not to have considered the political and legal impact of its decisions with regard to the relationship with third countries.

In this perspective, the contrast between the territorial limits of enforcement jurisdiction and the global nature of the Internet is evident. Only two solutions seem to be possible: one can tolerate the lack of effectiveness of the mechanisms of protection of fundamental rights on the Internet with the only palliative of geo-blocking, or one can impose the rules of the game of one's own constitutional order on third states. From 2014–15, the ECJ has chosen the second path, and, together with the enactment of the GDPR, has inaugurated and 'proposed' a strong model of data protection and right to privacy online – especially the right to be forgotten – which has deeply influenced some third countries that have started to consider the ECJ case law,[65] or to enact laws incorporating similar rights.[66] It is clear how the

[64] Giovanni De Gregorio, 'The e-Commerce Directive and GDPR: Towards Convergence of Legal Regimes in the Algorithmic Society?' (2019) Robert Schuman Centre for Advanced Studies Research Paper No RSCAS 2019/36, cadmus.eui.eu/bitstream/handle/1814/63044/RSCAS%202019_36.pdf?sequence=1&isAllowed=y, accessed 26 April 2020.

[65] See *ex multis* the Canadian case: *Equustek Solutions Inc v Jack*, [2014] BCSC 1063 (Can).

[66] It is possible to enumerate some examples, between them: Canada, Colombia, Chile, Israel, Peru, Mexico, Kenya, Russia and Indonesia. Cf Oskar J Gstrein, 'The Judgment That Will Be Forgotten. How the ECJ Missed an Opportunity in Google vs CNIL (C-507/17)' (*Verfassungsblog.de*, 25 September 2019)

new interpretation of fundamental rights and the new balance between the right to digital privacy and other rights have indirectly paved the way for manipulating the standard of adequate protection of personal data in order to require a substantially equivalent one in third countries.

Against this background, some decisions of the ECJ seem to have changed its data-centric jurisprudence, generating a quite uncommon self-restraint, which could be interpreted as a silent overruling or a slowdown, waiting for a legitimisation of further steps from the political power. Indeed, even if the *Schrems II* case still reflects the European path towards digital privacy, the ECJ seems to have followed a simple motto in other recent decisions, 'I would like to, but I can't'. It is probable that the Court has simply been more careful – following the opinions of the Advocates General – and has considered the broader scenario on which its decisions are likely to impact. From this perspective, if this trend is inaugurating a new horizontal dialogue with other jurisdictions, this phenomenon could help to build a more shared model of digital privacy beyond European borders, encouraging a transatlantic dialogue with the US. However, the references to the law-maker could be read as waiting for a green light to proceed. Further, a sort of extraterritorial effect could arise in the field of free speech where EU soft laws are increasingly trying to regulate freedom of expression online in the most divisive issues, such as hate speech and fake news.

In conclusion, it is undoubted that the issue of the territorial scope of fundamental rights is an expression of the broader conflict between local law and global law, which characterises (judicial) globalisation. As undisputable is the extraterritorial effect that the GDPR and the ECJ case law have generated. However, according to the latest decisions of the ECJ, the process of expansion of European fundamental rights into a global scope seems to be frozen in the privacy field. Nevertheless, new trends in the free speech field could inject a new vibrancy in the conflict between different digital sovereignties.

www.verfassungsblog.de/the-judgment-that-will-be-forgotten/, accessed 26 April 2020 and David Erdos and Krzysztof Garstka, 'The "Right to be Forgotten" Online within G20 Statutory Data Protection Frameworks' (2019) University of Cambridge Faculty of Law Research Paper No 31/2019, dx.doi.org/10.2139/ssrn.3451269, accessed 26 April 2020.

7

Schrems I and *Schrems II*: Assessing the Case for the Extraterritoriality of EU Fundamental Rights

MARIA TZANOU

I. Introduction

The issue of the territorial and extraterritorial application of European Union (EU) data privacy rights has attracted significant attention in recent years. Questions of digital sovereignty and extraterritoriality have preoccupied regulators, the Court of Justice of the EU (CJEU) and commentators alike. The EU's centrepiece of data protection legislation, the GDPR,[1] has strengthened the extraterritorial scope of application of EU data protection law. However, the main focus of the EU data protection beyond borders debate has been on the CJEU's jurisprudence. In particular, the Court has generated significant attention in a first line of cases, such as *Google Spain*[2] and *Schrems I*,[3] that established the extraterritorial application of EU privacy rights worldwide. Conversely, more recent decisions, such as *CNIL v Google*,[4] have provoked further discussions as to whether the Court is exercising some kind of self-restraint with regard to the extraterritorial scope of EU data protection rights.

While the CJEU's seemingly confusing approach regarding the territorial application of EU data privacy rights continues to dominate the debate, scant attention has been paid to the *factors* which form the basis of the extraterritoriality of EU

[1] Regulation (EU) 2016/679 of the European Parliament and of the Council of 27 April 2016 on the protection of natural persons with regard to the processing of personal data and on the free movement of such data, and repealing Directive 95/46/EC (General Data Protection Regulation), OJ, L 119/1, 4 May 2016.

[2] Case C-131/12 *Google Spain SL v Agencia Española de Protección de Datos ('AEPD') and Costeja González*, ECLI:EU:C:2014:317.

[3] Case C-362/14 *Maximillian Schrems v Data Protection Commissioner*, ECLI:EU:C:2015:650.

[4] Case C-507/17, *Google LLC v Commission nationale de l'informatique et des libertés (CNIL)*, ECLI:EU:C:2019:772.

data protection rights. This refers to two fundamental problems: one *internal* and one *external*. The *internal* problem concerns the *interpretation* of EU fundamental rights and the *standards* of their extraterritorial *application*. The *external* problem refers to the *examination* of foreign law.

A clear articulation of the *internal* and *external* factors of extraterritoriality is important if the Court wishes to protect fundamental rights online without being accused of engaging in data protection imperialism. The present chapter examines this particular aspect of the extraterritoriality by focusing on the application of EU fundamental privacy rights to trans-border data flows in the *Schrems I* and the recently decided *Schrems II*[5] cases. The chapter raises two criticisms regarding the Court's structuring of the premises of extraterritoriality in *Schrems I*. It argues that the CJEU's analysis failed to meaningfully engage with issues relating both to the *interpretation* of EU fundamental rights in the context of their extraterritorial *application* and to the *examination* of foreign law. More particularly, regarding the *internal* dimension of the problem, I question the invocation of the 'essence of fundamental rights' for the determination of matters of extraterritorial significance undertaken without appropriate theoretical and doctrinal considerations. *Schrems I* is also problematic with regard to the *external* aspect of extraterritoriality, ie the examination of foreign law. The final part of the chapter focuses on the construction of the dimensions of extraterritoriality in *Schrems II*. It concludes that this ruling clarifies both the rules of *applicability* of EU data protection law beyond borders and its *substantive* requirements and, therefore, establishes EU digital rights protection on more solid grounds.

II. *Schrems I*: Dimensions of Extraterritoriality

A. Safe Harbour and Transatlantic Data Transfers

The *Schrems I* case arose from Edward Snowden's revelations that the National Security Agency (NSA) had been operating secret surveillance programmes that allowed it to pursue mass surveillance of EU citizens through direct access to the central servers of leading US tech giants, such as Facebook, Skype, Microsoft and Yahoo.[6] Max Schrems, an Austrian lawyer, had been a subscriber to the social network Facebook since 2008. He lodged a complaint with the Irish Data Protection Commissioner (DPC) in June 2013, asking it to prohibit Facebook Ireland from transferring his personal data to the US, where it could be subject to

[5] Case C-311/18 *Data Protection Commissioner v Facebook Ireland Limited and Maximillian Schrems*, Judgment of the Court (Grand Chamber) of 16 July 2020, ECLI:EU:C:2020:559.

[6] Glenn Greenwald and Ewen MacAskill, 'NSA Prism program taps in to user data of Apple, Google and others', *The Guardian*, 7 June 2013.

NSA surveillance. The Commissioner rejected Schrems' complaint as 'frivolous or vexatious' on the basis that it was unsustainable in law. Mr Schrems challenged the DPC's decision before the Irish High Court, which decided to stay the proceedings and refer the issue to the CJEU following the preliminary reference procedure. The CJEU issued its decision in 2015, concluding that the US authorities were able to access the personal data transferred from EU Member States and process it beyond what was strictly necessary and proportionate to the protection of national security.[7]

Before turning to the decision, it is worth taking a closer look at the legal background of *Schrems I* by placing this in the broader context of the EU's complex regulatory framework for trans-border data flows. Under EU data protection law there are broadly three mechanisms that allow for personal data to be transferred from the EU to a third state. First, transfers can be based on a Commission decision finding that the third state ensures an 'adequate level of protection'.[8] In the absence of such a decision, the transfer can take place when it is accompanied by 'appropriate safeguards'[9] (for example 'Standard Contractual Clauses' (SCCs) or Binding Corporate Rules (BCRs));[10] and in the absence of such safeguards, on the basis of certain derogations for specific situations.[11]

Among the systems adopted worldwide to regulate trans-border data flows, the EU's adequacy requirement has been characterised as 'gunboat diplomacy'[12] that has prompted many countries to change their data protection rules – or indeed introduce new ones – in order to be able to receive data transfers from the EU.[13] The Commission has recognised a number of countries or jurisdictions as providing adequate protection.[14]

There has been no formal adequacy finding regarding the US data privacy regime, but the general approach is that the US lacks adequate protection.[15] This

[7] For a discussion, see Maria Tzanou, 'European Union Regulation of Transatlantic Data Transfers and Online Surveillance' (2017) 17(3) *Human Rights Law Review* 545.

[8] Article 45 GDPR.

[9] Article 46 GDPR.

[10] Article 47 GDPR.

[11] Article 49 GDPR.

[12] Vagelis Papakonstantinou and Paul de Hert, 'The PNR Agreement and Transatlantic Anti-Terrorism Co-Operation: No Firm Human Rights Framework on Either Side of the Atlantic' (2009) 46 *Common Market Law Review* 885, 901.

[13] See Michael Birnhack, 'The EU Data Protection Directive: An Engine of a Global Regime' (2008) 24(6) *Computer Law & Security Report* 508.

[14] The following countries have been recognised to provide adequate protection: Andorra, Argentina, Canada (commercial organisations), Faroe Islands, Guernsey, Israel, Isle of Man, Japan, Jersey, New Zealand, Switzerland and Uruguay.

[15] See Maria Tzanou, 'The EU-US Data Privacy and Counterterrorism Agreements: What Lessons for Transatlantic Institutionalisation?' in E Fahey (ed), *Institutionalisation of EU-US Relations: Multi-disciplinary Perspectives on Transatlantic Trade and Data Privacy* (Springer, 2018), 55; Paul Schwartz, 'The EU-U.S. Privacy Collision: A Turn to Institutions and Procedures' (2013) 126 *Harvard Law Review* 1966; Article 29 Working Party, *Opinion 1/99 Concerning the Level of Data Protection in the United States and the Ongoing Discussion Between the European Commission and the United States Government*, 26 January 1999.

is mainly because the US privacy regime is piecemeal and included in different sources: the US Constitution, the Supreme Court case law, federal legislation, State legislation and the theory of torts.[16] The Constitutional protection of privacy is mainly based on the First Amendment (protection of free speech and freedom of assembly), the Fourth Amendment (protection from unreasonable searches and seizures), and the Fifth Amendment (privilege against self-incrimination).[17] The Fourth Amendment, which protects personal privacy 'against unwarranted intrusion by the State',[18] is limited in its scope by the so-called third-party doctrine that stipulates that the US Constitution does not protect 'what a person knowingly exposes to the public, even in his own home or office'[19] or any 'information in the hands of third parties'.[20] Moreover, the Fourth Amendment does not protect persons overseas, such as EU citizens.[21] At the federal level, there is no omnibus legislation; privacy protection is included in various sector-specific[22] legislative measures that are different for the public and the private sector.[23] Regarding the oversight of the US privacy legislation, 'the closest that the United States comes to a national data protection agency is the Federal Trade Commission (FTC)',[24] which faces significant limits in its enforcement powers.[25]

In order to allow for international trade, transatlantic data flows between the EU and the US were made possible[26] (between 2000 and 2015) through the Safe Harbour scheme.[27] Safe Harbour was based on a system of voluntary self-certification and self-assessment of US-based companies that they abide with certain data protection principles (the 'Safe Harbour principles'), combined with some intervention by the public authorities. In particular, under the scheme,

[16] Gregory Shaffer, 'Globalization and Social Protection: The Impact of EU and International Rules in the Ratcheting up of U.S. Data Privacy Standards' (2000) 25 *Yale Journal of International Law* 1, 22.

[17] Susan Brenner, 'Constitutional Rights and New Technologies in the United States' in R Leenes, BJ Koops and P De Hert (eds), *Constitutional Rights and new technologies: A comparative Study* (TMC Asser Press, Distributed by Cambridge University Press, 2008) 225, 230.

[18] *Schmerber v California*, 384 US 757 (1966). It should be noted, however, that the Fourth Amendment has not been interpreted to afford a 'comprehensive right to personal data protection'. See Francesca Bignami, 'The US legal system on data protection in the field of law enforcement. Safeguards, rights and remedies for EU citizens', Study for the LIBE Committee, PE 519.215, (European Union, Brussels, 2015), p 8, available at: https://www.europarl.europa.eu/RegData/etudes/STUD/2015/519215/IPOL_STU(2015)519215_EN.pdf; Maria Tzanou, *The Fundamental Right to Data Protection: Normative Value in the Context of Counter-Terrorism Surveillance* (Hart Publishing, 2017).

[19] *Katz v United States*, 389 US 347 (1967).

[20] Ibid.

[21] *United States v Verdugo-Urquidez*, 494 US 1092 (1990).

[22] Shaffer (n 16 above).

[23] Schwartz (n 15 above), 1974.

[24] Ibid, 1977.

[25] Ibid.

[26] Transatlantic data flows also take place through SCC and BCR.

[27] Commission Decision 2000/520/EC of 26 July 2000 pursuant to Directive 95/46/EC of the European Parliament and of the Council on the adequacy of the protection provided by the safe harbour privacy principles and related frequently asked questions issued by the US Department of Commerce (notified under document number C(2000) 2441), OJ 2000 L 215/7.

US companies were required to register their compliance with the Safe Harbour principles with the US Department of Commerce, while the FTC was responsible for enforcing the agreement. On the basis of this, the Commission issued the Safe Harbour Decision recognising the adequacy of protection provided by the Safe Harbour principles. Safe Harbour proved to be an important tool of transatlantic commercial relations, with over 3200 companies signing up to the scheme. It has also been argued that Safe Harbour has levelled up US privacy protection standards.[28] Nevertheless, it was found to suffer from major weaknesses in terms of compliance by the self-certified companies and enforcement and oversight by the US authorities,[29] and the Snowden revelations raised additional concerns about the systematic access of US law enforcement authorities to data held by the private companies certified under the scheme.[30]

As mentioned above, the Commission's Safe Harbour adequacy decision was eventually invalidated by the CJEU in its *Schrems I* judgment delivered on 6 October 2015. In that case, the Court took the opportunity to clarify the adequacy criterion. While noting that there was no definition provided in law of the concept of an adequate level of protection,[31] the CJEU observed that adequacy does not require a level of protection 'identical to that guaranteed in the EU legal order', but nevertheless protection of fundamental rights and freedoms that is 'essentially equivalent' to that of the EU.[32] This requires an assessment of the content of the applicable domestic and international law rules in the third country as well as the practice designed to ensure compliance with those rules. The 'essentially equivalent' criterion shows that the Court is trying to bring external legal systems as close as possible to the EU's internal data protection legal framework[33] in order to ensure that domestic data protection rules are not circumvented by transfers of personal data from the EU to third countries.[34]

This approach is closely linked to the elevation of data protection to the level of a fundamental right that makes the EU's exercise of jurisdiction 'not just … permissive (discretionary), but also *mandatory*'.[35] This necessarily means that trans-border data flows should be regarded as part of the EU institutions'

[28] Shaffer (n 16 above), 22.

[29] Communication from the Commission to the European Parliament and the Council on the Functioning of the Safe Harbour from the Perspective of EU Citizens and Companies Established in the EU, Brussels, 27 November 2013, COM(2013) 847 final.

[30] Communication from the Commission to the European Parliament and the Council, 'Rebuilding Trust in EU-US Data Flows', 27 November 2013, COM(2013) 846 final, 13.

[31] *Schrems I* (n 3 above), para 70.

[32] Ibid, para 73.

[33] Steve Peers, 'The party's over: EU data protection law after the Schrems Safe Harbour judgment', 7 October 2015, www.eulawanalysis.blogspot.com/2015/10/the-partys-over-eu-data-protection-law.html.

[34] *Schrems I* (n 3 above), para 73.

[35] Cedric Ryngaert and Mistale Taylor, 'Symposium on the GDPR and International Law: The GDPR as Global Data Protection Regulation?' (2019) *AJIL Unbound* 5, 6.

fundamental rights protective duty.[36] Indeed, the Court stated that individuals cannot be deprived of their fundamental rights by the transfer of their data to third countries.[37] A valid argument can be made, therefore, in favour of the extraterritorial application of EU data protection standards.[38] In *Schrems I*, the Court applied EU fundamental rights law to data processing in the US by identifying the problems of the Commission's adequacy decision, rather than directly challenging the US legislation.

B. Establishing the *Internal* Dimension of Extraterritoriality

There are a number of problems regarding the CJEU's interpretation of the law that determined the extraterritorial application of EU data privacy rights in *Schrems I*. I focus here on one that is particularly problematic: the Court's discussion of the 'essence' of fundamental rights.

It should be recalled that the CJEU found in *Schrems I* that the essence of both the fundamental rights to privacy in the European Union Charter of Fundamental Rights (Article 7 EUCFR) and to effective judicial protection (Article 47 EUCFR) had been breached. According to the CJEU, the essence of the fundamental right to privacy was breached because the US mass online surveillance programmes grant access on a generalised basis not only to communications metadata but to the actual content of electronic communications.[39] The essence of the right to effective judicial protection was compromised because the US legislation does not provide EU persons with sufficient guarantees and effective legal remedies to exercise their data access, rectification and erasure rights.[40] The CJEU applied, in the *Schrems I* case, Article 52(1) EUCFR which is one of the horizontal provisions of the Charter detailing its interpretation and application and which states: 'Any limitation on the exercise of the rights and freedoms recognised by this Charter must … respect the essence of those rights and freedoms'.

The CJEU analysis in *Schrems I* regarding the essence of the right to privacy raises both theoretical and practical questions. Starting from the theoretical questions, what exactly is the 'essence of fundamental rights', and how is this essence

[36] See Christopher Kuner, *Transborder Data Flows and Data Privacy Law* (Oxford University Press, 2013), 129–33. It should be noted that unlike international human rights treaties such as the European Convention on Human Rights (ECHR), the European Union Charter of Fundamental Rights (EUCFR) does not have a limiting jurisdictional clause.

[37] *Schrems I* (n 3 above), para 58.

[38] Christopher Kuner, 'Extraterritoriality and Regulation of International Data Transfers in EU Data Protection Law' (2015) 5(4) *International Data Privacy Law* 235; Mistale Taylor, 'The EU's human right obligations in relation to its data protection laws with extraterritorial effect' (2015) 5(4) *International Data Privacy Law* 246; Maja Brkan, 'The Unstoppable Expansion of the EU Fundamental Right to Data Protection: Little Shop of Horrors?' (2016) 23(5) *Maastricht Journal of European and Comparative Law* 812.

[39] *Schrems I* (n 3 above), para 94.

[40] Ibid, para 95.

to be determined? Does the concept of the essence signify a maximum or a minimum[41] level of protection?[42] Is the essence of fundamental rights to be considered 'absolute', meaning that it 'can claim validity in all legal systems'[43] or is this a relative concept that can have a different meaning in each particular case? Besides the theoretical problems, there are also practical questions regarding the essence of fundamental rights: Who is to determine this and how? Are the courts the ones to determine the essence of rights? If so, which courts exactly? Specialised human rights courts, like the ECtHR and constitutional courts or every court? How are courts to determine the essence of a fundamental right? Do they do this following their own intuition or is there another way? What happens if the courts get the essence of a fundamental right wrong? How can a legal system (local or global) deal with conflicting judgments regarding the essence of fundamental rights?

These theoretical and practical questions are valid in general; however, they are compelling in the context of trans-border data flows that might entail the extraterritorial application of fundamental rights. Until now, both these sets of questions seemed quite philosophical, but in *Schrems I*, by finding a violation of the essence of two rights, the CJEU made this discussion very real. Admittedly, in *Digital Rights Ireland*[44] the CJEU had already indicated what constitutes the essence of the right to privacy: the access to the content of the data. Nevertheless, *Schrems I* constitutes a landmark, because while in the past the CJEU had indeed spoken in a number of cases about the essence of fundamental rights and more specifically in what I am more interested here – the essence of the rights to privacy and data protection – it had never found an actual breach of these.

Going back to the questions raised earlier, the issue becomes particularly problematic when these are examined in the context of trans-border data flows and the extraterritorial application of fundamental rights.

First, one might wonder why the Court did not follow the path it had taken in its previous *Digital Rights Ireland* judgment that was decided on the basis of a proportionality assessment, but it went straight to find a breach of the essence of the right to privacy, without discussing proportionality at all. Different authors have given different answers to this. Some have argued that the triggering of the essence of fundamental rights at issue really determined the outcome of the case,

[41] Understood as preventing the complete diminishing or negation of a right. See for instance the ECtHR cases *Baka v Hungary*, Application No 20261/12, para 121 and *Christine Goodwin v United Kingdom*, Application No 28957/95, paras 99–101.

[42] See Maja Brkan, 'The concept of essence of fundamental rights in the EU legal order: peeling the onion to its core' (2018) *European Constitutional Law Review* 332; Katharine G. Young, 'The Minimum Core of Economic and Social Rights: A Concept in Search of Content' (2008) 33 *Yale Journal of International Law* 113.

[43] Robert Alexy, 'The Absolute and the Relative Dimensions of Constitutional Rights' (2017) 37(1) *Oxford Journal of Legal Studies* 31. See also Robert Alexy, *A Theory of Constitutional Rights* (Oxford University Press, 2004).

[44] Joined Cases C-293/12 and C-594/12 *Digital Rights Ireland Ltd v Minister for Communications, Marine and Natural Resources and Others* (C-293/12) and *Karntner Landesregierung and Others* (C-594/12), ECLI:EU:C:2014:238.

without there being 'any need to examine the content of the safe harbour principles', 'address any other legal arguments made' or having to balance between privacy and security. This explanation appears tautological: the CJEU is assumed to recognise an infringement of the essence of a right when it sees it and, therefore, a discussion of proportionality is simply not needed.[45] However, I argue that there might be other reasons underpinning the Court's essence of fundamental rights analysis.[46] In my view, these may be related with the extraterritorial application of EU fundamental rights.[47] The Court, indeed, confirmed in *Schrems I* the application of the fundamental rights to privacy and effective judicial protection outside the EU territorial boundaries, but it is possible that it opted to limit this extraterritorial reach to serious circumstances in which the 'essence' of EU fundamental rights was affected.[48]

In this respect, the use of the 'essence' of EU fundamental rights as a *factor* to establish the extraterritoriality of these rights and invalidate a trans-border data transfer that violates these appears somewhat paradoxical: on the one hand, the essence of fundamental rights is the most serious infringement of fundamental rights that can be established (signifying a *maximum* level of protection). On the other hand, this can be seen as an exercise of self-restraint by the Court when it deals with extraterritorial questions: foreign laws would be considered problematic and invalidated only when they impinge on the very essence of EU fundamental rights (signifying a *minimum* level of protection within the context of trans-border data flows).

Secondly, the lack of depth of the CJEU's analysis of the essence of the fundamental to privacy is particularly troubling. The Court did not come up with a clear methodological approach or a comprehensive doctrinal justification why the essence of this right was breached in that case. It just drew a supposed red line – first laid down in *Digital Rights Ireland* – between generalised access to the content of communications and access to metadata, and concluded that the former constitutes the essence of the fundamental right to privacy. This conclusion can be criticised as erroneous, as it clearly disregards the fact that in the context of the Internet and modern digital technologies such a distinction between accessing the *content* of communications and the *metadata* is often artificial and very problematic. It is artificial because in the online, digital world, many Internet metadata, such as a simple Google search or the subject of an email, already reveals the

[45] Martin Scheinin, 'Towards Evidence-based Discussion on Surveillance: A Rejoinder to Richard A. Epstein' (2016) 12(2) *European Constitutional Law Review* 341 at 343.

[46] See Loïc Azoulai and Marijn van der Sluis, 'Institutionalizing personal data protection in times of global institutional distrust: *Schrems*. Case C-362/14, *Maximillian Schrems* v *Data Protection Commissioner*, joined by *Digital Rights Ireland*, judgment of the Court of Justice (Grand Chamber) of 6 October 2015, EU:C:2015:650' (2016) 53 *Common Market Law Review* 1343, 1365; David Cole et al (eds), *Surveillance, Privacy and Trans-Atlantic Relations* (Hart Publishing, 2017).

[47] See also Brkan (n 42 above), 354.

[48] See Kuner (n 36 above), 242–43.

content of the communication as well.[49] It is extremely problematic because metadata using modern data mining and algorithmic techniques can often reveal more precise and sensitive information than the data subjects are aware of themselves.[50]

I submit that the essence of fundamental rights should not be a mere symbolic, abstract idea of human rights protection, but it should be something that can come into play in real cases. That being said, the CJEU should resist the temptation of reformulating simply any fundamental rights issues – admittedly very serious ones – as an infringement of the essence of fundamental rights, even if these issues *do* cause a public outrage. The essence of fundamental rights is necessarily a vague notion and should to an extent remain so. Here, I agree with Robert Alexy about the abstractness of human rights in general. As Alexy has noted, 'human rights refer to abstract subject matter, like liberty and equality, life and property, freedom of speech and protection of personality.'[51] In contrast, the CJEU in *Schrems I* pinpointed in a dangerously accurate manner not just the content, but the very essence of the right to privacy, to the access to content of communications as opposed to metadata. Such an approach is problematic because not only it is based on an artificial distinction but because it also ends up prescribing in definitive – and possible incorrect – terms the essence of privacy, that will probably do more harm than good to digital privacy protection and the claim for informational sovereignty in the Internet context.

C. Establishing the *External* Dimension of Extraterritoriality

The CJEU's construction of extraterritoriality in *Schrems I* is problematic in its *external* dimension as well. This refers to the problem of the examination of the *foreign law*.

Scholars, particularly, on the other side of the Atlantic, have been very critical of the CJEU's assessment of US law in *Schrems I*.[52] In particular, it seems that the finding of a breach of the essence of rights spared the Court from dealing with the issue of how complete information concerning the third country's surveillance can be obtained and used in a judgment. The Court has been accused by mainly American scholars of relying 'on sources that took at face value news articles

[49] See *Digital Rights Ireland* (n 44 above), para 27; Joined Cases C-203/15 and C-698/15 *Tele2 Sverige and Watson and Others*, ECLI:EU:C:2016:970; and Opinion of AG Saugmandsgaard Øe in Case C-311/18 *Data Protection Commissioner v Facebook Ireland Limited, Maximillian Schrems*, delivered on 19 December 2019, ECLI:EU:C:2019:1145, para 257.

[50] See also *Malone v United Kingdom*, Application No 8691/79, 2 August 1984, [1984] ECHR 10, para 84; *Ben Faiza v France*, Application No 31446/12, 8 February 2018, para 66.

[51] Alexy (n 43 above), 34.

[52] Richard A Epstein, 'The ECJ's Fatal Imbalance: Its Cavalier Treatment of National Security Issues Poses Serious Risk to Public Safety and Sound Commercial Practices' (2016) 12(2) *European Constitional Law Review* 330; Russell A Miller (ed), *Privacy and Power: A Transatlantic Dialogue in the Shadow of the NSA-Affair* (Cambridge University Press, 2017).

containing substantial falsehoods regarding US surveillance'; of engaging 'in a series of errors'; and, of being driven 'by EU perceptions that ignore reality'.[53]

These accusations should be taken seriously when considering the extraterritorial impact of the Court's decision. To put it differently, the essence of fundamental rights cannot be used as a quick, easy-fix solution that bars the Court from seriously considering foreign law,[54] just because the case concerns a particularly sensitive issue involving a third country that provoked public outrage. A careful and thorough examination of foreign law is necessary if a valid argument is to be made that EU fundamental rights override this. The temptation of finding that politically sensitive cases trigger the essence of fundamental rights opens up the risk of producing inaccurate or incorrect conclusions that go beyond a particular case: they undermine the very foundations of the claim for digital sovereignty and expose this as a disguised case of data privacy imperialism.

III. *Schrems II*: A More Robust Case for The Extraterritoriality of EU Data Privacy Rights

A. Privacy Shield

Privacy Shield[55] was adopted in July 2016 to replace Safe Harbour, invalidated by the CJEU in *Schrems I*. It comprised a 'byzantine compilation of documents'[56] that included the European Commission's adequacy decision, the US Department of Commerce Privacy Shield Principles (Annex II) and the US government's official representations and commitments on the enforcement of the arrangement (Annexes I and III to VII).

Similarly to its predecessor, Privacy Shield was based on a system of self-certification by which US organisations committed to a set of privacy principles. However, unlike Safe Harbour that contained only a general exception for the purposes of national security, the Privacy Shield decision included a section on the access and use of personal data transferred under the agreement by US public

[53] David Bender, 'Having mishandled Safe Harbor, will the CJEU do better with Privacy Shield? A US perspective' (2016) 6(2) *International Data Privacy Law* 117, 118.

[54] It should be noted that the CJEU dealt with the validity of the Commission's Safe Harbour adequacy decision, on which it has jurisdiction to rule, rather than directly challenging the US legislation. See Tzanou (n 7 above), 553.

[55] Commission Implementing Decision of 12.7.2016 pursuant to Directive 95/46/EC of the European Parliament and of the Council on the adequacy of the protection provided by the EU-U.S. Privacy Shield, Brussels, 12 July 2016, C(2016) 4176 final.

[56] Elaine Fahey, 'Introduction: Institutionalisation beyond the Nation State: New Paradigms? Transatlantic Relations: Data Privacy and Trade Law' in E Fahey (ed), *Institutionalisation beyond the Nation State: Transatlantic Relations: Data Privacy and Trade Law* (Springer, 2018) 1.

authorities for national security and law enforcement purposes.[57] In this, the Commission found that

> there are rules in place in the United States designed to limit any interference for national security purposes with the fundamental rights of the persons whose personal data are transferred from the EU to the US to what is strictly necessary to achieve the legitimate objective in question.[58]

This conclusion was based on the representations and assurances provided by the Office of the Director of National Surveillance (ODNI) (Annex VI), the US Department of Justice (Annex VII) and the US Secretary of State (Annex III), which describe the limitations, oversight and opportunities for judicial redress under the US surveillance programmes.

Serious concerns have been raised as to whether Privacy Shield complies with EU data protection and privacy standards.[59] As I have argued elsewhere,[60] the Commission based its Privacy Shield adequacy analysis merely on a detailed description of US law – found in the US assurances – without any substantive commitments (with the exception of the Ombudsperson) being undertaken by the US authorities to comply with EU fundamental rights requirements as laid down by the CJEU in *Schrems I*. Privacy Shield has also been criticised for the lack of oversight of US surveillance programmes, the lack of judicial redress and the shortcomings of the Ombudsperson mechanism.[61]

B. The Judgment

The CJEU confirmed in *Schrems I* a new *procedural* safeguard regarding the extraterritoriality of EU data protection rights: national Data Protection Authorities (DPAs) were granted the power to investigate individuals' complaints alleging a third country's non-compliance with EU fundamental rights – despite the Commission's adequacy decision on the matter – and, if they consider them well-founded, to initiate proceedings before national courts, which must then make a preliminary reference to the CJEU on the validity of the Commission's decision.

[57] See Tzanou (n 7 above); Tzanou (n 15 above).

[58] Privacy Shield (n 55 above), recital 88.

[59] See WP29, Opinion 1/2016 of 13 April 2016 on the EU-U.S. Privacy Shield draft adequacy decision WP 238; Resolution of the Parliament of 6 April 2017 on the adequacy of the protection afforded by the EU-US Privacy Shield, P8_TA(2017)0131, para 17; Report of the Parliament of 20 February 2017 on fundamental rights implications of big data: privacy, data protection, non-discrimination, security and law-enforcement A8-0044/2017, paragraph 17; European Parliament Resolution of 5 July 2018 on the adequacy of the protection afforded by the EU-US Privacy Shield, P8_TA(2018)0315, para 22.

[60] Tzanou (n 7 above), 561–63.

[61] See, WP29, EU-U.S. Privacy Shield – First Annual Joint Review, 28 November 2017, WP 255; European Parliament Resolution of 5 July 2018 on the adequacy of the protection afforded by the EU-US Privacy Shield, P8_TA(2018)0315 (paragraph 22); and EDPB, EU-U.S. Privacy Shield – Second Annual Joint Review, 22 January 2019.

Schrems II arises from this new *procedural* DPA power. The factual background of this case is very similar to the 2016 *Schrems I* case. Following the invalidation of Safe Harbour, Max Schrems asked the DPC to suspend the transfer of his personal data held by Facebook Ireland to Facebook, Inc, its parent company established in the USA, on the basis that these could be made available to US authorities, such as the NSA and the Federal Bureau of Investigation (FBI), in the context of surveillance programmes that impede the exercise of the rights guaranteed in Articles 7, 8 and 47 EUCFR. The legal background of the claim this time concerned data transfers in the US under SCCs on the basis of Decision 2010/87.[62] As the DPC took the view that the assessment of Mr Schrems' complaint was conditional on the validity of Decision 2010/87, it initiated proceedings before the Irish High Court and requested that this made a preliminary reference to the CJEU to seek clarification on that point.

Advocate General Saugmandsgaard Øe delivered a lengthy Opinion in the case in December 2019.[63] The AG focused primarily on the validity of Decision 2010/87. The AG concluded that the SCC decision was valid and invited the CJEU not to deal with the validity of Privacy Shield even though the High Court had submitted several preliminary questions in this regard.[64] Nevertheless, the AG went on to offer some 'alternative observations' relating to the effects and the validity of Privacy Shield, finding that this did not conform with Article 45(1) GDPR, read in the light of Articles 7, 8 and 47 EUCFR and Article 8 ECHR.

In a landmark judgment delivered on 16 July 2020, the CJEU agreed with the AG that the SCC decision remains valid,[65] but annulled the Privacy Shield adequacy decision despite the AG's call for restraint. The invalidation of Privacy Shield raises significant questions regarding the future of transatlantic data flows. Indeed, *Schrems II* has important theoretical and practical ramifications that go well beyond transatlantic relations. The judgment constructs new requirements for legal mechanisms for trans-border data transfers other than adequacy decisions, such as for instance SCCs. While the validity of SCCs was confirmed by the Court in the case, the conditions for their use in third states that require government access to personal data become significantly complicated and raise questions about the role of private companies, such as Facebook, in assessing that the legal regimes of third countries 'do not go beyond what is necessary … to safeguard … national security'[66] and in providing 'additional safeguards'[67] to those offered by

[62] Commission Decision of 5 February 2010 on standard contractual clauses for the transfer of personal data to processors established in third countries under Directive 95/46/EC of the European Parliament and of the Council (OJ 2010 L 39/5), as amended by Commission Implementing Decision (EU) 2016/2297 of 16 December 2016 (OJ 2016 L 344/100, 'Decision 2010/87').

[63] Opinion of AG Saugmandsgaard Øe (n 49 above).

[64] Ibid, paras 173, 178 and 180–183.

[65] *Schrems II* (n 5 above), para 149.

[66] Ibid, para 141.

[67] EDPD, Frequently Asked Questions on the judgment of the Court of Justice of the European Union in Case C-311/18 – *Data Protection Commissioner v Facebook Ireland Ltd and Maximillian Schrems*, Adopted on 23 July 2020.

the SCCs where necessary;[68] as well as the powers of the DPAs[69] and the European Data Protection Board (EDPB). These issues fall outside the scope of this chapter, which focuses instead on the construction by the Court of the *internal* and *external* dimensions of the extraterritoriality of EU fundamental rights in the context of the examination of Privacy Shield.

C. Privacy Shield and the Construction of the Extraterritoriality of EU Data Privacy Rights

The CJEU's assessment of Privacy Shield is more carefully elaborated compared to the assessment of Safe Harbour in *Schrems I*. Overall, the Court's analysis in *Schrems II* pays closer attention to the *internal* and *external* dimensions of extraterritoriality and their respective interlinks. This is demonstrable for a number of reasons.

First, the Court clearly established the standard of protection under which the validity of the Privacy Shield decision should be ascertained: this should comply 'with the requirements stemming from the GDPR read in the light of the Charter'.[70] This pronouncement is significant because it provides legal certainty regarding the legal standard under which the Commission's adequacy decisions (and foreign law) are to be judged. It also clarifies that the GDPR

> applies to the transfer of personal data for commercial purposes by an economic operator established in a Member State to another economic operator established in a third country, irrespective of whether, at the time of that transfer or thereafter, that data is liable to be processed by the authorities of the third country in question for the purposes of public security, defence and State security.[71]

The possibility, therefore, that personal data transferred between two economic operators for commercial purposes might undergo, at the time of the transfer or thereafter, processing for the purposes of national security by the authorities of a third country 'cannot remove that transfer from the scope of the GDPR'.[72]

Second, the substantive examination of the *internal* dimension of extraterritoriality steers clear of the analysis on the 'essence' of the rights to privacy and to effective judicial protection and the confusion that arose thereof in *Schrems I*. The Court made clear, however, that US national security requirements cannot be given primacy over data protection principles.[73] *Schrems II* thus aligns with established case law concerning internal cases of surveillance where individuals' data

[68] *Schrems II* (n 5 above), para 134.
[69] Ibid, para 121.
[70] Ibid, para 161.
[71] Ibid, para 89.
[72] Ibid, para 86.
[73] Ibid, para 164. See also *Schrems I* (n 3), para 86.

privacy rights are the point of departure to ascertain the constitutional legitimacy of any interference posed by public policy objectives such as national security.[74] This confirms that the normative starting point for the examination of external surveillance measures should be the same as that on the basis of which internal surveillance measures are examined.

Third, the examination of the *external* dimension of the extraterritoriality is more carefully crafted in this case than in *Schrems I*. In particular, the Court in *Schrems II* laid down with sufficient clarity the factors that should be considered when assessing *external* limitations to fundamental rights in light of Article 52(1) EUCFR. These factors are (i) such limitations must be provided for by law; (ii) the legal basis which permits the interference with fundamental rights must itself define the scope of the limitation on the exercise of the right concerned;[75] (iii) to satisfy the requirement of proportionality, the legislation in question must lay down 'clear and precise rules governing the scope and application' of the relevant measures and 'imposing minimum safeguards, so that the persons whose data has been transferred have sufficient guarantees to protect effectively their personal data against the risk of abuse';[76] and, (iv) the third country must provide 'effective and enforceable data subject rights' for persons whose personal data is transferred.[77] These requirements construct a four-prong fundamental rights test, applicable to the *merits* of the examination of foreign surveillance programmes, thus providing legal certainty in an area of law that has remained unpredictable since the invalidation of the Safe Harbour principles in *Schrems I*.

Having established a reasonably clear test on the substantive requirements that foreign surveillance measures should satisfy in order to comply with EU fundamental rights, the Court proceeded to apply this in the context of US surveillance programmes. First, the CJEU held that neither section 702 of the Foreign Intelligence Surveillance Act (FISA),[78] nor Executive Order 12333,[79] read in conjunction with Presidential Policy Directive 28 (PPD-28) Signals Intelligence

[74] See Maria Tzanou 'The Future of EU Data Privacy Law: Towards a More Egalitarian Data Privacy' (2020) 7(2) *Journal of International and Comparative Law (Symposium Special Issue)* (forthcoming December 2020).

[75] *Schrems II* (n 5 above), para 175.

[76] Ibid, para 176.

[77] Ibid, para 177.

[78] 50 USC § 1881. Section 702 FISA allows the targeting of persons reasonably believed to be located outside the United States to acquire 'foreign intelligence information' and provides the basis for the PRISM and UPSTREAM surveillance programmes. Under the PRISM programme, Internet service providers are required to supply the NSA with all communications to and from a 'selector', some of which are also transmitted to the FBI and the Central Intelligence Agency (CIA). Under the UPSTREAM programme, telecommunications undertakings operating the 'backbone' of the Internet – the network of cables, switches and routers – are required to allow the NSA to copy and filter Internet traffic flows in order to acquire communications from, to or about a non-US national associated with a 'selector'.

[79] EO 12333: United States Intelligence Activities, Federal Register Vol. 40, No 235 (8 December 1981). EO 12333 allows the NSA to access data 'in transit' to the United States, by accessing underwater cables on the floor of the Atlantic Ocean, and to collect and retain such data before arriving in the United States and being subject there to the FISA.

Activities, correlate to 'the minimum safeguards' required to satisfy the principle of proportionality.[80] This is because section 702 FISA 'does not indicate any limitations on the power it confers to implement surveillance programmes for the purposes of foreign intelligence or the existence of guarantees for non-US persons potentially targeted by those programmes';[81] and, EO 12333 that allows for access to data in transit does not 'delimit in a sufficiently clear and precise manner the scope of … bulk collection of personal data'.[82] Second, the Court examined data subjects' rights in the US and found that these subjects 'have no right to an effective remedy'[83] because neither PPD-28 nor EO 12333 grant data subjects 'rights actionable in the courts against the US authorities',[84] the Ombudsperson does not have the power to adopt decisions that are binding on intelligence services[85] and the latter's independence can be undermined by the executive.[86]

Overall, the Court's analysis in *Schrems II* is 'unprecedented for the level of detail'[87] with which the CJEU interrogates the US surveillance programmes. This is explained by the fact that, unlike Safe Harbour, a detailed description of US national security and surveillance law was included in the Commission's Privacy Shield adequacy decision. It can, therefore, be argued that the *external* dimension of extraterritoriality, namely the examination of foreign law, was an easier task for the Court with respect to Privacy Shield than with Safe Harbour, as the former explicitly contained the legal bases regarding US authorities' access to personal data. The invalidation of Privacy Shield can be seen, therefore, less as a claim of data imperialism and more as 'punishing' the Commission for its failure to address the problems identified in Safe Harbour and reach a robust adequacy finding.

It has been pointed out that the extraterritorial application of data privacy rights must be based on 'rules that are reasonably clear and predictable, both with regard to the threshold question of *applicability* and with regard to the *merits*' (emphasis added).[88] *Schrems II* achieves both these requirements. It first establishes the *applicability* of EU data protection law to adequacy decisions for trans-border data flows under 'the GDPR read in the light of the Charter'.

Regarding the examination on the *merits* of the extraterritorial application of EU fundamental rights, the CJEU could have proceeded in two ways: One approach would be to apply the analytical framework of Article 52(1) EUCFR, as developed internally, to external cases of interference with privacy and data

[80] *Schrems II* (n 5 above), para 184.
[81] Ibid, para 180.
[82] Ibid, para 183.
[83] Ibid, paras 181, 182 and 192.
[84] Ibid, para 192.
[85] Ibid, para 196.
[86] Ibid, para 195.
[87] Kristina Irion, 'Schrems II and Surveillance: Third Countries' National Security Powers in the Purview of EU Law', *European Law Blog*, 24 July 2020, www.europeanlawblog.eu/2020/07/24/schrems-ii-and-surveillance-third-countries-national-security-powers-in-the-purview-of-eu-law/#more-6410.
[88] Marko Milanovic, 'Human Rights Treaties and Foreign Surveillance: Privacy in the Digital Age' (2015) 56 *Harvard International Law Journal* 81, 132.

protection rights (I call this the *inflexible* approach). A second way would be to flesh out an amended test on the *merits* for external surveillance – 'if the differences between the internal and external settings so warrant'[89] (I call this the *flexible* approach). In *Schrems I* the CJEU seemed to have followed the *inflexible* approach: it assessed the interference of US surveillance measures with the EUCFR on the basis of the 'essence' of EU fundamental rights. As seen above, this raised questions as to whether it implied a maximum or a minimum level of protection of rights in the extraterritorial context.

In *Schrems II* the CJEU adopted the *flexible* approach: it constructed a four-pronged test applicable to external interferences by interpreting Article 52(1) EUCFR in this context. The substance of the test illustrates that the Court is willing to recognise potential differences between the internal and the external settings: the test requires that foreign law imposes '*minimum* safeguards', so that the persons whose data has been transferred to third countries have some enforceable rights and sufficient protection 'against the risk of *abuse*' (emphasis added). Swire argues that '[f]or national security experts, it is puzzling in the extreme to think that citizens of one country have a right to review their intelligence files from other countries'.[90] This is not what the CJEU is requiring with its newly-devised merits test. The insistence on minimum guarantees and general requirements to prevent abuse demonstrates that the Court is well aware of the external constraints. It applies fundamental rights requirements more flexibly in the external context, while being cautious at the same time not to deprive them of their substance[91] by rendering their application so flexible 'that it ceases to have any impact or compromises the integrity of the whole regime'.[92]

IV. Potential Criticisms

Despite the Court's attempt to be flexible in the extraterritorial context, a crucial question remains: Does the CJEU's new test for external interference with data privacy rights show a 'reasonable degree of pragmatism in order to allow interaction with other parts of the world'?[93] Does it recognise adequately that while 'the protection of personal data … within the European Union meets a particularly high standard' 'the law of the third State of destination may reflect its own scale of values according to which the respective weight of the various interests involved may diverge from that attributed to them in the EU legal order'?[94]

[89] Ibid, 138.

[90] Peter Swire, '"Schrems II" backs the European legal regime into a corner – How can it get out?', International Association of Privacy Professionals (IAPP), 16 July 2020, www.iapp.org/news/a/schrems-ii-backs-the-european-legal-regime-into-a-corner-how-can-it-get-out/.

[91] Opinion of AG (n 49 above), para 249.

[92] Milanovic (n 88 above), 132.

[93] Opinion of AG Saugmandsgaard Øe (n 49 above), para 7.

[94] Ibid, para 249.

Initial reactions by American commentators show that this is not the case. *Schrems II* is a decision that has not been received with enthusiasm on the other side of the Atlantic. Indeed, an American commentator declared that the ruling is 'gobsmacking in its mix of judicial imperialism and Eurocentric hypocrisy' and noted that 'it is astonishing that a European court would assume it has authority to kill or cripple critical American intelligence programs by raising the threat of massive sanctions on American companies'.[95] But even less angry voices consider that 'the CJEU provides very little room for effective protection against military action' that is premised on 'needed intelligence activities'.[96]

I argue that in order to answer the above questions one needs to take a step back and delve deeper into the claim for extraterritoriality of privacy rights. What is the rationale behind the claim for the extraterritoriality of privacy? Or, to put it more simply, why is the extraterritoriality of privacy rights needed? So far, this claim has been examined within the context where (the GDPR) and the CJEU has placed it in the *Schrems I* and *II* judgments. For the Court, the answer to 'Why extraterritoriality of EU privacy rights?' is simple: personal data transferred to third countries should be followed by adequate data privacy protections. Extraterritoriality is therefore essentially linked to the *trans-border/ extraterritorial* personal data *flow* element; since data travels, data protection laws (the GDPR) are applicable as well. This centring of extraterritoriality on *trans-border data flows*, however, disregards another important aspect of the *Schrems* cases that justifies the need for the extraterritoriality of EU privacy rights: *extraterritorial surveillance.* US *extraterritorial surveillance* is designed to target non-US persons and is founded on the basis that US citizenship, residence or the presence of an individual on US soil, are 'criteria of categorical normative relevance with regard to the enjoyment of the right to privacy'.[97] Indeed, US surveillance programmes are 'inherently discriminatory on grounds of nationality'.[98] It is misplaced, therefore, to accuse the CJEU of impeding critical intelligence activities when it requires some minimum safeguards against abuse and enforceable rights for the protection of individuals that are subject to US extraterritorial surveillance without any guarantee of effective privacy protections.

V. Conclusion

The CJEU confirmed in *Schrems I* the effects of the extraterritorial application of EU fundamental rights by invalidating Safe Harbour. While this gave a clear message, the decision failed to establish the *conditions* for extraterritoriality, both *internally*

[95] Stewart Baker, 'How Can the U.S. Respond to Schrems II?', *Lawfare*, 21 July 2020, www.lawfareblog.com/how-can-us-respond-schrems-ii.

[96] Swire (n 90 above).

[97] Milanovic (n 88 above), 89.

[98] Tzanou (n 7 above), 556.

and *externally*. *Internally*, the 'essence' of the fundamental right to privacy was used as the benchmark to assess the US surveillance measures, with the unfortunate consequence of confining this concept to a minimum level of protection that entailed incorrect assumptions about the way modern surveillance is undertaken. *Externally*, the infringement of the essence of EU fundamental rights barred any serious discussion of US law – as it was considered redundant – and left the Court open to criticisms from the other side of the Atlantic. As such, the claim for extraterritoriality of EU privacy rights remained weak.

Schrems II presents a more robust *internal* and *external* approach to extraterritoriality that brings legal certainty and clarity both with regard to the question of *applicability* of EU law and with regard to the *merits* of assessing external interference with EU fundamental rights. The CJEU avoided an analysis based on the 'essence' of EU fundamental rights and undertook a more careful examination of US law. It showed willingness to follow a more flexible approach with respect to extraterritoriality by constructing a test of minimum safeguards against abuse that takes into account the specificities of external settings.

It remains to be seen how *Schrems II* fits in with the Commission's ambition to promote 'convergence of data protection standards at international level' and the goal to

> ensure that when companies active in the European market are called on the basis of a legitimate request to share data for law enforcement purposes, they can do so without facing conflicts of law and in full respect of EU fundamental rights.[99]

While conflicts of law seem unavoidable, *Schrems II* takes a first step towards a more reasonable, clear and principled way to addressing these.

[99] Communication From the Commission to the European Parliament and the Council, 'Data protection as a pillar of citizens' empowerment and the EU's approach to the digital transition – two years of application of the General Data Protection Regulation', Brussels, 24 June 2020, COM(2020) 264 final, p 13.

PART III

Cooperation

8

Clouds on the Horizon: Cross-Border Surveillance Under the US CLOUD Act

STEPHEN W SMITH

I. Introduction

On 3 October 2019, the United States and the United Kingdom (UK) executed the first bilateral Executive Agreement contemplated by a 2018 Congressional enactment known as the Clarifying Lawful Overseas Use of Data (CLOUD) Act. The legislation was hailed as a significant breakthrough in the ability of law enforcement authorities to obtain electronic data stored abroad. Advocates described it as a necessary antidote for the tendency of multinational tech companies to house their vast troves of communication data in server farms located in foreign countries beyond easy reach of local law enforcement. Discussion about the law has typically been framed as enabling law enforcement agencies to gain access to inconveniently stored data. Far less attention has been paid to another law enforcement-friendly aspect of the CLOUD Act – the enabling of real-time surveillance in a foreign country.[1]

This chapter takes a closer look at those provisions of the CLOUD Act that authorise, expressly or (perhaps) implicitly, ongoing monitoring of activities by criminal suspects and others abroad. One major concern is that the language of the Act is in many respects deeply ambiguous, most notably with regard to the types of surveillance implicitly authorised. While pen registers[2] and wiretaps are explicitly covered, two other common and extremely intrusive law enforcement techniques – real-time cellphone tracking and remote access (hacking) of computers – are not mentioned at all. Given the acknowledged role of the US Department of Justice (DOJ) in crafting the legislation, one may presume the omissions were not an oversight. The question is: What are we to infer from their absence? That these

[1] The focus of this chapter is law enforcement criminal investigations, rather than national security-related activities, such as those carried out under the Foreign Intelligence Surveillance Act of 1978 (FISA).

[2] See n 37 below.

techniques are not covered at all? Or that they are covered, but buried under ambiguous verbiage unlikely to attract attention and generate opposition?

At this point it is not obvious which is more likely to be the case. As a matter of strict statutory interpretation, the former alternative is the more compelling: existing US legal authorities would have to be bent out of shape to bring these two surveillance techniques under the CLOUD Act umbrella. Yet the DOJ has a history of aggressive (and creative) pushback against legislative constraints on its investigative authority, and its efforts have not infrequently found a sympathetic judicial ear.

This uncertainty is unsettling for many reasons. First of all, there is an inherent tension with the international law norm of territorial sovereignty, which traditionally proscribes extraterritorial law enforcement jurisdiction, absent consent of the foreign state. To the extent that the CLOUD Act authorises US law enforcement to unilaterally engage in surveillance[3] on foreign soil, it disregards international law.

Second, the CLOUD Act enables a new form of cross-border law enforcement cooperation: a network of bilateral executive agreements between the United States and selected partner countries, intended to streamline access to foreign-located electronic data relevant to domestic criminal investigations. Under a CLOUD Act executive agreement, the partner country agrees to allow US law enforcement expedited access to electronic data within the partner's territory, in exchange for reciprocal access to data located in the US. The chief feature of this expedited access is the elimination of the responding government's role in approving the requesting government's order; so long as that order satisfies the legal process of the *requesting* state, it is entitled to enforcement immediately upon service to the provider. Before a CLOUD Act agreement can be approved, the US must certify that the domestic law of its prospective partner affords what it deems to be appropriate levels of due process and civil liberties protection.[4] Presumably our negotiating partners will want to be assured that US law does the same with regard to the intrusive investigative techniques at issue. To the extent that US jurisprudence is unsettled as applied to particular surveillance techniques, such as cellphone tracking, then a foreign partner might be disinclined to enter into such an agreement.

Finally, the extraterritorial impact of modern electronic surveillance can be dramatic, especially in the case of remote access to foreign servers and devices. Wiretapping and cellphone tracking are highly intrusive activities, even when conducted on purely domestic targets.

But computer hacking is in a special category all its own, because it combines all the various surveillance functionalities – wiretaps, video surveillance, pen register, location tracking, online monitoring – into a single super-surveillance tool. Even

[3] For purposes of this chapter, the term 'surveillance' is used to denote real-time, ongoing monitoring of targeted persons, things, or activities. Unless otherwise indicated, the term does not refer to a discrete one-time search or seizure of property or information.

[4] See section II below, text to nn 26–30.

more consequential than the privacy intrusion, however, is the systemic risk to the Internet posed by the practice of exploiting cyber-vulnerabilities in software and operating systems. Experience has shown how difficult it is for even the most proficient of computer experts to confine the damage done by 'zero-day exploits' to the intended targets of the malware.[5] Most troubling of all, given that most critical infrastructure is now controlled and monitored by computers, the risk is ever-present that a government-sponsored cyber-operation on foreign-located servers or devices might be regarded as a hostile act, thereby triggering countermeasures ultimately leading to armed conflict.[6]

In all these various ways, cross-border surveillance techniques can have serious and troubling extraterritorial consequences. In its current form, the CLOUD Act does not come to grips with these dangerous possibilities. This ambiguity lends itself to applications in tension with international law, and thereby tending to destabilise US foreign relations, whether with friend or foe.

Section I examines the background leading to passage of the CLOUD Act, as well as an overview of its provisions, including the standards to be met by any executive agreement negotiated with a foreign government. Section II considers the modes of surveillance explicitly and implicitly covered by the CLOUD Act. It begins with wiretapping – the one form of real-time surveillance expressly covered by the Act – and attempts to understand the rationale for its inclusion. Next, this section evaluates the possibility that the CLOUD Act implicitly covers cellphone tracking, and examines the current controversy regarding which of two rival statutory regimes – the Tracking Device Statute or the Stored Communications Act (SCA) – governs this increasingly common technique. This section concludes with a look at so-called 'network investigative techniques', the DOJ's anodyne term for computer hacking. It highlights the failure of current US law to impose meaningful restrictions on this massively intrusive technique, and concludes with a recent comparative study commissioned by the EU describing the extensive regulations governing law enforcement hacking by six Member States. Section III explains the extraterritorial impact of the cross-border surveillance techniques arguably authorised by the CLOUD Act, and the resulting tension with international law principles restricting law enforcement jurisdiction. This section also flags the special risks to the security of the Internet and to territorial sovereignty posed by remote access to foreign-located computers. Section IV concludes with some observations about the inadequacy of US law on cellphone tracking and government hacking, as well as recommendations for future executive agreements under the CLOUD Act.

[5] See discussion in section IV below, text to nn 92–99.

[6] See Ahmed Ghappour, 'Searching Places Unknown: Law Enforcement Jurisdiction on the Dark Web' (2017) 69 *Stanford Law Review* 1075, 1084 (hereafter 'Ghappour'). This excellent article comprehensively examines the foreign relations impact of law enforcement hacking, and what follows here draws heavily upon the insights of that work.

II. Background to the Cloud Act

The ease and rapidity with which electronic data can be moved around the planet, completely unhampered by national borders and custom controls, has created headaches for law enforcement.[7] As a 2018 Congressional Research Report explains:

> Because the architecture of the internet allows technology companies to store data at a great distance from the physical location of their customers, electronic communications that could serve as evidence of a crime often are not housed in the same country where the crime occurred. This disconnect has caused governments around the world, including the United States, to seek data outside their territorial jurisdictions.[8]

The primary obstacle has been that law enforcement agencies are typically constrained not only by practical considerations but also by international law, to operate within their own territorial boundaries. Laws governing criminal investigations generally are subject to a presumption against extraterritoriality.[9]

Territorial sovereignty is regarded as a primary norm of international law.[10] In the context of criminal law, international law permits a state to criminalise conduct occurring beyond its borders so long as the prescribed conduct has domestic territorial effects.[11] But a state's jurisdiction to *prescribe* criminal conduct occurring abroad does not imply jurisdiction to *enforce* that law by the same means used to investigate, arrest, or prosecute domestic wrongdoers.[12] 'Thus, while Congress may criminalize conduct that occurs wholly overseas so long as it has domestic "effects," international law forbids U.S. investigators from directly exercising law enforcement functions in other countries without first obtaining consent.'[13] In practice, this means that execution of ordinary search and seizure warrants, authorising law enforcement agents to employ coercive force when necessary, would be impermissible on foreign soil. Unfortunately for law enforcement, the traditional consent-based mechanisms for obtaining foreign-located information – letters rogatory and mutual legal assistance treaties (MLATs) – are widely acknowledged to be slow, cumbersome, and inadequate to deal with the huge amounts of data now residing in cloud-based servers.[14]

[7] See generally, Jennifer Daskal, 'The Un-Territoriality of Data' (2015) 125 *Yale Law Journal* 326.

[8] Stephen P Mulligan, *Cross-Border Data Sharing under the CLOUD Act*, Congressional Research Service R45173, at 1 (23 April 2018) (hereafter 'Mulligan').

[9] See *Morrison v National Australia Bank Ltd*, 561 US 247, 266 (2010).

[10] See Ahmed Ghappour, 'Tallinn, Hacking, and Customary International Law' (2017) 111 *AJIL Unbound* 224, 225.

[11] See *United States v Aluminum Co. of America*, 148 F2d 416, 443 (2d Cir 1945); International Bar Association, Report of the Task Force on Extraterritorial Jurisdiction 11–16 (2009).

[12] See *Federal Trade Commission v Compagnie de Saint-Gobain-Pont-a-Mousson*, 636 F2d 1300, 1316 (DC Cir 1980) ('Unlike a state's prescriptive jurisdiction, which is not strictly limited by territorial boundaries, enforcement jurisdiction by and large continues to be strictly territorial.')

[13] Ghappour, above n 6, at 1100 (footnotes omitted), citing Restatement (Third) of the Foreign Relations Law of the United States § 432(2).

[14] US Department of Justice, CLOUD Act White Paper at pp 2–3 (April 2019), available at: www.justice.gov/CLOUDAct.

Matters came to a head in 2016, when Microsoft refused to comply with a US warrant seeking a subscriber's emails stored in its datacentre in Ireland. Microsoft argued that the law purporting to authorise the warrant – the Stored Communications Act – had no effect outside the territory of the United States, and therefore did not authorise the seizure of emails stored exclusively on foreign servers. The US government contended that the warrant should be regarded as a mere subpoena directed to a corporation properly subject to the jurisdiction of a US court, and therefore enforceable. A federal appeals court sitting in New York agreed with Microsoft,[15] setting the stage for a showdown at the Supreme Court. After the case was briefed, argued, and awaiting decision, Congress stepped in to resolve the dispute. It passed the Clarifying Lawful Overseas Use of Data (CLOUD) Act on 23 March 2018. The Supreme Court dismissed the case as moot shortly thereafter.[16]

Despite its surprisingly quick passage, the CLOUD Act had been in the works for a while. Many of its most significant provisions had already been drafted by the Department of Justice,[17] including the proposed amendment to the SCA expressly stating that a service provider must comply with the law's disclosure mandates when the data is in the provider's possession, custody, or control – regardless of whether the data is located within or outside of the United States.[18] Besides defining the extraterritorial reach of SCA warrants, the CLOUD Act contains provisions to help resolve potential conflicts of law arising when the United States seeks data stored in a foreign state with laws forbidding its disclosure. Providers caught in that trap now have a procedural mechanism to obtain relief from US courts using a modified comity analysis.[19]

The second major facet of the CLOUD Act addresses the reciprocal issue of a foreign government's ability to access data in the United States as part of its investigation and prosecution of crimes. Because technology companies headquartered in the United States hold most of the world's electronic communications on their servers,[20] foreign law enforcement frequently needs to obtain data held by US companies. These efforts have been impeded by certain US laws ('blocking statutes') prohibiting providers from disclosing certain data directly to foreign governments,[21] which in turn forced them to rely on the increasingly inefficient MLAT and letters rogatory mechanisms.

To deal with this problem, the CLOUD Act amended the pertinent sections of the Wiretap Act,[22] the Stored Communications Act,[23] and the Pen/Trap Statute[24]

[15] *Matter of Warrant to Search a Certain E-Mail Account Controlled and Maintained by Microsoft Corp*, 829 F3d 197 (2d Cir 2016).

[16] *United States v Microsoft*, 138 S Ct 1186 (2018) (per curiam).

[17] See Mulligan, above n 8, at 7–8.

[18] Ibid at 8.

[19] 18 USC § 2703(h).

[20] See Mulligan, above n 8, at 10.

[21] Ibid at 10–11.

[22] 18 USC § 2511(2).

[23] 18 USC §§ 2702(b)(9), 2707(e)(3).

[24] 18 USC §§ 3121(a), 3124.

to modify the blocking provisions which might have otherwise prevented US providers from responding to data requests from foreign governments. Those provisions are not eliminated entirely, but are effectively suspended for certain qualified foreign governments. A new form of international data sharing arrangement, the so-called CLOUD Act Agreement, is also authorised by the Act.[25] Under these bilateral executive agreements, select foreign governments can seek data directly from US technology companies without individualised review by any branch of the US government. Such agreements must satisfy certain conditions imposed by the Act.[26] Before a CLOUD Act Agreement enters into force, the US Attorney General with the concurrence of the Secretary of State, must make four written certifications to Congress, which must be reviewed every five years.[27]

Perhaps the most significant of these certifications is that

> the domestic law of the foreign government, including the implementation of that law, affords *robust substantive and procedural protections for privacy and civil liberties* in light of the data collection and activities of the foreign government that will be subject to the agreement. (emphasis added)[28]

Among the factors to be considered in making this certification is whether the foreign government

> has clear legal mandates and procedures governing those entities of the foreign government that are authorized to seek data under the executive agreement, including procedures through which those authorities collect, retain, use, and share data, and effective oversight of these activities.[29]

The final required certification imposes substantive limitations on court orders covered by CLOUD Act Agreements. These include specific targeting requirements and a minimum legal threshold: the order must be premised on 'reasonable justification based on articulable and credible facts, particularity, and severity regarding the conduct under investigation.'[30]

[25] 18 USC § 2523.

[26] Ibid. Among those conditions are that the Agreement only applies in cases involving 'serious crimes', that the data requests do not target US persons, and that the foreign nation's laws adequately protect privacy and civil liberties. Other conditions apply specifically to wiretap requests, basically incorporating the requirements of US wiretap law.

[27] 18 USC § 2523(e).

[28] 18 USC § 2523(b)(1).

[29] 18 USC § 2523(b)(1)(B)(iv).

[30] Ibid. In October 2019, the US and UK signed the first of what is expected to be a series of CLOUD Act agreements to be negotiated with US-aligned nations. *Agreement Between the Government of the United Kingdom of Great Britain and Northern Ireland and the Government of the United States of America on Access to Electronic Data for the Purpose of Countering Serious Crime* (3 October 2019), available at: www.justice.gov/dag/cloud-act-agreement. The Agreement became effective on 8 July 2020.

III. Modes of Surveillance Under the Cloud Act

The CLOUD Act does not contain a definition or specification of the types of electronic data to which it applies. The closest one can find are the prefatory Congressional findings in the statute. The first and third findings refer to data 'held by communications-service providers.'[31] The second finding is more specific, referring to 'data stored outside the United States that is in the custody, control, or possession of communications-service providers'.[32] In the same vein, findings four and five refer to the potential conflicting legal obligations of communications service providers when served with orders to disclose electronic data.[33] This focus on provider-held electronic data is echoed in the US-UK CLOUD Act Agreement, which limits 'Covered Data' to that which is 'possessed or controlled by a private entity acting in its capacity as a Covered Provider' (emphasis added).[34] From these provisions one might reasonably infer that providers under the CLOUD Act have no duty to *create* data at the behest of law enforcement, or to disclose data not maintained in the ordinary course of that provider's business.

This inference is consistent with the Stored Communications Act itself, the statutory authority at the centre of the Microsoft case. The SCA is the legal framework for law enforcement access to stored electronic communication and transaction records in the hands of electronic service providers. Passed in 1986, it was a part of the comprehensive Electronic Communications Privacy Act.[35] Unlike other components of that law, which regulate wiretaps, pen registers, and tracking devices, the SCA was not explicitly designed to govern ongoing surveillance.[36]

A. Wiretapping

Yet, in at least one respect, the CLOUD Act clearly extends beyond disclosure of data 'held' by providers. The Act has several provisions dealing with wiretaps, that is, the interception and monitoring of live communications.[37] This electronic data

[31] Clarifying Lawful Overseas Use of Data Act, part of the Consolidated Appropriations Act of 2018, Pub L 115–141, Division V, Section 102(1), (3).

[32] Ibid, at 102(2).

[33] Ibid, at 102(4).

[34] US-UK CLOUD Act Agreement art 1(3).

[35] Pub L 99–508, 100 Stat 1848 (codified at various sections of 18 USC).

[36] See *In re Order Authorizing Prospective and Continuous Release of Cell Site Location Records*, 31 F Supp 3d 889, 895–96 and fn 30 (SD Tex 2014). As discussed below, however, the DOJ has recently argued, with some success, that the SCA does authorise at least one form of ongoing surveillance – real-time GPS cellphone tracking. See *United States v Ackies*, 918 F 3d 190 (1st Cir), cert denied 140 S Ct 662 (2019).

[37] The CLOUD Act amends the Wiretap Act to set out specific requirements for an interception order under a CLOUD Act executive agreement: such an order must be (1) for a fixed, limited duration;

is captured in real time by law enforcement agents with the technical assistance of the provider.[38] The 'listening post' that intercepts the communication is typically staffed by law enforcement agents, rather than provider personnel.[39] Once recorded, the content is entirely within the custody and control of law enforcement and the presiding judge.[40] At no point in time does this evidence constitute a 'business record' of the provider, subject to its own custody, control, or discretion about where it would be stored.

It is not intuitively obvious why the CLOUD Act should have had anything to do with this form of real-time surveillance. To be sure, other nations have for some time complained that the bulk of global communications was controlled or facilitated by US companies, thereby placing foreign law enforcement at a comparative disadvantage. A guiding rationale of the CLOUD Act executive agreement provisions was to encourage reciprocity, levelling the playing-field so that law enforcement of trusted partners would enjoy substantially the same access to US-based evidence as US law enforcement had in those countries.[41]

But this reciprocity rationale does not explain why wiretapping surveillance should be singled out for CLOUD Act coverage. According to available statistics published by the Administrative Office of the US Courts, wiretapping is probably the least-used of all surveillance techniques available to US law enforcement, probably due to the stringent legal requirements imposed by the Wiretap Act. In 2018, a total of 1684 wiretaps were issued by federal judges, compared to 116,190 search warrants.[42] How many of these wiretaps, if any, targeted individuals abroad is unknown. The incidence of wiretapping in the UK is on a similar scale, though perhaps higher on a per capita basis – in 2017 there were 2306 wiretap warrants issued for serious crime.[43] Neither the US nor the UK reporting makes clear how many of these wiretaps were directed to email or social media providers – in either case the numbers would be only a subset of the relatively small totals.

In sum, a convincing justification for wiretap coverage in the CLOUD Act is hard to identify – to the extent such an argument was ever articulated, it received little attention during the rush to enactment in the spring of 2018. If in fact the rationale is that real-time intercepts of communications are to be considered electronic data 'held' by providers, then the question naturally arises – what other

(2) not longer than reasonably necessary to accomplish the approved purposes of the order; and (3) issued only if the same information could not reasonably be obtained by another less intrusive method. 18 USC § 2523. Other CLOUD Act provisions make clear that pen registers – a less intrusive form of real time surveillance yielding only non-content attributes of a communication such as numbers dialled – may also be the subject of a CLOUD Act court order. See 18 USC § 3121(a).

[38] 18 USC §§ 2518(4), 2252.

[39] See *United States v Rodriguez*, 968 F 2d 130, 135 (2d Cir), cert denied, 506 US 847 (1992).

[40] 18 USC §§ 2517, 2518.

[41] See Peter Swire and Jennifer Daskal, 'Frequently Asked Questions About the U.S. Cloud Act,' posted at Cross-Border Data Forum on 14 January 2019, at 9, available at https://ssrn.com/abstract=3469829.

[42] See Administrative Office of the United States Courts, 2018 Wiretap Report, Table 6; Judicial Business of U.S. Courts 2019 Report, Table M-3.

[43] See Annual Report of the UK Investigatory Powers Commissioner 2017, at 42.

forms of surveillance might also fall within that expansive view? When providers assist law enforcement in GPS monitoring of cellphone movements, or enable government hacking by providing decryption assistance, are those surveillance activities likewise within CLOUD Act coverage because the data obtained is notionally 'held' by those providers? No one seems to have posed such questions, until now.

B. Real-Time Cellphone Tracking

While the law enforcement technique of tracking cellphone users is not as old as wiretapping,[44] it is far more commonly employed. In fact, cellphone tracking orders are rapidly becoming as common as traditional bricks-and-mortar search warrants. Court records from the federal district court in Houston (where I once sat) demonstrate the trend:

FY	Standard Search Warrants	Cellphone Tracking Warrants
2013	226	112
2014	284	87
2015	355	137
2016	214	204
2017	284	171
Total	1363	711

Over the entire five-year period, the ratio of cellphone tracking warrants to traditional warrants was 52 per cent; in one of those years (2016) the ratio climbed to 95 per cent.[45] There is no reason to believe this trend will reverse itself anytime soon.

Even though cellphone tracking is commonplace, there has been a long-simmering debate about the appropriate legal regime governing its use. The Supreme Court in *Carpenter* expressly declined to consider the Fourth Amendment status of real-time cellphone tracking.[46] One view, shared by many if not most magistrate judges, is that cellphone tracking is subject to the requirements of the Tracking Device Statute (TDS), and the related provisions of Federal Rule of

[44] The Wiretap Act was passed in 1968. Congress's first explicit recognition of the cellphone's ability to track user location was in 1994, when it passed the Communications Assistance and Law Enforcement Act. Susan Freiwald and Stephen W Smith, 'The Carpenter Chronicle: A Near-Perfect Surveillance' (2018) 132 *Harvard Law Review* 205, 231.

[45] Records on file with author. The AO does not gather aggregate nationwide statistics on cellphone tracking warrants. Although Houston is one of several hundred federal courts around the country, I have no reason to believe its experience is unusual or unrepresentative.

[46] *Carpenter v United States*, 138 S Ct 2206, 2220 (2018).

Criminal Procedure 41, setting out procedures for tracking warrants.[47] The TDS, passed in 1986 as part of the broader Electronic Communications Privacy Act, defines a tracking device in broad, technologically neutral terms: 'an electronic or mechanical device which permits the tracking of the movement of a person or object.'[48] The statute imposes a venue provision that allows monitoring of a tracking device outside the jurisdiction of the authorising court, so long as it is installed within the court's jurisdiction. Rule 41 adds additional procedural guidance for courts issuing tracking warrants, including the probable cause standard, a 10-day installation period, and a 45-day monitoring period, as well as return and notice requirements.[49] It also repeated the venue limitation imposed by the TDS, and incorporated the broad statutory definition of 'tracking device'. Significantly for our purposes, Rule 41 tracking warrants have no extraterritorial reach, and do not authorise operations on foreign soil.[50]

Even so, and not for the first time in its history, the DOJ resisted this effort to cabin its use of surveillance technology in criminal investigations. Instead, they argued that such warrants were authorised under section 2703 of the Stored Communications Act, which allows law enforcement to compel an electronic service provider 'to disclose a record or other information pertaining to a subscriber to or customer of such service' by obtaining a warrant issued using the procedures described in the Federal Rules of Criminal Procedure.[51] The DOJ much prefers these so-called 'SCA warrants' to the more rigorous tracking device warrants, because the SCA lacks procedural restrictions such as the venue limitation, installation and monitoring periods, and notice to the target.[52]

Until last year, no appellate court had ruled on this question, and it is fair to say that the DOJ's position on the use of SCA warrants to track cellphones had enjoyed only limited support among magistrate and district judges. In early 2019, however, the First Circuit sided with the government on this question in *United States v Ackies*.[53] A detailed critique of the court's reasoning is beyond the scope of this chapter.[54] Suffice to say that the result is questionable. At a minimum, the First Circuit's refusal to recognise cellphones as tracking devices is in tension with the Supreme Court's opinion in *Carpenter*, which equated cellphones with ankle

[47] See eg, *In re Application*, 396 F Supp 2d 747 (SD Tex 2015).

[48] 18 USC § 3117(b).

[49] https://www.law.cornell.edu/rules/frcrmp/rule_41.

[50] In 1990 the Supreme Court disapproved a proposed amendment to Rule 41 that would have authorized warrants to search property outside the United States. See Advisory Committee Notes to 1990 Amendments to Federal Rule of Criminal Procedure 41.

[51] 18 USC 2703(c)(1)(A).

[52] The only element an SCA warrant has in common with a tracking warrant is a required showing of probable cause.

[53] 918 F 3d 190 (1st Cir), cert denied, 140 S Ct 662 (2019).

[54] I have extensively criticised the *Ackies* holding in a series of posts at Stanford's cyberlaw blog. See eg, www.cyberlaw.stanford.edu/blog/2019/12/why-are-precise-location-warrants-thing.

monitors, the quintessential tracking device.[55] But for the time being, US law regarding cellphone tracking is in a state of flux.

Uncertainty over whether the SCA covers real-time cellphone tracking translates into uncertainty about the scope of the CLOUD Act itself: if this form of surveillance is authorised by the SCA, then it is also given extraterritorial reach by the provisions of the CLOUD Act.[56] We discuss the potential ramifications of this expanded enforcement jurisdiction in section III below.

C. Network Investigative Techniques (Hacking)

Unlike wiretapping and cellphone tracking, government hacking into target computers is largely a twenty-first-century development. Over the years law enforcement has used a wide variety of descriptions for this technique, but their preferred term today is the euphemism 'network investigative technique' or NIT.[57] As Professor Ahmed Ghappour explains, this term

> describes a law enforcement surveillance method that entails remotely accessing and installing malware on a computer without the permission of its owner or operator. Network investigative techniques are especially useful in the pursuit of criminal suspects who use anonymizing software to obscure their location. By accessing the target computer directly and converting it into a surveillance device, use of network investigative techniques circumvents the need to know a target's location … Once installed, the right malware can cause the computer to perform any task the computer is capable of performing. Malware can force the target computer to covertly upload files to a server controlled by law enforcement or instruct the computer's camera or microphone to gather images and sound.[58]

In short, government hacking is the Swiss army knife of surveillance. It combines multiple surveillance functions – audio, visual, email, texts, communications metadata, online activity, location tracking – into one powerful tool. Any human activity enabled, assisted or recorded by computer (that is, practically everything we do these days) is now subject to remote, ongoing and surreptitious monitoring via this single method.

Such a potent investigative tool inevitably poses exceptional risk and opportunity for abuse. Like other surveillance techniques, government hacking intrudes upon reasonable expectations of privacy in our daily lives. But unlike other techniques, this form of surveillance is inherently difficult to confine to national borders. For example, a single NIT warrant issued by a Virginia federal court in

[55] Known in the UK as electronic tagging. Unfortunately, the Supreme Court declined to review the case on a petition for certiorari. 140 S Ct 662 (2019). Such denials are not precedential, and are not uncommon when other circuits have yet to weigh in on the issue. The *Ackies* decision is binding precedent in only one of the dozen circuit courts across the country.

[56] See 18 USC § 2713.

[57] Ghappour, above n 6, at 1079.

[58] *Ibid* at 1079–80.

2015 caused malware to be installed in over 8000 computers in 120 countries.[59] This means that government hacking carries a unique potential for disruptive extraterritorial consequences, including real harm to foreign relations with both friendly and non-friendly states.[60]

Given the stakes, one might expect the legal process for authorising this form of surveillance to be more rigorous than for run-of-the-mill searches and seizures.[61] Indeed that is the case in the European Union. In the words of a 2017 survey report commissioned by the European Parliament:

> Hacking techniques are extremely invasive, particularly when compared with traditionally invasive investigative tools (e.g. wiretapping). Thus, their use is inherently in opposition to international, EU and national-level legislation protecting the fundamental right of privacy.[62]

The Report concluded that government hacking should be tightly regulated, with specially tailored legal process restricting its use.[63] A survey of six EU Member States found a variety of such legal restrictions in place (or soon to take effect). Many of those resemble the 'super warrant' provisions of US wiretap law: enumerated serious offences only, a fixed duration period, the lack of effective alternatives, and minimisation of non-pertinent information.[64] Other restrictions go far beyond any super warrant analogue: a detailed operational log, securely documented; provisions for malware removal, without impairing the security of the target device or system; comprehensive reporting and oversight of the technical 'exploits' or vulnerabilities used to obtain access (eg a national Trojan registry holding a 'fingerprint' of each version of deployed malware).[65]

By stark contrast, the US has so far taken a laissez faire approach to government hacking. Federal law enforcement agencies have sought and obtained court approval for network investigative techniques in all sorts of criminal investigations.[66] DOJ policy appears to concede that remote access to a target computer requires a search warrant based on probable cause, but courts have yet to weigh in on whether the Constitution might require greater safeguards, as in the case of wiretaps.[67] Congress has enacted no statutory scheme comparable to the Wiretap

[59] Ghappour, above n 6, at 1106 fn 156.

[60] These extraterritorial consequences are discussed in more detail below in section IV.

[61] See Jonathan Mayer, 'Government Hacking' (2018) 127 *Yale Law Journal* 570, 641-43 (making policy arguments in favour of imposing so-called 'super warrant' requirements for a NIT warrant).

[62] Directorate General for Internal Policies, *Legal Frameworks for Hacking by Law Enforcement: Identification, Evaluation and Comparison of Practices* (2017) [hereafter 'EU Report']. The EU countries surveyed were France, Germany, Italy, the Netherlands, Poland, and the United Kingdom.

[63] Ibid at 66. So-called 'grey area' legal provisions (ie general search and seizure rules, or rules aimed at other techniques such as wiretapping) 'are considered insufficient to adequately protect the right to privacy.' Ibid at 67.

[64] Ibid at 41–61.

[65] Ibid.

[66] See eg, *In re Warrant to Search a Computer at Premises Unknown*, 958 F Supp 2d 753 (SD Tex 2013) (fraud and identity theft); Ghappour, above n 8, at 1130 ('The DOJ has made it clear that it intends to use hacking techniques for all crimes, regardless of the potential cross-border implications.').

[67] See *Berger v New York*, 388 US 41 (1967).

Act or Pen Trap Statute to regulate its use. Nor has there been any effort to restrict government hacking by new rules of criminal procedure.

To the contrary, in 2016 Rule 41 was amended to make it easier to obtain hacking warrants. This rule change was prompted by a 2013 court decision of mine rejecting a hacking warrant application on jurisdictional grounds.[68] At that time Rule 41 generally required that the search warrant be issued by a magistrate judge in the district where the search was to occur.[69] Because the government candidly acknowledged that the location of the target device was unknown, that territorial restriction could not be satisfied in this case.

Rather than challenge the ruling by direct appeal, the DOJ formally requested the Rules Committee to amend Rule 41(b) by easing the territorial restrictions for remote access searches of out-of-district computers.[70] For two years the Committee considered various fixes for the problem, including proposals from civil rights groups and providers to impose meaningful restrictions on the use of this powerful investigative tool.[71] At the end of the day the Committee was content simply to ease the territorial limits on 'remote access' searches, 'leaving the application of … constitutional standards to ongoing case law development.'[72] As approved and effective 1 December 2016, the amendment reads in pertinent part:

> (6) a magistrate judge with authority in any district where activities related to a crime may have occurred has authority to issue a warrant to use remote access to search electronic storage media and to seize or copy electronically stored information located within or outside that district if:
>
> (A) the district where the media or the information is located has been concealed through technological means …[73]

The rule's parsimonious language raises troublesome issues. Exactly what is meant by the phrase 'concealed through technological means'? No definition is given in the rule, although the Committee notes offer 'anonymizing software' as an example.[74] Whether other common cyber-security measures such as encryption or two-factor authentication passwords would count as technological concealment will have to await future case law. What happens if, despite the presence of encryption or anonymising software, law enforcement has good reason to believe that the target device is in a foreign country? Does the rule now effectively authorise US law enforcement to hack into foreign computers? Nothing in the text of the amended rule precludes that result.

[68] *In re Warrant to Search a Computer at Premises Unknown*, 958 F Supp 2d 753 (SD Tex 2013).

[69] Ibid at 756–58.

[70] Ghappour, above n 6, at 1081.

[71] Ibid at 1082.

[72] See Advisory Committee Notes to 2016 Amendments to Federal Rule of Criminal Procedure 41, Subdivision (b)(6).

[73] Federal Rule of Criminal Procedure 41(b)(6)(A). Subsection (B) imposes a slightly different condition for investigations of a specific crime related to botnets.

[74] Advisory Committee Notes, Federal Rule of Criminal Procedure 41, 2016 Amendments.

Even if the amended rule is applied restrictively, US law enforcement has other creative legal arguments at its disposal. As we have already seen in the case of cellphone tracking, SCA warrants issued 'using the procedures described' in Rule 41 are not bound by the venue limitations of that rule, at least according to one appellate court.[75]

If the SCA can be found to authorise real-time GPS tracking of cellphone users, it can just as easily be said to cover real-time hacking of computers. And after the CLOUD Act amendments to the SCA, such orders now have extraterritorial reach.

Only a few reported US cases to date have dealt with this technique in any detail. Those cases have so far involved warrant applications for law enforcement to directly deploy its own technical facilities, without the compelled assistance of technology companies.[76] However, it is not difficult to imagine that future applications could seek to compel the assistance of a provider in decrypting[77] or bypassing security features of targeted devices in order to enable malware installation. If provider assistance is sufficient to bring wiretaps under the umbrella of the CLOUD Act, then the same logic would work for NIT warrants as well.

In sum, US law effectively imposes no meaningful restriction on government hacking, aside from the basic probable cause standard applicable to every run-of-the-mill search and seizure application. The special Rule 41 venue provision for remote access imposes only a modest constraint on permissible targets, and even that constraint goes away if the warrant is issued under SCA section 2703.[78] In that respect, remote access search warrants may be *easier* to get than ordinary search warrants for home or office, because Rule 41 limits those searches to US territory.

IV. Extraterritorial Impact of Cloud Act Surveillance

To the extent that the CLOUD Act authorises ongoing surveillance overseas, there are unsettling implications on several fronts: tension with (and possible violation of) settled norms of international law; diminished privacy protections for individuals around the world; and destabilised relations with foreign governments.

As we have seen,[79] a fundamental norm of international law is the protection of territorial sovereignty. This norm forbids US investigators from *directly* exercising

[75] See *United States v Ackies*, 918 F 3d at 201-2, and discussion above in section III.B.

[76] See eg, *United States v Henderson*, 906 F 3d 1109, 1112 (9th Cir 2018) (describing 'watering hole' technique in which government seized and operated servers hosting child pornography); see generally Ghappour, above n 8, at 1097-98 (summarising various hacking techniques).

[77] The CLOUD Act requires that the executive agreement be 'decryption neutral' – creating neither an obligation that providers be capable of decrypting data, nor a limitation that prevents providers from doing so. 18 USC § 2523(b)(3).

[78] *United States v Ackies*, 918 F 3d at 202 ('Rule 41(b) does not apply to § 2703 warrants.')

[79] Above at 4 n 10.

law enforcement functions in other countries without first obtaining consent.[80] Thus Rule 41 search and seizure warrants, authorising law enforcement to act coercively when necessary, may only be executed with respect to persons and property that touch the United States.[81] However, indirect evidence collection methods, such as subpoenas and disclosure orders directed at domestic parties subject to the court's jurisdiction, do not violate the territorial sovereignty principle. Such indirect evidence collection methods are deemed to comply with international law because 'the steps of the collection act – accessing and extracting foreign-located data – are performed by third parties, not state actors.'[82] Moreover, any court-imposed sanctions for non-compliance will be assessed only against persons or property within the court's jurisdictional reach.[83]

Application of these legal principles to conventional evidence-gathering methods is relatively straight-forward. In the digital realm, however, things become complicated, because the location of stored electronic data is often difficult to pin down.[84] And when it comes to digital surveillance – that is, data-in-motion, as opposed to data-at-rest – the picture is more complicated still. The direct vs. indirect collection distinction tends to collapse, because the actors principally involved in remote monitoring of suspected criminal activity – via wiretaps, video surveillance, cellphone tracking, or computer hacking – are law enforcement agents, not private third parties.

It is true that most forms of electronic surveillance require technical assistance from service providers, to a greater or lesser degree.[85] In the case of service providers, this assistance typically takes the form of flipping switches or activating software to allow law enforcement agencies access to the provider's network. Sometimes, the requested technical assistance is less routine and more controversial, as in the case of compelled decryption of secure devices.[86] But once law enforcement has accessed the targeted system or device, and surveillance begins, the third party typically drops from the picture. Law enforcement agents perform the day-to-day monitoring, and control the collection, extraction, and recording of relevant data from the target, even when that target is located on foreign soil.[87]

[80] See Ghappour, above n 6, at 1099–1108 for a detailed examination of international law rules governing criminal law enforcement jurisdiction.

[81] Federal Rule of Criminal Procedure 41(b). There are a few exceptions, but none explicitly authorise extraterritorial searches.

[82] Ghappour, above n 6, at 1103, 1105.

[83] Ibid at 1102.

[84] See generally Jennifer Daskal, 'The Un-Territoriality of Data' (2015) 125 *Yale Law Journal* 326.

[85] See 18 USC § 2518(4) (requiring 'a provider of wire or electronic communication service, landlord, custodian or other person' to provide technical and other assistance necessary to accomplish interception of communications); 18 USC § 3124 (requiring the same assistance to install and operate a pen register or trap and trace device).

[86] *In re Apple, Inc*, 149 F Supp 3d 341 (EDNY 2016).

[87] See *In re Warrant to Search a Target Computer at Premises Unknown*, 958 F Supp 2d 753, 756 (SD Tex 2013).

Consequently, any non-consensual surveillance that involves real-time monitoring by law enforcement of targeted communications (wiretaps and pen registers), individuals (cellphone tracking), or online activities (hacking) in other countries would seem contrary to established principles of territorial sovereignty. To the extent that the CLOUD Act amendments to the SCA are construed to authorise such offshore surveillance, the US could find itself on the wrong side of international law. This is not mere theoretical conjecture. The 2004 Convention on Cybercrime (Budapest Convention) – the first (and to date the only) multilateral agreement to directly address the issue – explicitly refused to authorise remote access cross-border searches by law enforcement.[88] A more recent report by the Council of Europe's Project on Cybercrime declared:

> [I]nvestigative activity of law enforcement authorities of a State Party in international communication networks or in computer systems located in the territory of another state may amount to a violation of territorial sovereignty of the State concerned, and therefore cannot be undertaken without prior consent of the State concerned.[89]

It is true that CLOUD Act executive agreements provide a bilateral consent mechanism for US partners to engage in such cross-border surveillance. As the US-UK Agreement illustrates, the consent will be limited; a party is not permitted to use such means to intentionally target a person located in the territory of the other party.[90] However, as my colleague Al Gidari has pointed out,[91] the Agreement provides no similar targeting limitations for individuals located in a *non-party* third country. For example, a British court might order a US provider to direct its foreign subsidiary/affiliate to enable a wiretap on a criminal suspect in that foreign country. The US-UK Agreement makes no provision for notifying that foreign country and obtaining prior consent for this cross-border intrusion.

Professor Gidari has dubbed this the 'interception flaw' in the CLOUD Act Agreement, but the same notice/consent problems could occur with other forms of third-country targeted surveillance, such as tracking and hacking. Ironically then, an unintended consequence of CLOUD Act executive agreements may be an increase, rather than a reduction, in non-consensual cross-border searches.

Of the various modes of surveillance potentially unleashed by the CLOUD Act, government hacking poses the greatest risk of negative extraterritorial consequences.[92] As computer professionals routinely stress, it is nearly impossible to

[88] See Budapest Convention art 32, 2296 UNTS 167 (entered into force 1 July 2004). The United States Senate ratified the Budapest Convention in September 2006. Senate Treaty Doc No 108-11 (2006).

[89] See Henrik WK Kaspersen, *Cybercrime and Internet Jurisdiction* (Discussion paper) p 26 (2009).

[90] See US-UK CLOUD Act Agreement, art 4.3. Of course, this provision implicitly contemplates (and allows) incidental collection of non-targeted individuals within the receiving party's territory.

[91] Albert Gidari, 'The Big Interception Flaw in the US-UK CLOUD Act Agreement' (18 October 2019), available at: www.cyberlaw.stanford.edu/blog/2019/10/big-interception-flaw-us-uk-cloud-act-agreement.

[92] See generally Ghappour, above n.6, at 1108–1122.

write error-free code.[93] Malware is no exception. 'Poorly designed malware could cause destruction of data or the corruption of the whole operating system.'[94] Nor is the collateral damage limited to targeted devices or systems. Once released in the wild, even the most sophisticated malware is difficult to control, possibly generating a global digital pandemic. A prime example is Stuxnet, a computer worm that infiltrated Iranian nuclear facilities in 2010. This cyberattack is widely believed to have been a joint project between US and Israeli intelligence agencies, although neither country has claimed responsibility. Despite its expert pedigree, the malware had notable spillover effects outside Iran, likely infecting more than 100,000 computers worldwide.[95]

An especially problematic aspect of government hacking is the exploitation of software vulnerabilities, a process known as 'zero-day' exploits. A zero-day vulnerability is invaluable because it 'provides the capability to penetrate any device in the world running the affected software until the developer rolls out a software update that patches the security flaw.'[96] Law enforcement agencies, primarily interested in offensive use of these exploits, are typically not eager to disclose the zero-day vulnerability to the software vendor for patching. Of course, this is not in the best interest of non-criminal users, whose systems or devices remain insecure as long as the vulnerability remains unrepaired. In addition, the government's use of malware risks exposing these vulnerabilities to criminals or malicious state actors, who may be able to reverse engineer the malware and convert it to their own regrettable purposes.[97] Thus, the systemic risk to internet security posed by minimally-regulated US government hacking is substantial.

Perhaps the most serious of all extraterritorial concerns is the risk of countermeasures by affected countries. International law recognises the right of a state to 'self-help' measures in response to a violation of its sovereignty by another state.[98] Such countermeasures must be necessary and proportionate to the harm suffered. Given the interconnectedness of any developed country's infrastructure – financial, energy, transportation, communications, industrial – the potential harm done by a misguided hacking operation could be catastrophic. It is not difficult to imagine a scenario – say, malware that takes down critical infrastructure such as the country's electrical grid – in which the affected country perceives itself to be

[93] See Steven M Bellovin, Matt Blaze, Sandy Clark, and Susan Landau, 'Lawful Hacking: Using Existing Vulnerabilities for Wiretapping on the Internet' (2014) 12 *Northwestern Journal of Technology and Intellectual Property* 1, 28.

[94] Richard M Thompson II, Congressional Research Service, R44547, *Digital Searches and Seizures: Overview of Proposed Amendments to Rule 41 of the Rules of Criminal Procedure* at 9 (2016).

[95] Erica Borghard and Shawn Lonergan, 'The Logic of Coercion in Cyberspace' (2017) 26 *Security Studies* 452.

[96] Ghappour, above n 6, at 1110.

[97] Ibid at 1111.

[98] Michael N Schmitt, '"Below the Threshold" Cyber Operations: The Countermeasures Response Option and International Law' (2014) 54 *Virginia Journal of International Law* 697, 699.

under a cyber 'armed attack', thereby triggering self-defence measures, up to and including military force.[99]

Of course, cyberspace operations are now seen as a vital component of national security, and therefore carefully coordinated and overseen at the highest levels of government and the military. However, this is not true of cyber-operations in the realm of ordinary law enforcement. As Professor Ghappour observes, rank-and-file law enforcement officials are allowed 'to make decisions that have direct foreign policy implications without meaningful guidance or oversight.'[100] He urges the adoption of a new framework for regulating law enforcement hacking, which would reallocate decision-making away from rank-and-file prosecutors who lack perspective on the disruptive foreign relations implications of this technique:

> Law enforcement's use of hacking techniques to pursue criminal suspects on the dark web will result in overseas cyber-exfiltration operations that may violate the sovereignty of other nations. The risks associated with such techniques are enormous: disability of U.S. foreign relations, exposure of the United States and its citizens to countermeasures, and exposure of the investigators performing overseas searches and seizures to prosecution by foreign nations.[101]

V. Conclusion

The impetus behind the CLOUD Act's passage in 2018 was a reaction to a legitimate and urgent law enforcement concern – electronic records necessary to investigate local crime were increasingly stored in foreign countries, beyond the jurisdictional reach of investigators. The newly-created mechanism of CLOUD Act executive agreements is a rational response to those concerns, and a welcome alternative to the inefficient MLAT and letters rogatory procedures.

Less understandable is the need to include real-time surveillance techniques in these cross-border data-sharing agreements. In the case of wiretaps, for example, it is not obvious how a tech company's business decision to store its data in offshore servers could diminish or impede law enforcement's ability to intercept live communications.

The picture becomes even more puzzling in the case of more common surveillance techniques like cellphone tracking and computer hacking. Neither of these techniques are explicitly mentioned anywhere in the CLOUD Act. However, the imprecise language of the Stored Communications Act may provide sufficient wiggle room for a future Supreme Court to hold that the CLOUD Act authorises law enforcement agencies to track cellphones and hack computers on foreign soil.

[99] Ahmed Ghappour, 'Symposium on Sovereignty, Cyberspace, and Tallinn Manual 2.0: Tallin, Hacking, and Customary International Law' (2017) 111 *AJIL Unbound* at 226.

[100] Ghappour, above n 6, at 1122–23.

[101] Ibid at 1136.

The case of government hacking is the most troubling of all. To date, the US has failed to impose any legal restrictions on this surveillance technique, beyond those applicable to any garden-variety search warrant. By contrast, EU countries have recognised the dangers posed by government hacking – to privacy, internet security, and foreign relations – and have developed a panoply of protections and restrictions to mitigate those risks.

Ironically, one of the required certifications for a CLOUD Act agreement is that the domestic law of the foreign government affords 'robust substantive and procedural protections for privacy and civil liberties in light of the data collection and activities of the foreign government that will be subject to the agreement.'[102] In the case of government hacking, US domestic law currently falls embarrassingly short of its own standard.

In sum, the CLOUD Act should be amended to unambiguously exclude coverage of real-time surveillance techniques. Until that is accomplished, any executive agreements under the CLOUD Act should be negotiated with a clear mutual understanding of the types of surveillance orders allowed. Our negotiating partners should be made aware of the limits and uncertainties of US law concerning tracking and hacking, and insist upon robust substantive and procedural rules appropriate to those privacy intrusive techniques.

[102] 18 USC § 2523(b)(1).

9

Voluntary Disclosure of Data to Law Enforcement: The Curious Case of US Internet Firms, their Irish Subsidiaries and European Legal Standards

TJ McINTYRE

I. Introduction

Voluntary[1] disclosure of data by online service providers[2] is by some distance the most common form of cross-border access to data for law enforcement purposes.[3] Irish law is particularly important for this issue due to the number of providers headquartered in the state. Despite this, there has been almost no assessment of the Irish practice by which providers can give user data directly to foreign authorities for criminal investigations, without either a Mutual Legal Assistance (MLA) request or other mandatory requirement under Irish law.[4]

[1] For the purposes of this chapter I treat disclosures to a law enforcement agency in a third country as voluntary, notwithstanding that there may be a binding order under the law of that third country, as such an order will not be binding as a matter of Irish law. See Articles 6(3) and 48 of the General Data Protection Regulation (GDPR), and Part IV of this chapter.

[2] 'Provider' is used in this chapter as a catch-all for most internet services, including eg webmail and messaging providers, hosting providers, domain name registrars, search engines, online gaming services, online marketplaces, and other information society services. However I do not consider the position of providers of 'electronic communications networks' and 'electronic communications services', which generally are prohibited from making voluntary disclosures under the ePrivacy Directive (Directive 2002/58/EC of the European Parliament and of the Council of 12 July 2002 concerning the processing of personal data and the protection of privacy in the electronic communications sector).

[3] See eg European Commission, 'Non-Paper: Improving Cross-Border Access to Electronic Evidence: Findings from the Expert Process and Suggested Way Forward' (22 May 2017) p 3: ec.europa.eu/home-affairs/sites/homeaffairs/files/docs/pages/20170522_non-paper_electronic_evidence_en.pdf, accessed 21 May 2020.

[4] I leave to one side the question when another Member State will have jurisdiction to issue a production order to a provider headquartered in Ireland.

In this chapter I provide the first detailed scrutiny of this system.[5] I outline the legal environment which encouraged its use, including the Irish state's failure to legislate for cross-border data access, and describe how it transplanted standards from the US Electronic Communications Privacy Act into an Irish setting. I assess the requirements of the General Data Protection Regulation (GDPR) in relation to voluntary disclosure and argue that the stated policies of several large providers fail to meet those requirements. I develop the case that the permissive Irish approach to voluntary disclosure violates the European Convention on Human Rights (ECHR) on legality grounds, given its lack of safeguards against arbitrary interference with individual rights. I conclude by assessing the future of voluntary disclosure in light of wider developments including the European Electronic Communications Code[6] (EECC) and the proposed e-Evidence Package.[7]

II. Context

For a small country, Ireland plays a disproportionately large role in relation to the world's data. An influx of firms has seen internet giants such as Apple, Facebook, Google, Microsoft and Twitter set up Irish headquarters.[8] These are generally structured so that an Irish subsidiary is the data controller for and provides services to users throughout Europe.[9] These firms consequently treat Irish law as governing (at least some) government requests for access to data. This was highlighted in the *Microsoft Ireland* case, in which Microsoft successfully challenged a warrant issued by a US court under the Electronic Communications Privacy Act, on the basis that such a warrant could not act extraterritorially to compel production of emails stored in a Dublin datacentre.[10]

[5] The chapter focuses on access for criminal justice purposes rather than the less problematic area of emergency requests for personal data to prevent death or physical harm, which are more likely to be permitted by Articles 6(1)(d) and 49(1)(f) GDPR.

[6] Directive (EU) 2018/1972 of the European Parliament and of the Council of 11 December 2018 establishing the European Electronic Communications Code.

[7] European Commission, 'Proposal for a Regulation of the European Parliament and of the Council on European Production and Preservation Orders for electronic evidence in criminal matters' COM/2018/225 final; European Commission, 'Proposal for a Directive of the European Parliament and of the Council laying down harmonised rules on the appointment of legal representatives for the purpose of gathering evidence in criminal proceedings' COM/2018/226 final.

[8] Pamela Newenham (ed), *Silicon Docks: The Rise of Dublin as a Global Tech Hub* (Liberties Press, 2015).

[9] 'Privacy Policy' (*Apple*, 31 December 2019), www.apple.com/ie/legal/privacy/en-ww/, accessed 23 May 2020; 'Data Policy' (*Facebook*, 19 April 2018), www.facebook.com/policy.php, accessed 21 May 2020; 'Privacy Policy – Privacy & Terms' (*Google*, 31 March 2020), policies.google.com/privacy?hl=en-US#intro, accessed 21 May 2020; 'Privacy Statement' (*Microsoft*, April 2020), privacy.microsoft.com/en-US/privacystatement#mainhowtocontactusmodule, accessed 23 May 2020; 'Privacy Policy' (*Twitter*, 1 January 2020), twitter.com/content/twitter-com/legal/en/privacy.html, accessed 21 May 2020.

[10] For context see Jennifer Daskal, '*Microsoft Ireland*, the CLOUD Act, and International Lawmaking 2.0' (2018) 71 *Stanford Law Review Online* 9.

The presence of these firms makes Irish law central to the privacy of hundreds of millions of users throughout Europe and elsewhere, but the state has dragged its heels when it comes to meeting this responsibility. This is well known in relation to the overall data protection framework and I have described elsewhere how a weak legislative scheme and underfunding of the Data Protection Commissioner (DPC) led to widespread international criticism and belated reforms.[11] The same pattern of legislative lethargy and under-resourcing can also be seen in relation to cross-border access to data – but so far without any significant reform.

The starting point is the lack of a specific legal framework regarding law enforcement access to data.[12] Ireland has, despite making repeated commitments, failed to ratify the Cybercrime Convention. The substantive offences required by the Convention were eventually created by the Irish legislature in 2017,[13] but neither the procedural law provisions in Chapter II of the Convention nor the international cooperation provisions in Chapter III have been legislated for. While domestic laws provide some ad hoc powers, there is no general legislation on access to data, or on other aspects of the Convention such as expedited preservation of stored computer data or real-time collection of computer data.

The position is similar when we consider Irish (non)participation in EU initiatives to expedite cross-border access to data. Ireland did not transpose the European Evidence Warrant and opted out of the European Investigation Order (EIO). More recently Ireland has agreed to take part in the e-Evidence proposals, but apparently reluctantly: a leaked memorandum to government from the Department of Justice and Equality argued for participation in largely transactional terms, noting that 'Ireland is relying on the solidarity and support of other EU member states' in the context of Brexit, there was already 'clear disappointment' at the Irish failure to take part in the EIO, and that:

> with the imminent departure of the UK from the EU, Ireland needs to build new relationships and alliances with like-minded EU states. A decision not to opt into relevant measures that [are] clearly welcomed by the other member states may be interpreted as a lack of willingness by Ireland to play a constructive part in the development of the union.[14]

[11] TJ McIntyre, 'Regulating the Information Society: Data Protection and Ireland's Internet Industry' in David Farrell and Niamh Hardiman (eds), *Oxford Handbook of Irish Politics* (Oxford University Press, forthcoming).

[12] The only exception is in relation to the telecommunications sector where data retention and interception of communications are available in relation to 'authorised undertakings' (but not over-the-top (OTT) services) under the Interception of Postal Packets and Telecommunications Messages (Regulation) Act, 1993 and the Communications (Retention of Data) Act 2011. The validity of the 2011 Act has recently been referred to the CJEU: see *Dwyer v Commission of An Garda Síochána and others* [2020] IESC 4.

[13] Criminal Justice (Offences Relating to Information Systems) Act 2017.

[14] Fiach Kelly, 'Government Told to "Properly Regulate" Internet Giants', *Irish Times* (9 July 2018), www.irishtimes.com/news/ireland/irish-news/government-told-to-properly-regulate-internet-giants-1.3558281, accessed 7 August 2018.

Cross-border access to data in Ireland has, therefore, been left without any specific legislative basis other than the general mutual legal assistance process.[15] Even there, however, there have been criticisms that Irish handling of MLA requests is slow. There are no official statistics regarding the time it takes to fulfil requests but in 2018 the European Commission's Impact Assessment for the e-Evidence package noted that 'stakeholders have reported an increase in the time needed to access e-evidence, presumably due to the high number of requests to Irish authorities'.[16]

III. Development of Voluntary Disclosure

Given this limited legislative framework, it is unsurprising that foreign law enforcement authorities took advantage of the opportunity to make voluntary disclosure requests directly to providers headquartered in Ireland.[17] As the Commission's *Non-Paper on Improving Cross-Border Access to Electronic Evidence* notes:

> Direct cooperation between Member States' authorities and service providers based in another jurisdiction on a voluntary basis has *de facto* become the main channel for law enforcement and judicial authorities to obtain non-content data. While US-based service providers are able to provide non-content data to foreign law enforcement under US law, in the EU, only service providers based in Ireland are able to do the same. These two countries account for a large proportion of the total volume of requests.[18]

This, however, presents an obvious yet surprisingly neglected issue. Why is Irish practice so different when all other Member States (who share the same obligations under the ECHR, the Charter of Fundamental Rights (CFR) and the GDPR) either do not permit or explicitly prohibit service providers from responding to direct requests from foreign law enforcement authorities?[19]

[15] Regulated in Ireland by the Criminal Justice (Mutual Assistance) Act 2008. For an overview of the Irish MLA process see Marco Stefan, 'JUD-IT Handbook' (Centre for European Policy Studies, 2020) 15–19, www.ceps.eu/ceps-publications/jud-it-handbook/, accessed 20 May 2020.

[16] European Commission, 'Impact Assessment Accompanying the document Proposal for a Regulation of the European Parliament and of the Council on European Production and Preservation Orders for Electronic Evidence in Criminal Matters and Proposal for a Directive of the European Parliament and of the Council Laying down Harmonised Rules on the Appointment of Legal Representatives for the Purpose of Gathering Evidence in Criminal Proceedings', SWD/2018/118 Final, para 2.2.

[17] European Commission (n 3 above) 3–4.

[18] ibid 3.

[19] See eg European Commission, 'Non-Paper: Progress Report Following the Conclusions of the Council of the European Union on Improving Criminal Justice in Cyberspace' (2 December 2016) para 2.2.1, data.consilium.europa.eu/doc/document/ST-15072-2016-INIT/en/pdf, accessed 29 June 2017.

A. Section 8(b) of the Data Protection Act 1988

The starting point is the Data Protection Act 1988[20] which was enacted to allow Ireland to ratify 'Convention 108'.[21] Section 8(b) of that Act created an extremely wide exemption in relation to criminal matters, providing that:

> Any restrictions in this Act on the disclosure of personal data do not apply if the disclosure is–
>
> …
>
> (b) required for the purpose of preventing, detecting or investigating offences, [or] apprehending or prosecuting offenders … in any case in which the application of those restrictions would be likely to prejudice any of the matters aforesaid …

This provision entirely disapplied the data protection rules – purpose limitation, legal basis and restrictions on transfers to third countries – which would otherwise have precluded voluntary disclosures.[22] Note, however, that section 8(b) did not *compel* or *authorise* disclosure, but merely disapplied restrictions stemming from data protection law. Restrictions imposed by other legal rules (such as obligations of bank secrecy or professional confidentiality) were not affected, and it remained the responsibility of the data controller to determine whether the basis for disclosure was met.[23]

B. Data Protection Commissioner Endorses Voluntary Disclosure

Section 8(b) came to be used extensively in Ireland, both by the *Garda Síochána* (the Irish police force) and by internet firms who saw in it the opportunity to replicate their existing voluntary cooperation practices in their new Irish subsidiaries. As is well known, in the United States the Electronic Communications Privacy Act of 1986[24] permits online service providers to make wide disclosure of information relating to customers (other than the contents of a communication) and on foot of this many firms developed practices of voluntarily providing 'non-content

[20] Later amended and styled as the Data Protection Acts 1988 and 2003, and since largely repealed by the Data Protection Act 2018.

[21] Convention for the Protection of Individuals with regard to Automatic Processing of Personal Data (CETS 108, 1981).

[22] In *CRH Plc, Irish Cement Ltd & others v The Competition and Consumer Protection Commission* [2017] IESC 34 the Supreme Court subsequently confirmed that section 8(b) created a blanket exclusion.

[23] 'Disclosures Permitted under Section 8 of the Data Protection Act' (*Office of the Data Protection Commissioner*), www.dataprotection.ie/docs/Disclosures-Permitted-under-Section-8-of-the-Data-Protection-Act-Section/237.htm, accessed 29 April 2016.

[24] Specifically 18 USC § 2702.

data' (such as 'basic subscriber data') to foreign law enforcement agencies outside the MLA process.[25] As Irish subsidiaries began to take on responsibility for user data, section 8(b) was the obvious legal tool to ensure that these practices could continue.

This first came to public attention in 2011 when the DPC carried out an audit of Facebook Ireland.[26] In the course of the audit, Facebook set out its policy as permitting voluntary disclosure of non-content data provided that requests (i) met 'legal standards in the originating jurisdiction', (ii) were 'intended to protect Facebook or [its] users', and (iii) were 'consistent with internationally recognised standards'.[27] The DPC endorsed this practice and accepted that Facebook Ireland could provide data to both Irish and foreign law enforcement (including law enforcement agencies outside the EEA) on the basis that:

> Under Section 8(b) of the Acts, [Facebook Ireland] is enabled to provide personal data following a lawful request if it is satisfied that to not do so could prejudice the prevention, detection or investigation of an offence.[28]

The only significant change recommended by the audit was that Facebook introduce a standard request system, seeking more detail as to why data is sought in each case, and that it should seek to have such requests signed by a designated senior officer within each police force.[29] Crucially, however, this was merely a 'best practice recommendation' – the DPC did not require Facebook to implement any limits on disclosure. On the DPC's reasoning, if section 8(b) applied, then any additional safeguards (such as the limitation to non-content data) were a matter for Facebook's discretion rather than Irish law.

The audit did not comment on Facebook's claims that it could also make voluntary disclosure, including to law enforcement agencies in third countries, on two alternative grounds – user consent based on acceptance of its terms of use, and its legitimate interest in cooperating with law enforcement authorities.[30] With the benefit of hindsight, this was a missed opportunity: while there was little reality to the claim that terms of use could constitute valid consent, an assessment of Facebook's legitimate interest argument could have helped to develop a more

[25] For a snapshot of these practices as of 2016 see Cybercrime Convention Committee Cloud Evidence Group, 'Criminal Justice Access to Data in the Cloud: Cooperation with "Foreign" Service Providers', rm.coe.int/168064b77d, accessed 31 May 2016.

[26] Data Protection Commissioner, 'Facebook Ireland Report of Audit' (2011) 98–100, www.dataprotection.ie/documents/facebook%20report/final%20report/report.pdf accessed 28 June 2017; Data Protection Commissioner, 'Facebook Ireland Report of Audit: Appendices' (2011) 216–21, www.dataprotection.ie/documents/facebook%20report/final%20report/Appendices.pdf, accessed 21 March 2018.

[27] Data Protection Commissioner, 'Facebook Ireland Report of Audit' (n 26 above) 98.

[28] ibid.

[29] Data Protection Commissioner, 'Facebook Ireland Ltd Report of Re-Audit' (2012) 34–35, www.dataprotection.ie/documents/press/Facebook_Ireland_Audit_Review_Report_21_Sept_2012.pdf, accessed 28 August 2018.

[30] See appendix 5 of Data Protection Commissioner, 'Facebook Ireland Report of Audit' (n 26 above).

nuanced assessment of voluntary disclosure as an alternative to the 'all or nothing' approach of section 8(b).

The voluntary disclosure aspect of the Facebook audit prompted little comment at the time, but deserved more scrutiny. In just three pages of a 150-page audit the DPC, without any public consultation, gave the green light for an industry-wide practice implicating the rights of hundreds of millions of users based on a dubious reading of a dubious provision.

Section 8(b) itself was very likely an improper transposition of Convention 108 and the Data Protection Directive. Both instruments did allow derogations where necessary for the 'suppression of criminal offences'[31] or 'the prevention, investigation, detection and prosecution of criminal offences'.[32] In each case, however, such derogations had to be proportionate.[33] Convention 108 expressly required that any 'such derogation … constitutes a necessary measure in a democratic society',[34] while under the Directive the CJEU had read in a requirement that any derogation 'requires compliance with the requirement of proportionality with respect to the public interest objective being pursued'.[35] Section 8(b), on the other hand, permitted disclosure of *any* personal data in relation to *any* crime, whether or not the alleged offence was a serious one, regardless of the extent or intrusiveness of the information sought, and with no assessment of the proportionality of disclosure in the individual case.[36]

In addition, the DPC's wide interpretation of section 8(b) was questionable at best. Hogan, for example, argues that: 'the exemption … only applies in respect of offences under Irish law … As such, from an Irish law perspective, any disclosure of personal data to foreign law enforcement would need to comply with the Data Protection Acts'.[37] This was surely correct: by construing section 8(b) to include foreign offences the DPC authorised significant interference with the rights of individuals without any requirement of dual criminality.

Similarly, the DPC failed to consider the possibility of alternative means of accessing data, notwithstanding the statutory prerequisite that processing must

[31] Convention 108 (n 21 above), Article 9.

[32] Data Protection Directive, Article 13(1)(d).

[33] As to the validity of derogations see generally Dominique Moore, 'Article 23: Restrictions' in Christopher Kuner and others (eds), *The EU General Data Protection Regulation (GDPR): A Commentary* (OUP, 2020).

[34] Convention 108 (n 21 above), Article 9(2).

[35] Joined cases C-465/00, C-138/01 and C-139/01 *Rechnungshof v Österreichischer Rundfunk and Others* and *Christa Neukomm and Joseph Lauermann v Österreichischer Rundfunk* ECLI:EU:C:2003:294, para 91.

[36] Indeed section 8(b) was systematically used to access retained communications data in relation to non-serious offences. See John Murray, 'Review of the Law on the Retention of and Access to Communications Data' (Department of Justice and Equality 2017), www.justice.ie/en/JELR/Review_of_the_Law_on_Retention_of_and_Access_to_Communications_Data.pdf/Files/Review_of_the_Law_on_Retention_of_and_Access_to_Communications_Data.pdf, 45.

[37] Annette Hogan, 'The Interception of Communications in Ireland – Time for a Re-Think' (2014) 7(5) *Data Protection Ireland* 8.

be '*required* for the purpose' of investigating, etc, crime and that a data protection restriction 'would be *likely to prejudice*' that purpose (emphasis added). By permitting voluntary disclosures to the *Garda Síochána* even though a court order would be available, and permitting voluntary disclosures to another jurisdiction with which a MLAT was in place, the DPC replaced a test of necessity with one of official convenience.

C. Other Irish Subsidiaries Adopt Voluntary Disclosure

There is no direct evidence as to how the Facebook audit finding influenced other large US service providers in their approaches to their Irish subsidiaries, or what legal grounds they relied upon in their internal decision-making. However, most appear to have adopted a similar approach to Facebook. In 2016 the Council of Europe Cybercrime Convention Committee surveyed the law enforcement guidelines of Apple, Facebook, Google, Microsoft, Twitter and Yahoo.[38] All bar Google and Yahoo identified Irish law as applying to at least some of the information they held, and all drew a distinction between non-content data and content data, with the former being made available on the basis of a 'valid legal request' and the latter requiring a mutual legal assistance request or other binding legal process.

IV. Voluntary Disclosure Under The GDPR

I argue above that voluntary disclosure was already questionable as a practice when it was endorsed by the DPC in 2011. It became even more so following the adoption of the GDPR and its implementation in Irish law through the Data Protection Act 2018 (DPA 2018). The 2018 Act disapplied section 8(b) of the Data Protection Acts 1988 and 2003, and with the loss of that shield voluntary disclosure now faces three difficult questions. First, is it compatible with the purpose limitation principle? Second, is there a legal basis under Article 6 GDPR? Third, in the case of a request from a third country is there a legal basis for the transfer of data under Chapter 5 GDPR?

A. Purpose Limitation

The purpose limitation principle requires data to be collected for specified, explicit and legitimate purposes and not further processed in a manner that is incompatible with those purposes.[39] In some cases voluntary disclosure may be compatible

[38] Cybercrime Convention Committee Cloud Evidence Group (n 25 above).
[39] Article 5(1)(b) GDPR.

with the purpose for which data is collected – for example, where a provider detects fraud in relation to its own service and reports it to law enforcement.[40] However, applying the five criteria in Article 6(4) GDPR suggests that in many cases (probably the overwhelming majority) voluntary disclosure at the request of law enforcement will constitute further processing for an incompatible purpose.[41] First, the disclosure will generally be unrelated to the primary purpose of delivering the service.[42] Second, users will usually have a reasonable expectation of privacy in information about their use of a service; and the balance of power will be in favour of the controller, with the data subject having no real choice but to provide the information. Third, the data disclosed will very often be particularly intrusive (even for non-content data, where an IP address may be enough to provide access to an individual's real name, home address and communications history).[43] Fourth, the impact on the data subject may be particularly severe (criminal prosecution). Finally, disclosures within the EU will be safeguarded by the Law Enforcement Directive[44] but disclosures to a third country will not, with a particular risk that the data may be used for other purposes or further disclosed to other third countries.

As a result, many voluntary disclosures will be prohibited by Article 5(1)(b) GDPR unless either the data subject consents or the disclosure is permitted by a Union or Member State law restricting the purpose limitation principle.[45] Under Article 23 GDPR, such a restriction must be a legislative measure, constituting a necessary and proportionate measure in a democratic society, containing specific

[40] As contemplated by Recitals 47 and 50 GDPR.

[41] See Article 29 Data Protection Working Party, 'Opinion 03/2013 on Purpose Limitation' (2 April 2013) 23–27, www.ec.europa.eu/justice/article-29/documentation/opinion-recommendation/files/2013/wp203_en.pdf, accessed 17 June 2020.

[42] Some data (such as network logs for security purposes as envisaged by Recital 49 GDPR) will be processed with disclosure as a possible purpose, but the fact that providers specify in their privacy policies that user data *may be disclosed* to law enforcement does not itself mean that all such user data are collected *for the purpose of being disclosed*. The purpose limitation principle cannot be entirely disapplied in this way, though such a provision may affect the data subject's reasonable expectation of privacy.

[43] Compare the analysis of the Article 29 Working Party in relation to use of retained telecommunications data, which concluded that disclosure of such data was 'a clear example of incompatible purpose': Article 29 Data Protection Working Party (n 41 above) 68.

[44] Directive (EU) 2016/680 of the European Parliament and of the Council of 27 April 2016 on the protection of natural persons with regard to the processing of personal data by competent authorities for the purposes of the prevention, investigation, detection or prosecution of criminal offences or the execution of criminal penalties, and on the free movement of such data, and repealing Council Framework Decision 2008/977/JHA.

[45] See Article 29 Data Protection Working Party (n 41 above) 3; Els De Busser, 'Private Companies and the Transfer of Data to Law Enforcement Authorities: Challenges for Data Protection' (2016) 23 *Maastricht Journal of European and Comparative Law* 478, 488; Adrian Haase and Emma Peters, 'Ubiquitous Computing and Increasing Engagement of Private Companies in Governmental Surveillance' (2017) 7 *International Data Privacy Law* 126, 134; Nadezhda Purtova, 'Between the GDPR and the Police Directive: Navigating through the Maze of Information Sharing in Public–Private Partnerships' (2018) 8(1) *International Data Privacy Law* 52, 66.

provisions regarding (inter alia): the categories of personal data affected, the scope of the restriction, the safeguards to prevent abuse or unlawful access or transfer, the controller or categories of controllers to whom it applies, the storage periods and applicable safeguards for the disclosed data, and the right of data subjects to be informed about the restriction.[46]

Irish law does purport to disapply the purpose limitation principle in relation to criminal matters, with section 41 DPA 2018 providing that:

> the processing of personal data and special categories of personal data for a purpose other than the purpose for which the data has been collected shall be lawful to the extent that such processing is necessary and proportionate for the purposes–
>
> …
>
> (b) of preventing, detecting, investigating or prosecuting criminal offences.

However, although this provides for a test of proportionality, it does not specify the categories of data to which it applies, or the controllers to which it applies; nor does it address any of the other specific provisions or safeguards against abuse required by Article 23 GDPR. While some safeguards against abuse may be provided for in other legislation – such as the implementation of the Law Enforcement Directive in DPA 2018 – the blanket nature of this provision makes it very unlikely to be compatible with Article 23 GDPR, leaving voluntary disclosure still generally in breach of the purpose limitation principle.[47]

B. Legal Basis for Voluntary Disclosure under Article 6 GDPR

(i) Disclosure to Law Enforcement in the EU

Voluntary disclosure, as with any form of processing of personal data, must have a legal basis, under Article 6 GDPR. Consider first the case of voluntary disclosure to law enforcement *within* the EU – what is the legal basis for such disclosure?

This point was recently considered by the European Data Protection Board (EDPB) and European Data Protection Supervisor (EDPS) in their joint assessment on the impact of the US CLOUD Act on EU law, which concluded that the only possible legal bases for voluntary disclosure are GDPR Articles 6(1)(d) (to protect the vital interests of a natural person) and 6(1)(f) (legitimate interests

[46] See Waltraut Kotschy, 'Article 6: Lawfulness of Processing' in Christopher Kuner and others (eds), *The EU General Data Protection Regulation (GDPR): A Commentary* (OUP, 2020) 343.

[47] Though compare *R (Open Rights Group & the3million) v Secretary of State for the Home Department* [2019] EWHC 2562 (Admin) upholding the somewhat similar immigration exemption under the UK Data Protection Act 2018 as compatible with Article 23 GDPR. For a more convincing argument that the immigration exemption is contrary to both the GDPR and ECHR see Matthew White, 'Immigration Exemption and the European Convention on Human Rights' (2019) 5 *European Data Protection Law Review* 26.

of the data controller or a third party).[48] This is also the consensus in the academic literature.[49] Disclosures under Article 6(1)(d) – typically in emergency situations – are beyond the scope of this chapter, leaving us to consider only Article 6(1)(f). When will this permit voluntary disclosures?

The GDPR itself contemplates that some voluntary disclosures to law enforcement may fall within the concept of legitimate interests and Recital 50 provides in part that:

> Indicating possible criminal acts or threats to public security by the controller and transmitting the relevant personal data in individual cases or in several cases relating to the same criminal act or threats to public security to a competent authority should be regarded as being in the legitimate interest pursued by the controller. However, such transmission in the legitimate interest of the controller or further processing of personal data should be prohibited if the processing is not compatible with a legal, professional or other binding obligation of secrecy.

However, this part of Recital 50 GDPR does not support the wide practice of voluntary disclosure as it has developed in Ireland. The language is framed narrowly to 'individual cases or … several cases relating to the same criminal act or threats' and does not endorse any general or systematic practice of voluntary disclosure. By referring to '[i]ndicating *possible* criminal acts or threats to public security'[50] it envisages the controller taking the initiative to notify the competent authority of the existence of a possible crime or threat – it does not address the situation where the competent authority is already aware and seeks further information from the controller, which could be done by a court order or other formal process.[51]

Recital 50 GDPR also notes that further processing should be prohibited where there is 'a legal, professional or other binding obligation of secrecy', and this imposes a further constraint on voluntary disclosures. Consider, for example, a webmail account belonging to a journalist. Disclosure of data from such an account would, if it was sought to identify a source, amount to a violation of the implied requirement in Article 10 ECHR that such disclosures should take place

[48] European Data Protection Board and European Data Protection Supervisor, 'Joint Response to the LIBE Committee on the Impact of the US Cloud Act on the European Legal Framework for Personal Data Protection' (European Data Protection Board, 12 July 2019), edpb.europa.eu/our-work-tools/our-documents/letters/edpb-edps-joint-response-libe-committee-impact-us-cloud-act_en, accessed 27 May 2020.

[49] Thomas Kopp and Valentin Pfisterer, 'Between a Rock and a Hard Place – Legal Pitfalls of Voluntary Cooperation of German Companies with German and Foreign Regulatory and Law Enforcement Authorities' (2016) 2 *Compliance Elliance Journal* 24; Busser (n 45 above); Haase and Peters (n 45 above); Purtova (n 45 above).

[50] In the French text 'révéler l'existence d'éventuelles infractions pénales ou de menaces pour la sécurité publique'.

[51] Compare the statement by the Canadian Supreme Court in *R v Spencer* [2014] SCR 212 at para 64: 'I also note with respect to an ISP's legitimate interest in preventing crimes committed through its services that entirely different considerations may apply where an ISP itself detects illegal activity and of its own motion wishes to report this activity to the police.'

only on the basis of an ex ante review by an independent body,[52] and would not be permissible under Article 6(1)(f) GDPR. Similar considerations would apply to voluntary disclosure of other material such as that protected by legal professional privilege.

In any event, such disclosure under GDPR Article 6(1)(f) must not take place if the interest of the controller is 'overridden by the interests or fundamental rights and freedoms of the data subject'[53] and application of this balancing test requires an individualised assessment of the need for disclosure and the impact on the data subject.[54] This is an under-appreciated point: the implication is that any disclosure will necessarily amount to a violation of Article 6 unless the decision to disclose was taken by reference to all relevant factors such as the position of the data subject, the nature of the alleged crime, the nature of the data sought and the necessity and proportionality of disclosure.[55] Blanket disclosure policies – such as those stating that data will be disclosed on the basis of a request signed by a Chief Superintendent in the *Garda Síochána*, or on the grounds of 'a valid request from a law enforcement authority' – are per se unlawful; the controller must carry out and document an independent assessment of the proportionality of disclosure *in each case*.

(ii) Disclosure to Law Enforcement in Third Countries

Unlike disclosures within the EU, there appears to be no legal basis for voluntary disclosure to a law enforcement authority in a third country.[56] The starting point is that providers cannot rely on Article 6(1)(c) GDPR (compliance with a legal obligation) as a legal basis, even if they are subject to a warrant or similar legal obligation in the third country.[57] Similarly, the EDPB and EDPS have taken the view that a provider subject to a warrant in a third country cannot fall back on Article 6(1)(f) GDPR. While they accept that a provider may in principle have a legitimate interest in complying with a request to disclose data by a foreign law enforcement authority, particularly if failure to do so would result in sanctions,

[52] See *Telegraaf Media Nederland Landelijke Media BV and others v The Netherlands* [2012] ECHR 1965.

[53] The test becomes more stringent if the data subject has exercised their right to object to processing under Article 21 GDPR, at which point the controller must demonstrate 'compelling legitimate grounds for the processing which override the interests, rights and freedoms of the data subject' to justify disclosure.

[54] Article 29 Data Protection Working Party, 'Opinion 06/2014 on the Notion of Legitimate Interests of the Data Controller under Article 7 of Directive 95/46/EC', www.ec.europa.eu/justice/article-29/documentation/opinion-recommendation/files/2014/wp217_en.pdf, accessed 15 February 2019.

[55] Compare European Data Protection Board, 'Guidelines 3/2019 on Processing of Personal Data through Video Devices' (29 January 2020) 12, www.edpb.europa.eu/sites/edpb/files/files/file1/edpb_guidelines_201903_video_devices.pdf, accessed 29 May 2020; Kopp and Pfisterer (n 49 above) 63–64.

[56] Leaving aside disclosures to protect the vital interests of a natural person under Article 6(1)(d) GDPR.

[57] See European Data Protection Board and European Data Protection Supervisor (n 48 above) 4.

they stress that such authorities are not public or competent authorities established under and subject to EU law. Consequently, in the absence of a framework provided by an international agreement such as a MLAT, the impact on the rights of the data subject will override the interest of the controller.[58]

In addition, the EDPB and EDPS note that there are severe practical difficulties in applying Article 6(1)(f) to demands which are compulsory under the law of a third country: the provider would be unable to carry out a balancing exercise when provided with only limited information as to why information is sought, and would be unable to facilitate the data subject's exercise of their right to object under Article 21(1) GDPR. They therefore conclude that 'the difficulty of applying such [a] balance of interests is a strong argument against leaving the performance of such tests to private operators'.[59]

C. Voluntary Disclosure to a Third Country and Article 49 Derogations

In addition to the lack of a legal basis to make a voluntary disclosure to a law enforcement authority in a third country, where the transfer of data would otherwise be prohibited under Chapter 5 GDPR it is very unlikely that it could be brought within any of the relevant Article 49 derogations.[60] User 'consent' in terms of use would not meet the requirements of prior information and explicit consent under Article 49(1)(a) GDPR. The Article 49(1)(e) derogation for transfers 'necessary for the establishment, exercise or defence of legal claims' is most likely limited to cases in which the data controller is closely involved rather than cases where the controller merely holds some evidence,[61] but in any event transfers for merely *investigative* purposes would not fall within that derogation.[62] The 'important reasons of public interest' derogation under Article 49(1)(d) is very unlikely to apply – the EDPB has taken the view that the public interest at stake must be identified by national or EU law.[63]

Finally, the last paragraph in Article 49(1) permitting transfers for 'compelling legitimate interests pursued by the controller which are not overridden by the interests or rights and freedoms of the data subject' will not apply to systematic

[58] ibid 5; though compare Peter Swire, 'When Does GDPR Act as a Blocking Statute? The Relevance of a Lawful Basis for Transfer' in Randal S Milch, Sebastian Benthall and Alexander Potcovaru (eds), *Cybersecurity and Privacy in a Globalized World – Building Common Approaches* (NYU Center for Cybersecurity, 2019) pt 6.

[59] European Data Protection Board and European Data Protection Supervisor (n 48 above) 6.

[60] Bearing in mind that Article 49, as an exception to the general rule, must be interpreted strictly: compare Case C-119/12, *Josef Probst v mr.nexnet GmbH*, ECLI:EU:C:2012:748 at para 23.

[61] European Data Protection Board, 'Guidelines 2/2018 on Derogations of Article 49 under Regulation 2016/679' p 11, www.edpb.europa.eu/sites/edpb/files/files/file1/edpb_guidelines_2_2018_derogations_en.pdf, accessed 17 February 2019.

[62] Kopp and Pfisterer (n 49 above) 73; European Data Protection Board (n 61 above) 11.

[63] European Data Protection Board (n 61 above) 10.

practices of voluntary disclosure. That derogation applies only if 'the transfer is not repetitive', only if it 'concerns only a limited number of data subjects', only if 'the controller has assessed all the circumstances surrounding the data transfer and has on the basis of that assessment provided suitable safeguards with regard to the protection of personal data', and only if the controller 'inform[s] the data subject of the transfer'. The exceptional nature of this derogation is not compatible with routine and therefore repetitive disclosures; a provider is not in a position to 'provide suitable safeguards' in relation to controlling the use which a third country law enforcement agency may make of personal data; and in many investigations the provider will be precluded by a gagging order from informing the data subject of the transfer.[64] While the European Commission has suggested that this provision might apply to some voluntary disclosures to comply with a third country court order,[65] the better view is that of the European Privacy Law Scholars amicus brief in the *Microsoft Ireland* litigation which points out that:

> [A] data controller's interest in complying with non-EU law is identical to an interest in not complying with the GDPR. Moreover, Article 48 addresses precisely those situations in which a non-EU country seeks data stored in the European Union, so the data controller will always have an interest in complying with such a request. It makes no sense to read Article 49's 'compelling legitimate interest' derogation to swallow Article 48.[66]

V. Assessing Providers' Practices

In the previous section I identified ways in which the GDPR has significantly restricted the scope for voluntary disclosures, particularly to third countries. Without empirical research it is impossible to say whether this has been reflected in a change of practice by providers: the DPC has not publicly examined the issue since the 2011/2012 Facebook audit, and the providers themselves publish little detail.[67] However, a preliminary assessment of privacy policies, law enforcement guidelines and transparency reports suggests that it is still business as usual, with prominent providers still claiming the right to make voluntary disclosures in a way which would violate the GDPR.

[64] European Data Protection Board and European Data Protection Supervisor (n 48 above) 7.

[65] Patrick W Pearsall and Adam G Unikowsky, 'Brief of the European Commission on Behalf of the European Union' (13 December 2017), blogs.microsoft.com/wp-content/uploads/sites/149/2018/01/Brief-of-the-European-Commission-on-Behalf-of-the-EU.pdf, accessed 30 May 2020.

[66] Daniel M Sullivan, 'Brief of EU Data Protection and Privacy Scholars as *Amici Curiae* in Support of Respondent' (18 January 2018) 12, www.blogs.microsoft.com/datalaw/resource/initiative/microsofts-search-warrant-case/, accessed 23 May 2020.

[67] Transparency reports generally do not identify voluntary requests for data (with the exception of emergency requests) and police/judicial authorities do not usually publish these statistics. See eg 'SIRIUS EU Digital Evidence Situation Report 2019: Cross Border Access to Electronic Evidence' (Europol 2019) 8, www.europol.europa.eu/sirius.

Facebook, for example, still differentiates between the 'contents of an account', which 'may require' a MLA request,[68] and non-content data which may be disclosed if a request is legally binding in another jurisdiction.[69] Twitter's Privacy Policy claims a broad discretion to disclose user data in response to a 'governmental request', whether or not it is legally binding.[70] This is narrowed somewhat by the Twitter Guidelines for Law Enforcement[71] which require a 'valid legal process' but still seem to permit voluntary disclosure of non-content data.[72] Google appears to rule out voluntary disclosure to Irish law enforcement authorities but seems to leave the option open in relation to other jurisdictions.[73] Finally, Apple's Legal Process Guidelines differentiate between content data (subject to US law, and requiring a MLA request) and non-content data which can be disclosed on foot of a 'legally valid request' with a 'precise legal basis in the domestic law of the requesting country and […] pertaining to the bona-fide prevention, detection or investigation of offences'.[74]

This is necessarily a limited assessment, and there are no doubt more detailed internal policies which might address some of the issues I have identified. But from the information provided, these voluntary disclosure practices appear to be unlawful: none of these providers distinguish between requests from Member States and requests from third countries; nor do they indicate that they will carry out the balancing test required by Article 6(1)(f) GDPR before giving voluntary disclosure on the basis of legitimate interest. While they do state that they will refuse requests which are overbroad or which undermine freedom of expression, there is no commitment to examining the proportionality of disclosures generally. The requirement that there be a legal basis in the requesting jurisdiction is not enough: the balancing test cannot be outsourced, much less offshored.

A particular problem is that these policies still rely on the content/non-content distinction borrowed from the US Electronic Communications Privacy Act, despite a series of recent cases which recognise significant privacy interests in non-content data. It appears that providers view non-content data as less sensitive, so that restricting disclosure to non-content data serves as an alternative to an individualised balancing test. However, as the ECtHR noted in *Benedik v Slovenia*:

> [W]hat would appear to be peripheral information sought by the police, namely the name and address of a subscriber, must in situations such as the present one be treated

[68] 'Information for Law Enforcement Authorities' (*Facebook*), www.facebook.com/safety/groups/law/guidelines/, accessed 5 June 2020.

[69] 'Data Policy' (n 9 above).

[70] 'Privacy Policy' (n 9 above).

[71] Which, incidentally, still refer to section 8 of the Data Protection Acts 1988 and 2003.

[72] 'Guidelines for Law Enforcement' (*Twitter*), www.help.twitter.com/en/rules-and-policies/twitter-law-enforcement-support> accessed 21 May 2020; see also 'Information Requests – January to June 2019' (*Twitter*), www.transparency.twitter.com/en/information-requests.html, accessed 5 June 2020.

[73] 'How Google Handles Government Requests for User Information' (*Google*), www.policies.google.com/terms/information-requests, accessed 21 May 2020.

[74] 'Legal Process Guidelines: Government & Law Enforcement Outside the United States' (*Apple*), www.apple.com/legal/privacy/law-enforcement-guidelines-outside-us.pdf, accessed 27 May 2020.

> as inextricably connected to the relevant pre-existing content revealing data … To hold otherwise would be to deny the necessary protection to information which might reveal a good deal about the online activity of an individual, including sensitive details of his or her interests, beliefs and intimate lifestyle.[75]

VI. Voluntary Disclosure and the ECHR

Disclosure of personal data engages the Irish state's responsibility under Article 8 ECHR.[76] As the Committee of Ministers noted in its 2013 *Declaration on Risks to Fundamental Rights stemming from Digital Tracking and other Surveillance Technologies*, this responsibility includes both a negative obligation to refrain from interference with privacy rights and also a positive obligation to actively protect these rights against non-state actors such as online service providers.[77] In the present case both positive and negative obligations are involved: Ireland has not only failed to prevent voluntary disclosure to other states, but has endorsed such disclosure through the DPC's audit of Facebook (as well as itself making use of voluntary disclosure requests by the *Garda Síochána*).

To comply with Article 8 ECHR, therefore, disclosure practices must be 'in accordance with the law'. This requires the nature of the law to be compatible with the rule of law: the law must provide protection against arbitrary interference with an individual's rights and must be sufficiently clear in its terms to give individuals an adequate indication as to the circumstances in which public authorities are entitled to use a measure which interferes with those rights.[78]

What this test of legality requires in a particular case depends on the nature of the interference with an individual's rights; for example, different considerations may apply to disclosure of location data as distinct from content data. There is therefore no uniform set of standards; the safeguards required will depend on the nature of the provider and the information to be disclosed. However in one of the most important areas for voluntary disclosure – over the top communications services such as webmail or WhatsApp – we can identify a specific set of rules established by the ECtHR in an extensive line of cases regarding communications data. To (over)simplify, for state access to communications data to be 'in accordance with the law' there must be a legislative framework which: regulates the types of crimes which may give rise to access; establishes some form of independent oversight providing effective and continuous control of access (preferably with judicial involvement, whether ex ante or ex post); provides for notification

[75] *Benedik v Slovenia* [2018] ECHR 363 at paras 109–110.

[76] This section focuses on the ECHR but the same points can be made mutatis mutandis in relation to the CFR which will also be engaged.

[77] Committee of Ministers of the Council of Europe, 'Declaration of the Committee of Ministers on Risks to Fundamental Rights Stemming from Digital Tracking and Other Surveillance Technologies' (11 June 2013).

[78] *Khan v United Kingdom* [2000] ECHR 194, para 26.

of affected individuals or an equivalent safeguard against abuses; and provides controls on the use and deletion of acquired data.[79] To the extent that the CFR is also engaged, then the higher standards articulated in *Tele2/Watson*[80] (restriction to serious crime, ex ante authorisation by an independent body and mandatory notification of affected individuals) will also apply where the disclosure of data creates a 'serious interference' with fundamental rights – that is, where the data allows 'precise conclusions to be drawn concerning the private lives of the persons whose data is concerned.'[81]

Applying these standards, it is clear that voluntary disclosure in the Irish context – by giving providers a largely unfettered discretion without any statutory framework, and by allowing police to seek data without any independent authorisation or oversight – is inconsistent with the legality requirements of Article 8, and especially so in relation to communications data. Indeed, the problematic nature of voluntary disclosure was identified by the ECtHR long before the modern internet. In its 1984 judgment in *Malone v United Kingdom*[82] the Court considered the UK practice of the Post Office giving to the police 'metering' data (information about the numbers dialled and the time/duration of each call) without any statutory basis to do so, holding that:

> [N]o rule of domestic law makes it unlawful for the Post Office voluntarily to comply with a request from the police to make and supply records of metering … [A]part from the simple absence of prohibition, there would appear to be no legal rules concerning the scope and manner of exercise of the discretion enjoyed by the public authorities. Consequently, although lawful in terms of domestic law, the interference resulting from the existence of the practice in question was not 'in accordance with the law'.[83]

It is unfortunate that, nearly 40 years later, this still has to be reiterated.

VII. Conclusion

In this chapter I have argued that voluntary disclosure of personal data by online service providers is an import of US standards under the Electronic Communications Privacy Act which is incompatible with European legal norms. Previously it was protected from scrutiny by section 8(b) of the Irish Data Protection Acts 1988 and 2003; with that shield taken away it will come under increasing challenge by civil society and by individuals whose data has been disclosed. It will be interesting to see how providers respond; it may not take long

[79] On these requirements see eg TJ McIntyre, 'Judicial Oversight of Surveillance: The Case of Ireland in Comparative Perspective' in Martin Scheinin, Helle Krunke and Marina Aksenova (eds), *Judges as Guardians of Constitutionalism and Human Rights* (Edward Elgar, 2016).

[80] Joined Cases C-203/15 and C-698/15 *Tele2 Sverige/Watson*, ECLI:EU:C:2016:970.

[81] Case C-207/16 *Ministerio Fiscal*, ECLI:EU:C:2018:788, para 60.

[82] *Malone v United Kingdom* [1985] ECHR 5.

[83] Ibid, para 87.

for the risk of GDPR fines to curtail voluntary disclosure. If so, this will reflect a wider international trend restricting disclosures of private information to law enforcement without statutory safeguards.[84] Probably the best known example is the judgment of the Supreme Court of Canada in *R v Spencer*,[85] holding that it was a violation of section 8 of the Canadian Charter of Rights and Freedoms for an internet access provider to disclose subscriber data without prior judicial authorisation. The same concerns can also be seen in other contexts such as disclosure by genetic genealogy firms, where initial willingness to provide data to police has been curtailed by a significant public backlash.[86]

Regulatory convergence will also undermine voluntary disclosure in the near future. From December 2020 the new European Electronic Communications Code[87] will expand the scope of the ePrivacy Directive by widening the definition of 'electronic communications services' beyond traditional voice telephony, SMS messages and emails, to include also a number of over the top services such as voice over IP, messaging and chat services, and webmail services.[88] These services will then come within the stronger confidentiality rules of Article 5 of the ePrivacy Directive, which prohibits 'interception or surveillance of communications and the related traffic data without the consent of the users concerned' except where authorised by legislative measures, significantly restricting the scope for voluntary disclosure.

Finally, the likely decline of voluntary disclosure will further increase pressure to adopt new schemes for cross-border access to data, particularly the proposed e-Evidence package[89] and the related Commission mandate to enter into negotiations on an EU-US agreement to facilitate access to electronic evidence in criminal investigations.[90] The merits of these are beyond the scope of this chapter, but the point must be made that any reform should supplant, not merely supplement, voluntary disclosure: it must not be possible to evade the safeguards in new rules by falling back on old informal practices.

[84] See eg Ira S Rubinstein, Gregory T Nojeim and Ronald D Lee, 'Systematic Government Access to Private-Sector Data: A Comparative Analysis' in Fred H Cate and James X Dempsey (eds), *Bulk Collection: Systematic Government Access to Private-Sector Data* (Oxford University Press, 2017) 20 as well as the other chapters in that edited collection.

[85] *R v Spencer* [2014] SCR 212.

[86] Sevasti Skeva, Maarten HD Larmuseau and Mahsa Shabani, 'Review of Policies of Companies and Databases Regarding Access to Customers' Genealogy Data for Law Enforcement Purposes' (2020) 17 *Personalized Medicine* 141.

[87] See (n 6 above).

[88] Rosa Barcelo and Matthew Buckwell, 'New European Electronic Communications Code Means the Application of the EPrivacy Directive to OTTs' (*IAPP Privacy Tracker*, 2019), www.iapp.org/news/a/new-european-electronic-communications-code-means-the-application-of-the-eprivacy-directive-to-otts/, accessed 19 May 2020.

[89] See (n 7 above).

[90] European Commission, 'Joint statement on the launch of EU-U.S. negotiations to facilitate access to electronic evidence' (26 September 2019), www.ec.europa.eu/commission/presscorner/detail/en/STATEMENT_19_5890, accessed 26 June 2020.

10

European Law Enforcement and US Data Companies: A Decade of Cooperation Free from Law

ANGELA AGUINALDO AND PAUL DE HERT

I. Introduction

Online evidence has become indispensable in criminal matters but due to its transnational and volatile nature, law enforcement authorities are confronted with challenges in accessing, securing, and using it in their investigations and prosecutions of both online and ordinary crimes. Traditional routes of international cooperation such as mutual legal assistance have allegedly become more of stumbling blocks rather than instruments of efficiency and fluidity in ensuring that law enforcement authorities are not hampered in the fulfilment of their duties and obligations. It does not help that online evidence, and cyberspace matters in general, are intertwined with sensitive issues that ought to be addressed and yet no definite consensus has been made towards a solution.

Thus, it has not been surprising to see on the state, regional, and international levels that recourse to different methods has been made to overcome these challenges. There is, for instance, the phenomenon of data localisation or nationalisation, compelling service providers and tech companies to localise and keep data within the confines of a particular jurisdiction.[1] The evident objective of this state-centric approach is to create domestic-level information controls to shift governance away from international or pluralist governance models.[2]

[1] Christoph Burchard, 'Der grenzüberschreitende Zugriff auf Clouddaten im Lichte der Fundamental-prinzipien der internationalen Zusammenarbeit in Strafsachen – Teil 1' (2018) 7 *Zeitschrift für die internationale Strafrechtsdogmatik* 52, 52; Paul De Hert, Cihan Parlar and Johannes Thumfart, 'Legal Arguments Used in Courts Regarding Territoriality and Cross-Border Production Orders: From Yahoo Belgium to Microsoft Ireland' (2018) 9 *New Journal of European Criminal Law* 326, 326; Jonas Force Hill, 'Problematic Alternatives: MLAT Reform for the Digital Age', 28 January 2015, *Harvard Law School National Security Journal* 1.

[2] Ronald J Deibert and Louis W Pauly, 'Mutual Entanglement and Complex Sovereignty in Cyberspace' in Didier Bigo, Engin Isin and Evelyn Ruppert (eds), *Data Politics: Worlds, Subjects, Rights* (Routledge, 2019) 81, 81.

Also oversimplifying, at the cost of the blurred reality of the digital, is the resort to unilateralism or jurisdictional expansion – an expanding, deepening, and more elaborate extraterritorial projection of power which overstretches a state's jurisdiction over data regardless of where the same is located.[3] In connection to this, law enforcement authorities are finding ways to directly cooperate with service providers and tech companies – while attempting to legitimise their actions – to access online evidence without the hurdles posed by traditional international cooperation agreements.

Although initially not acknowledged, voluntary or not-so-voluntary cooperation between law enforcement authorities and service providers has been a reality for more than a decade as regards online evidence in criminal matters.[4] The Council of Europe, in its 2008 Guidelines,[5] tacitly recognised that direct liaison between foreign service providers and law enforcement authorities occurred, albeit that the said practice was highly discouraged.[6] In 2012 and 2013, statistics were provided by the biggest tech companies and service providers that further highlighted this trend.[7] In a 2014 report, the Council of Europe concluded that

> the prosecution or police services of many States contact foreign service providers directly, in particular those based in the United States, and these may respond positively under certain conditions. Such requests may take the form of domestic production orders. Some providers may respond directly to requests related to emergency situations. Overall, conditions for such direct contacts are unclear; in some countries information thus obtained may need to be validated through a subsequent mutual legal assistance (MLA)- request before use as evidence in court.[8]

[3] Burchard (n 1 above) 52; De Hert, Parlar and Thumfart (n 1 above) 326; Deibert and Pauly (n 2 above) 81; Hill (n 1 above) 1. For illustrations of unilateralism, see David Callaway and Lothar Determann, 'The New US Cloud Act – History, Rules, and Effects' (2018) 35 *The Computer & Internet Lawyer* 4; Paul De Hert and Monika Kopcheva, 'International Mutual Legal Assistance in Criminal Law Made Redundant: A Comment on the Belgian Yahoo! Case' (2011) 27 *Computer Law & Security Review* 291, 291–97.

[4] Micheál O'Floinn, 'It Wasn't All White Light before Prism: Law Enforcement Practices in Gathering Data Abroad, and Proposals for Further Transnational Access at the Council of Europe' (2013) 29 *Computer Law & Security Review* 610, 611.

[5] Guidelines for the Cooperation between Law Enforcement and Internet Service Providers against Cybercrime, adopted by the global Conference Cooperation against Cybercrime, 01-02 April 2008, Guideline 36.

[6] Ian Walden, 'Accessing Data in the Cloud: The Long Arm of the Law Enforcement Agent' in Siani Pearson and George Yee (eds), *Privacy and Security for Cloud Computing* (Springer, 2013) 47.

[7] In April 2013 Google published its annual transparency reports and disclosed how authorities would interact with the company by requesting content removal or user data. Of all the requests Google received, 40% were complied with. One-third of the requests received came from EU Member States. On the other hand, Microsoft released its Law Enforcement Requests Report that shows that in 2012 requests from EU Member States represented 47% of the total requests. See Gertjan Boulet and Nicholas Hernanz, 'Cross-Border Law Enforcement Access to Data on the Internet and Rule of Law Challenges in the EU' (2013) 6 SAPIENT Policy Brief (Deliverable 6.6).

[8] Cybercrime Convention Committee, 'T-CY Assessment Report: The Mutual Legal Assistance Provisions of the Budapest Convention on Cybercrime', *12th Plenary of the Cybercrime Convention Committee* (Council of Europe 2014) 124.

In September 2016, a survey was conducted by the European Commission that revealed a lack of common approach to obtaining cross-border access to digital evidence by Member States: either they accessed evidence by going directly to service providers with a request to cooperate or by means of direct cross-border access to digital evidence.[9]

Today law enforcement authorities are less coy on this kind of practice: in many countries they routinely turn to foreign service providers (often based in the US) and are provided with data from these providers, with the latter having readily available mechanisms to grant these requests.[10]

We start our contribution with a short section on the recent reforms to codify direct cooperation between law enforcement authorities and private actors (section II). After a discussion of the 2018 US CLOUD Act, we turn to the proposal of the European Union to facilitate cross-border access to electronic evidence, which was presented by the European Commission in April 2018 (e-evidence package) and the reform process at the Council of Europe to amend the 2001 Cybercrime Convention envisaging a similar mechanism and powers.

The following section discusses the current MLA framework that regulates cooperation in criminal matters and exchange of evidence between the US and Europe (section III). The MLA system allows cooperation between enforcement authorities but does not foresee any basis for direct cooperation with private actors in other states. Nonetheless this practice was dubiously accepted by the regulatory community on shaky interpretative grounds as permissible under Article 18 (on domestic production orders) and 32 (on extraterritorial data access relying on consent) of the Cybercrime Convention (see section IV).

We then proceed in section V with the challenges this kind of relationship poses for state interests and for public international law and the individual concerned that is deprived by these informal practices of certain checks and guarantees built into the formal MLA system as stated above. This discussion includes issues surrounding data protection that arise from the kind of relationship that allows law enforcement authorities to have direct access to online evidence through cooperating directly with service providers and tech companies (see section VI). After a brief reflection on the weight of privacy and data protection in criminal law matters, we identify the relevant dos and don'ts in data protection law and clarify the relationship between our subject matter and the outcomes of the two *Schrems* judgments of the CJEU. In particular, the combination of the teachings of *Schrems II* (decided on 16 July 2020) about the deficiencies in US law with those of the German Federal Constitutional Court on the proportionality of domestic production orders (BVerfG, 27 May 2020) might add to the relevance of data protection

[9] Els De Busser, 'The Digital Unfitness of Mutual Legal Assistance' (2017) 28 *Security and Human Rights* 161, 171. See for other reports, De Hert, Parlar and Thumfart (n 1 above) 328.

[10] Bert-Jaap Koops and Morag Goodwin, 'Cyberspace, the Cloud, and Cross-Border Criminal Investigation: The Limits and Possibilities of International Law' (Tilburg University, 2014) 58; O'Floinn (n 4 above) 61.

as an argument against informal trans-border co-operations (section VII). Lastly, we summarise our discussion and provide recommendations for further study and discussion (section VIII).

II. New Alternative Systems to The MLATs

In 2018, the United States enacted the Clarifying Lawful Overseas Use of Data (CLOUD) Act, allowing US federal law enforcement authorities to compel US-based data companies (via warrant or subpoena) to provide data, regardless of whether the data are stored in the US or on foreign soil.[11] With the Act the US now declares that it has the authority to reach into the data centres of US data companies in Europe without any need for international corporation or European judicial controls.[12] But there is also good news for Europe. The CLOUD Act also exempts international requests for data from US firms from the traditional framework of mutual legal assistance treaties in criminal law (MLATs). Rather than operating through treaties, the US executive branch is given the ability to enter into bi-lateral ('executive') agreements with foreign countries to provide requested data related to its citizens in a streamlined manner, as long as the Attorney General, with concurrence of the Secretary of State, agrees that the foreign country adheres to applicable international human rights obligations and has sufficient protections in place to restrict access to data related to US citizens. No special guarantees are built in for data relating to non-US citizens. Once such an agreement is there, direct contacts between foreign law enforcement authorities and US data companies are permitted in response to an order from a foreign government with which the United States has an executive agreement on data access, a provider may intercept or disclose the contents of a stored electronic communication or non-content records or information pertaining to a subscriber or customer.

Simultaneously, the same year, the European Union (EU) proposed similar sweeping changes which would allow European law enforcement agencies in Member States to preserve and collect cloud-based evidence outside of the MLAT system. This e-evidence package includes 'a proposed regulation for European Production and Preservation Orders' as well as 'a proposed directive' supplementary thereto, which will mandate the establishment of legal representatives of service providers within the EU that could be served with orders.[13] Like the

[11] The Act was signed by Trump on 23 March 2018 and amends the Stored Communications Act (SCA) of 1986 and the Electronic Communications Privacy Act of the same year.

[12] Lawrence Siry, 'Cloudy Days Ahead: Cross-Border Evidence Collection and Its Impact on the Rights of EU Citizens' (2019) 10 *New Journal of European Criminal Law* 227, 241.

[13] European Commission, Proposal for a Regulation of the European Parliament and of the Council on European Production and Preservation Orders for electronic evidence in criminal matters, COM(2018) 225 final; Council of Europe, 'Legal Opinion on Budapest Cybercrime Convention: Use of a Disconnection Clause in the Second Additional Protocol to the Budapest Convention on Cybercrime';

CLOUD Act, the EU proposals organise direct cooperation with service providers while taking away the need to go through the traditional route of mutual legal assistance.[14] These proposals are intended as fast-track alternatives vis-à-vis online evidence to make it 'easier to secure and gather electronic evidence for criminal proceedings stored or held by service providers in another jurisdiction'.[15] The main idea is that certificates of judicial orders will be transmitted directly to the legal representatives of online service providers. These will be obliged to respond within 10 days or, in urgent cases, within six hours.

Finally, there is the work of the Council of Europe (CoE), mother organisation of the 2001 Cybercrime Convention.[16] Currently, the organisation is drafting a second new Protocol to the Cybercrime Convention. The work on the Second Additional Protocol started in June 2017.[17] The Second Additional Protocol is meant to clarify matters on transnational access to electronic evidence and is supposed 'to set out, among other things, a clearer framework and stronger safeguards for existing practices of transborder access to data and safeguards, including data protection requirements',[18] including provisions for an efficient and effective mutual legal assistance, direct trans-border cooperation with providers, a framework and safeguards for practices of trans-border access to data, including trans-border searches, and data protection provisions.[19] With regard to mutual legal assistance, the Second Additional Protocol is intended to be the legal basis for international production orders or simplified MLA for subscriber information, direct cooperation between authorities, joint investigations, requests to be made in English, and emergency procedures.[20]

A detailed account of these regulatory initiatives can be found in other contributions to this volume,[21] but for purposes of the present discussion, it can be said that in terms of human rights and data protection concerns, much will depend on the implementation of the US CLOUD Act by the US executive, and on the details of the two European initiatives. In terms of state choice between unilateralism and

Sofie Depauw, 'Electronic Evidence in Criminal Matters: How About E-Evidence Instruments 2.0?' (2018) 8 *European Criminal Law Review* 62, 1–23; Ángel Tinoco Pastrana, 'The Proposal on Electronic Evidence in the European Union' (2020) 15 *EUCrim* 46, 46–50.

[14] See Proposed Regulation on the European Preservation and Production Orders, arts 2, 4–7.

[15] Other international cooperation instruments such as the European Investigative Order and mutual legal assistance will continue to exist. See the Explanatory Memorandum on the Proposed Regulation on the European Preservation and Production Orders.

[16] Convention on Cybercrime, Budapest, 23 November 2001, available at conventions.coe.int/Treaty/EN/Treaties/Html/185.htm.

[17] Europe (n 13 above); Cybercrime Convention Committee (T-CY), 'Preparation of the 2nd Additional Protocol to the Budapest Convention on Cybercrime: State of Play', p 2.

[18] See Depauw (n 13 above) 3; Luca Tosoni, 'Rethinking Privacy in the Council of Europe's Convention on Cybercrime' (2018) 34(6) *Computer Law & Security Review* 1197, 1210.

[19] De Hert, Parlar and Thumfart (n 1 above) 335; Alexander Seger, 'E-Evidence and Access to Data in the Cloud Results of the Cloud Evidence Group of the Cybercrime Convention Committee', *Handling and Exchanging Electronic Evidence Across Europe* (Springer, 2018).

[20] Seger (n 19 above) 40; Cybercrime Convention Committee (T-CY) (n 17 above) 2.

[21] See for a first analysis, Mirko Hohmann and Sophie Barnett, 'System Upgrade. Improving Cross-Border Access to Electronic Evidence', GPPI Policy Brief.

multilateralism to face extraterritorial challenges, the same 'wait and see' attitude is warranted. In particular, the US and the EU initiatives have an aggressive unilateral dimension in facilitating their law enforcement authorities to obtain data abroad, and it is likely that other states, including authoritarian ones, are going to seek the same kind of access.[22] If the US limits its executive agreements to 'like-minded states' in terms of human rights, without MLA reform to help out the others, these states will likely move ahead with their own national initiatives to access user data, including measures like forced data localisation or government-sponsored hacking. Such approaches can threaten user rights and hurt businesses.[23]

III. The MLA Framework with the US

MLA represents the classical treaty-based mechanism allowing for foreign law enforcement cooperation and assistance in ongoing criminal investigations and proceedings, while respecting the notions of jurisdiction and national sovereignty in criminal justice matters. MLA is mostly based on treaties between states that confirm that authorities can send each other requests for help (to search a house, to hear a witness, to send over a copy of a criminal record). These treaties then specify the modalities of cooperation based on requests and contain mechanisms that allow requested states to perform certain checks on the incoming requests before deciding whether to follow up with the request.[24] States can traditionally refuse cooperation when this would be detrimental to their interest or state sovereignty. The MLA system has gained its place in international public law. It is built on the idea of mutual respect between states and the principle of territoriality as the starting point of jurisdiction, giving states wide discretion in law enforcement within their territory but forcing them to request assistance when evidence is situated abroad or when suspects have evaded the territory. The doctrine of territoriality has successfully created trust among the actors involved, preventing states from enforcing their laws extraterritorially and infringing the sovereign territory of other states.[25]

Its success cannot nonetheless shield its shortcomings: not all states have signed MLATs; international public law is poor in enforcing the MLA system and the territoriality principle; it is not designed for handling a high number of requests;

[22] 'In general, the EU should be aware that the scope of the change to the system of international data access it proposes with the Regulation and the respective production orders is quite dramatic. If it gives its member states access to data stored by companies that are not incorporated in the EU, other states, including authoritarian ones, are going to seek the same kind of access. This does not mean that one should not establish such a system, but it is necessary to be aware of the consequences': Hohmann and Barnett (n 21 above) 25.

[23] Hohmann and Barnett (n 21 above) 25.

[24] De Busser (n 9 above) 162–63.

[25] Hohmann and Barnett (n 21 above) 17.

it does not distinguish between light and heavy assistance and does not foresee swift, but balanced procedures for 'light' requests about, for instance, subscriber data; MLATs frequently do not address fundamental issues like the balancing of defence rights or data protection and privacy with law enforcement's need for evidence,[26] and MLATs' strong link with territoriality when applied to data that is often unterritorial does not address contemporary understandings and 'questions of data jurisdiction, like how to treat data held overseas by a subsidiary of a domestic parent company'.[27]

The US has MLATs of a general nature with all Member States of the EU and with the EU itself, all of a recent nature,[28] with broadly formulated possibilities to request assistance suited in relation to many aspects, including obtaining data. It is true, however, that these treaties were conceived in the pre-Internet era, do not envisage contacts with private parties abroad, and do not formulate answers to most of the shortcomings identified in the previous paragraph.

The US has equally ratified, together with other European and non-European states, the more specific 2001 Cybercrime Convention.[29] Cooperation with private partners is featured in this convention,[30] but only at the national level, not at the international level. Most of the shortcomings of MLATs discussed *above* are also present. The Convention is poor on defence rights,[31] on privacy and data protection; is based on the territoriality principle and on the idea that data can be located in space; there is no 'light' MLA procedure for requests like obtaining subscriber data, and the text of this convention is bereft of any provision that permits law enforcement authorities to directly contact foreign service providers in pursuit of cross-border access and exchange of online evidence in criminal matters.

[26] 'MLATs frequently do not specify what constitutes "protected data" or under what conditions "content" differs from "metadata" for the purposes of information sharing. This hinders cooperation between states with differing domestic understanding of these terms': Hill (n 1 above) 2.

[27] Hill (n 1 above) 2; Jennifer Daskal, 'The Un-Territoriality of Data' (2015) 125 *Yale Law Journal* 326. Cf Hohmann and Barnett (n 21 above) 17. Under the territoriality principle the data's physical location determines the jurisdiction to which the data and thus the company holding the data is subject. The US CLOUD Act and the EU initiative focus on the locations of the user and the company – rather than that of the data – as the determinant of jurisdiction, in order to oblige companies to transfer data, irrespective of the place of storage. As such, they depart from the principle of territoriality.

[28] One national example: Agreement between the Kingdom of Belgium and the United States of America on mutual legal assistance in criminal matters, signed 28 January 1998, *Belgian Official Journal*, 8 December 1998, entry into force on 18 December 1999. At EU level; *Agreement on Mutual Assistance in Criminal Matters between the European Union and the United States of America*, 25 June 2003, OJ L 181/34–42, 19 July 2003. The agreement that was concluded in 2008 with the EU further harmonises the 27 Member State agreements. (OJ L 291, 7 November 2009).

[29] See the chart of signatures at: https://www.coe.int/en/web/conventions/full-list/-/conventions/treaty/185/signatures?p_auth=ZZawh58m.

[30] The convention invites Member States to create on behalf of their law enforcement authorities, powers to order providers to produce certain data, powers to order the preservation of data, and powers to search computers and networks.

[31] Jonathan Clough, 'A World of Difference: The Budapest Convention of Cybercrime and the Challenges of Harmonisation' (2014) 40 *Monash University Law Review* 698, 710.

IV. The Cybercrime Convention As a Basis for Direct Cooperation

The drafters of the Convention were well aware of the importance of these contacts with internationally based firms, but they only created 'domestic' production orders (and only) for subscriber data. Article 18 allows them to order 'a service provider offering its services in the territory of the Party to submit subscriber information relating to such services in that service provider's possession or control'. Contacting providers outside the territory is unforeseen in the Convention. Extraterritorial matters or cross-border access instead are covered by classical MLAT terms of cooperation *between* law enforcement authorities (Articles 25, 27, 31, 33, and 34), wherein a Party needs to send a request to another Party to obtain or access data found in the latter's territory. Article 32 is the only exception, and allows for domestic law enforcement authorities' trans-border access to stored computer data where publicly available, or to any data in another country if they obtain the 'lawful and voluntary consent of the person who has the lawful authority to disclose the data to the party through that computer system'.

Today it is felt that that the Cybercrime Convention is a missed opportunity to resolve jurisdictional issues or to regulate investigative measures in cyberspace.[32] In 2011, the Cybercrime Convention Committee (T-CY) discussed possible ways to enable or regulate trans-border access to data through the Cybercrime Convention through either an amendment or a protocol,[33] but, because of the time-consuming nature of this venture, it started focusing on expanding the interpretation of the Convention via interpretative soft law instruments. Thus, the so-called Guidance Notes entered the picture and they taught us that Article 18 on domestic production orders and the exception in Article 32 could work via consent, and be read in such a way as to make possible, legally speaking, coerced cooperation with companies offering services to Europeans (even when they work abroad) and voluntary cooperation with companies in case the data is in another country.[34] Bad faith

[32] Catherine Van De Heyning, 'The Boundaries of Jurisdiction in Cybercrime and Constitutional Protection: The European Perspective' in Oresto Pollicino and Graziella Romeo (eds), *The Internet and Constitutional Law: The Protection of Fundamental Rights and Constitutional Adjudication in Europe* (Routledge, 2016) 26, 41–42.

[33] Cybercrime Convention Committee (T-CY) Ad-Hoc Subgroup on Transborder Access and Jurisdiction, 'Transborder Access to Data and Jurisdiction: Options for Further Action by the T-CY', *8th Plenary of the Cybercrime Convention Committee* (Council of Europe, 2012); Koops and Goodwin (n 10 above) 37; O'Floinn (n 4 above) 611.

[34] We have elsewhere exhaustively discussed the details and clarifications proffered by *Guidance Note No 3* involving transnational access as provided in Article 32 (2014), and *Guidance Note No 10* involving domestic production orders as provided in Article 18 (2017) vis-à-vis trans-border access to online evidence in criminal matters in earlier contributions: see Angela Aguinaldo and Paul De Hert, 'The Council of Europe Machinery Influencing International Law Through Guidance Notes and a Proposed Second Additional Protocol' in Vanessa Franssen and Stanislaw Tosza (eds), *Cambridge Handbook of Digital Evidence in Criminal Investigations* (Cambridge University Press, 2020); Paul De Hert, Cihan Parlar and Juraj Sajfert, 'The Cybercrime Convention Committee's 2017 Guidance Note on Production

toward the original spirit and text of the Convention is apparent in these Guidance Notes, as they ignore how the Convention is structured and how it is based on the territoriality principle. Guidance Note No 10 specifically confuses the citizen's consent with the consent of the company processing this citizen's data. This 'guidance' worked nonetheless. In policy discussions of recent years, direct cooperation with providers in the US was generally accepted as compatible with the Cybercrime Convention, albeit lacking further clarification.[35]

V. Direct Contacts with Private Parties and Issues of Legality, Trust and MLA-Rights

Notwithstanding the practice of direct contacts being 'generally accepted', a lot of issues can be identified. Firstly, both the existence of informal practices and the attempt to shield behind the Cybercrime Convention are problematic with regard to legal analysis and coherence of international public law. Respectable as prosecutors and law enforcement authorities might be, things get troubled when they take a hard swing at the text of the Cybercrime Convention. Article 32 clearly targets consent of users, not of companies processing data of these users. Article 18 is part

Orders: Unilateralist Transborder Access to Electronic Evidence Promoted via Soft Law' (2018) 34 *Computer Law & Security Review* 327.

[35] In all relevant documents on direct cooperation and data transfers by data protection authorities, it is striking to note that all these authorities (Working Party 29, European Data Protection Board (EDPB) and European Data Protection Supervisor) either seem to accept the practice on the basis of Article 32 of the Convention or at least fail to contradict this view. Compare 'While the Commission highlights that the consent for access or to receive stored computer data, in the sense of Article 32(b) of the Budapest Convention does not refer to the consent of the individual for the processing of personal data, several references to "the affected person" seem to imply that for certain legislative options the consent of a data subject could be considered as a legal ground for access' (Statement of the Article 29 Working Party, 'Data protection and privacy aspects of cross-border access to electronic evidence', Brussels, 29 November 2017, pp 6-7 at: www.ec.europa.eu/newsroom/just/document.cfm?doc_id=48801) and 'With regards to trans-border direct access to stored computer data as per Article 32(b) of the Budapest Convention, the EDPB reaffirms in particular that data controller can normally only disclose data upon prior presentation of a judicial authorisation/warrant or any document justifying the need to access the data and referring to the relevant legal basis for this access, presented by a national law enforcement authority according to their domestic law that will specify the purpose for which data is required' (EDPB contribution to the consultation on a draft second additional protocol to the Council of Europe Convention on Cybercrime (Budapest Convention), Brussels, 13th November 2019, p 2 at: www.edpb.europa.eu/our-work-tools/our-documents/edpb-contribution-consultation-draft-second-additional-protocol-council_en). See also the Article 29 Working Party's comments on the issue of direct access by third countries' law enforcement authorities to data stored in other jurisdictions, as proposed in the draft elements for an additional protocol to the Budapest Convention on Cybercrime, 05/12/2013; EDPS Opinion 3/19 regarding the participation in the negotiations in view of a Second Additional Protocol to the Budapest Cybercrime Convention, at: www.edps.europa.eu/sites/edp/files/publication/19-04-02_edps_opinion_budapest_convention_en.pdf.

of a convention clearly based on the idea of territoriality of data and distinguishing between domestically held data (subject to domestic orders under Article 18) and MLA procedures for non-domestically held data. The Convention furthermore provides that all powers and procedures established in the Convention are subject to the conditions and safeguards under the domestic (constitutional) law of the Member States and the protection of human rights, in particular those entrenched in the ECHR.[36] Hence, a legal basis that includes safeguards is imperative for any cooperation with any private actor.

In light of the current practice, trust problems could arise. The MLA system has created trust amongst states due to its formalised nature and its respect for territorial sovereignty. The direct cooperation approach, as an expression of unilateralism, is a fundamental departure therefrom and can affect the trust between stakeholders and carry unexpected ramifications. Codification will only bring this issue to the forefront. The lauded success of direct cooperation might be premature or even fleeting. Hohmann and Barnett rightly point to the aggressiveness (in terms of international law) of the proposed EU e-evidence package: without distinction between democratic states with observation of the rule of law and others, it allows European authorities to demand access from all companies that provide services in their territory. These authors rightly wonder about the follow up by other states (democratic or not) that will demand such access too and will refer to the EU law as justification.[37]

Another trust issue is with civil society and human rights groups, representatives of which have already spoken out against the CLOUD Act and against the EU and CoE initiatives because, as stakeholders, they were evidently kept out of the policy loop in the informal co-creation of the direct contact system (built by law enforcement authorities together with US data firms) and in most of the regulatory work by the US and 'the two Europes'.[38]

[36] The Convention stresses the importance of a proper legal basis, of judicial and independent supervision and of limitations of scope and duration of the powers and procedures provided. Article 18 needs to be read together with, and refers explicitly to, Articles 14 and 15 of the same Convention. We repeat that Article 18 is only about *domestic* production orders and allows 'persons in the territory to be ordered to hand over all data and 'service providers offering services in the territory' to hand over subscriber data. The first important element is the duty for states to introduce specific legal provisions to allow these domestic orders: Member States should introduce a cooperation duty for service providers (Article 14). Only then can enforcement authorities compel ISPs to provide data within their possession or control. See Van De Heyning (n 32 above) 42–43. Given the reference to fundamental rights, in particular the ECHR, in the Convention (Article 15), this cooperation duty is to be developed with respect for the defence of privacy and data protection. The second element in Article 18 and its distinction between 'orders to persons' *in the territory* (Article 18 (1a) (emphasis added)) and 'orders to service providers' *offering services in the territory* (Article 18 (1b) (emphasis added)) is that more can be asked from the former than from the latter: all computer data can be requested from persons in the territory, but only subscriber data (hence, no traffic data or content data) can be requested from service providers *offering services in the territory*.

[37] Hohmann and Barnett (n 21 above) 22.

[38] Hohmann and Barnett (n 21 above) 25; Paul De Hert and Angela Aguinaldo, 'A Leading Role for the EU in Drafting Criminal Law Powers? Use of the Council of Europe for Policy Laundering' (2019) 10(2) *New Journal of European Criminal Law* 99. Interesting is the proposal to establish an expert

A third trust aspect concerns the involvement of private actors in the investigation of crimes and in assisting law enforcement authorities from all parts of the world. Legal experts have difficulties with this 'natural trend' to ask data from companies that are then supposed to assess and vet these requests from foreign authorities. What criteria will they use to say 'yes' or 'no' to requests? Hohmann and Barnett observe that there is a risk in privatising legal assistance, 'because companies will follow their own guidance and establish their own mechanisms for evaluating such requests, which are neither wholly transparent nor determined in democratic processes'.[39]

Further, as De Busser has opined, a service provider is a company and not an authority, so invoking grounds for refusal as one knows them from mutual legal assistance agreements and mutual recognition would not be a task for the provider.[40] De Busser further notes that it is not generally part of the interests of service provider companies to refuse cooperation based on, for example, double criminality or *ne bis in idem*, and in fact they cannot be expected to have the knowledge base or capacity to thoroughly assess such grounds and other issues.[41] Thus, it would not be surprising that, even if private companies were given the responsibilities to be aware of all the relevant data protection legislation, mutual legal assistance and other cooperation legislation, grounds of refusal, etc, as well as increased capacity to entertain requests coming from different countries, service providers would never grasp completely the idea of political and constitutional responsibility, let alone the common public spirit.[42]

VI. Privacy and Data Protection Repercussions

The confrontation between criminal procedural law and privacy or data protection seldom delivers groundbreaking results. Investigating crimes often trumps privacy and data protection concerns as long as there is a firm legal basis for investigatory powers and a graduated system of checks and balances proportional to the seriousness of the privacy infringements. In order to pass the European human rights standards of the European Court of Human Rights it helps – but it is not enough – to have a judge involved in the investigation either beforehand, during,

and stakeholder input process for non-governmental stakeholders to rebuild trust in the CLOUD Act system and the proposal to demand transparency reports from both US data firms and governments detailing the number of requests sent or received, respectively (including the number of requests that were declined) combined with regular reviews and audits to check whether governments as well as companies are complying with the legal framework.

[39] Hohmann and Barnett (n 21 above) 19.

[40] De Busser (n 9 above) 172.

[41] De Busser (n 9 above) 172.

[42] Christoph Burchard, 'Der Grenzüberschreitende Zugriff Auf Clouddaten Im Lichte Der Fundamental-Prinzipien Der Internationalen Zusammenarbeit in Strafsachen – Teil 2' (2018) 7/8 *Zeitschrift für die internationale Strafrechtsdogmatik* 249, 260.

or after the investigative measure of some importance is carried out.[43] Other measures can be left to the discretion of authorities. Serious privacy objections in criminal law will trigger serious guarantees, but usually lack the clout to block certain powers asked for by the law enforcement community permanently. Having said that, it is more than useful to discuss here privacy and data protection powers, in a law enforcement context, to set limits on what is collected, where, by whom, and to impose a duty of care on law enforcement authorities once the data is collected.

Data protection is essentially about guaranteeing a full cycle of control over data. Processing data of others is acceptable on legitimate grounds if one controls the flow, nature, and quality (including assessing the proportionality) of data. When, for instance, personal data is inaccurate or erroneous, it falls on the controller of this data to correct and to inform all others who have had access to the erroneous data about the inaccuracy. In transnational matters things become more complicated because one has to consider data protection laws in all countries involved. Nudging or forcing international companies to share data that is stored abroad is a clear violation of the protective rules of privacy and data protection under the domestic law of the state where the server storing the data is established.[44] Practices of direct cooperation, based on a misleading interpretation of the term 'consent' in the Cybercrime Convention, are simply antipodal to the American and European data protection obligations of the US data firms and to the standards of foreseeability identified by the European Court of Human Rights with regard to privacy intrusions.[45]

The informed reader might wonder how our theme relates to the CJEU's *Schrems I* decision invalidating an EU data protection agreement with the US (Safe Harbour Framework) in 2015, because of insufficiencies in US law that did not set forth any objective criteria for determining limits to the access and use of this personal data by US public authorities.[46] Resulting therefrom and the Snowden revelations, the European Commission replaced the Safe Harbour Framework

[43] Gianclaudio Malgieri and Paul De Hert, 'European Human Rights, Criminal Surveillance, and Intelligence Surveillance: Towards "Good Enough" Oversight, Preferably But Not Necessarily by Judges' in David Gray and Stephen Henderson (eds), *Cambridge Handbook of Surveillance Law* (Cambridge University Press, 2017).

[44] Van De Heyning (n 32 above) 42–43.

[45] The provider does not own the data of data subjects and needs the data subject's consent or an explicit legal basis in domestic law to give access. A demand by a foreign law enforcement actor is neither of both.

[46] Case C-362/14 *Maximillian Schrems v Data Protection Commissioner*, 6 October 2015, ECLI:EU:C:650. The judgment resulted from a complaint filed by Max Schrems with the Irish data protection authority against Facebook for allowing US law enforcement and intelligence authorities access to his personal data in violation of EU data protection law. The CJEU invalidated the EU 'data-deal' with the US – allowing US data firms to process data about EU citizens in the US – because of the general insufficiency, in the eyes of the Court, of US data protection laws to guarantee controlled data processing cycles in the US when confronted with data-hungry US law enforcement and intelligence agencies.

with a new one (the EU-US Privacy Shield Framework), and added Article 48 to the EU General Data Protection Regulation (GDPR) stating that:

> any judgment of a court or tribunal and any decision of an administrative authority of a third country requiring a controller or processor to transfer or disclose personal data may only be recognized or enforceable in any manner if based on an international agreement, such as a mutual legal assistance treaty, in force between the requesting third country and the Union or a Member State.[47]

Hence, 'no EU data for US law enforcement authorities without MLA', says the GDPR. Interestingly, while Article 48 GDPR addresses law enforcement authorities from non-EU nations, it does not impart any strong cautionary message directed to European law enforcement authorities which obtain data from non-EU firms such as those in the US. Neither does the rest of the GDPR nor the Law Enforcement Directive (EU) 2016/680 for Police and Criminal Justice Authorities, which entered into force on 5 May 2016.[48] Significantly, these two instruments are grounded on the message (which we already mentioned above) that data protection is quintessentially legalistic: regulate all data flows vis-à-vis all data protection principles enshrined in law. Thus, there is the need to formalise the informal (or unstated) and regulate it. This is hardly a fundamental objection!

VII. *Schrems II* and the Decision of the Bundesverfassungsgericht on Domestic Production Orders

With this being said, it is yet to be determined if this tone towards European law enforcement authorities would change in light of the *Schrems II* judgment or whether European policymakers will remain resilient in favouring law enforcement authorities.[49] The validity of standard contractual clauses (SCC) with the US notwithstanding,[50] the CJEU held as invalid the EU-US Privacy Shield Framework

[47] This 'blocking statute', that requires an international agreement for data to be shared with law enforcement officers in non-EU nations, is now being criticised as 'conflicting' since the EU is prohibiting broad access to data for others, while its e-evidence package will allow EU authorities broad access to data stored abroad. See Hohmann and Barnett (n 21 above) 25–26.

[48] The political agreement of the co-legislators on the Police and Criminal Justice Directive was, together with the General Data Protection Regulation (GDPR), reached just before Christmas 2015. Subsequently, the PCJ Directive and the GDPR were formally adopted on 14 April 2016, officially signed on 27 April 2016 and published in the Official Journal of the European Union on 4 May 2016.

[49] Case C-311/18 *Data Protection Commissioner v Facebook Ireland and Maximillian Schrems*, 16 July 2020.

[50] In said judgment, the CJEU upheld the validity of standard contractual clauses (SCC) as appropriate protection for EU personal data but enjoined EU organisations to take a proactive role in evaluating the existence of appropriate protection. Also, any inability to comply with the SCC by non-EU data importers must be reported immediately and EU data exporters ought to suspend transfer of data and/ or terminate the contract.

based on several factors: (1) the primacy of US law enforcement requirements over those of the Privacy Shield (paragraph 164); (2) a lack of necessary limitations and safeguards on the power of the authorities under US law, particularly in light of proportionality requirements (paragraphs 168–185); (3) the lack of an effective remedy in the US for EU data subjects (paragraphs 191–192); and (4) deficiencies in the Privacy Shield Ombudsman mechanism (paragraphs 193–197). In its evaluation of these issues, the Court paid particular heed to Articles 7, 8, and 47 of the EU Charter of Fundamental Rights. In light of these deficiencies, the Court found that the Privacy Shield Framework was invalid (paragraph 201) with immediate effect (paragraph 202).

With this judgment about the imperfect US system in mind, we are dumbfounded by the fact that the issue of direct contacts between law enforcement authorities and US data firms has not triggered intense debates from the data protection community, including the European data protection authorities. In their interventions and recommendations, we find an emphasis on a detailed legal basis, on effective remedies, on a duty to notify (if possible) the data subject after the data has been shared, on the danger of an uncritical distinction between content and non-content data,[51] but in general there has been no fundamental objection to the idea itself of seeking data amongst US-based companies.

We hope nonetheless that this improves in light of the recent decision of the German Federal Constitutional Court (*Bundesverfassungsgericht*) to the effect that direct contact of law enforcement authorities with service providers to obtain subscriber data is unconstitutional for violating the data subject's constitutional right to informational self-determination and privacy of telecommunications.[52] In deciding on the unconstitutionality of § 131 of the German Telecommunications Act that provides for this procedure under challenge, the Federal Constitutional Court states that while providing information on subscriber data is constitutionally permissible, there ought to be a proportionate legal basis for the transfer and retrieval of said data by authorities, which was not provided for in the contested law.[53]

[51] More in detail, Statement of the Article 29 Working Party (n 35 above), 1-4; EDPB contribution to the consultation on a draft second additional protocol to the Council of Europe Convention (n 35 above), p 4.

[52] BVerfG, Beschluss des Ersten Senats vom 27. Mai 2020–1 BvR 1873/13 – Rn. 1-275

[53] As the Court elucidated, 'The First Senate clarified that, in principle, despite the moderate weight of the interference, using the general powers to transfer and retrieve subscriber data in the context of maintaining public security and the activities of intelligence services requires there to be a specific danger in the individual case, and an initial suspicion of criminal conduct (*Anfangsverdacht*) in the context of the investigation and prosecution of offences. Where, with regard to maintaining public security or activities of intelligence services, the thresholds for the use of powers require less than a specific danger, this must be compensated for by establishing stricter requirements for the weight of the legal interests meriting protection. For the most part, the challenged provisions did not satisfy these requirements.'

Noteworthy is the suggestion by one of the data protection authorities to add more data protection guidance in the CoE draft proposals.[54] Most of their input on the current European e-evidence projects discussed earlier has to do with criminal law and MLAT principles, but not so much with data protection strictly speaking. For example, they invited the EU legislator to move prudently and step by step, taking into account previous measures, often of a recent nature. Hence they asked for consideration and assessment of the potential impact of the recent Directive on the European Investigation Order on the access to e-evidence located in another Member State, before moving forward with the proposal.[55] Other ideas suggested by the data protection authorities are equally not data-protection-specific: for example, the suggestion to allow direct contacts with private companies only for specific, serious crimes,[56] and to impose a double criminality requirement (no collaboration if the facts are not criminalised in both the requesting and requested state).[57]

In our opinion, these suggestions gain considerably in terms of weight in the light of a combined reading of *Schrems II* (16 July 2020) about deficiencies in US law and the ruling of the German Federal Constitutional Court on the proportionality of domestic production orders (BVerfG, 27 May 2020).

VIII. Conclusion

We started our contribution with a short discussion of the 2018 US CLOUD Act, the 2018 EU package to facilitate cross-border access to electronic evidence, and

[54] EDPB contribution to the consultation on a draft second additional protocol to the Council of Europe Convention (n 35 above), p 5: 'The EDPB considers that specific provisions on data protection safeguards shall reflect key principles and in particular lawfulness, fairness and transparency, purpose limitation, data minimisation, accuracy, storage limitation, integrity and confidentiality. These principles are also in line with the Council of Europe modernised Convention for the Protection of Individuals with Regard to the Processing of Personal Data (Convention 108+), to which many Parties to the Convention on Cybercrime are also Party'.

[55] Statement of the Article 29 Working Party (n 35 above), p 4.

[56] 'The EDPB recommends that the definition of subscriber information, as per Article 18.3 of the Convention, be further clarified in order to avoid inclusion of any traffic data or content data. Information needed for the purpose of identifying a subscriber of a service may indeed include certain Internet Protocol (IP) address information – for example, the IP address used at the time when an account was created, the most recent log-on IP address or the log-on IP addresses used at a specific time, which under EU law constitute traffic data relating to the transmission of a communication. In addition, the EDPB recalls that, in accordance with the relevant CJEU case law, to establish the existence of an interference with the fundamental right to privacy, it does not matter whether the information on the private lives concerned is sensitive or whether the persons concerned have been inconvenienced in any way. The CJEU has furthermore ruled in its judgment in joined cases C-203/15 and C-698/15 Tele2 Sverige AB that metadata such as traffic data and location data provides the means of establishing a profile of the individuals concerned, information that is no less sensitive, having regard to the right to privacy, than the actual content of communications' (EDPB contribution to the consultation on a draft second additional protocol to the Council of Europe Convention (n 35 above), p 4 with reference to CJEU Joined Cases C-203/15 and C-698/15, *Tele2 Sverige AB*, ECLI:EU:C:2016:970 – para 99).

[57] EDPB contribution to the consultation on a draft second additional protocol to the Council of Europe Convention (n 35 above), p 4.

the 2018 CoE reform process to amend the 2001 Cybercrime Convention. All three initiatives open the door for a formal recognition of public-private cooperative mechanisms. How was this legally possible without such frameworks? In section III we discussed the pre-existing MLA framework. This MLA system allowed for cooperation between enforcement authorities but did not foresee any basis for direct cooperation with private actors in other states. Nonetheless this practice was dubiously accepted by the regulatory community on shaky interpretative grounds as being permissible under Articles 18 (on domestic production orders) and 32 (on extraterritorial data access relying on consent) of the Cybercrime Convention (section IV).

We proceeded thereafter to highlight problems arising from the practice of direct contacts. We pointed out the problems about legality, trust, and rights concomitant to the MLA system, which are being wittingly or willingly disregarded (sections V–VII). This includes the dangers of privatising international cooperation and the safeguards that are sacrificed in this regard. Lastly, we pointed out the want of necessary discussion and debate about data protection and privacy vis-à-vis direct contacts. There are lessons to be learned from recent judgments of the CJEU and the German Federal Constitutional Court, but we have yet to determine how these would truly affect the direction policymakers would take in the discussion. This notwithstanding, the message of data protection is clear on formalising informal processes, delineating and defining the needed processes and parameters to be followed. For us, this is not highly objectionable and can be done to ensure safeguards are in place.

Having said this, the work is still not done. Despite our initial observations made herein, the practice of direct contacts between law enforcement authorities and service providers ought to be continually analysed together with the policies being currently pushed regarding it. Reflection is needed to ensure that direct contacts are not merely a quick fix with no long-term solutions. And more importantly, it would be prudent to determine whether direct contacts are the best solution in the first place to address the problems surrounding cross-border exchange of digital evidence.

11

Free-Flow of Data: Is International Trade Law the Appropriate Answer?

VINCENZO ZENO-ZENCOVICH*

I. Introduction: The Problem

The free-flow of data (FFD) is a major concern in international political and economic relations. In the last decade, there have been growing signs of 'data nationalism'[1] and of 'data balkanization'.[2] The normative formalisation of such trend is very well represented by Article 3 of EU Regulation 2016/679, the General Data Protection Regulation (GDPR)[3] according to which:

> 1. This Regulation applies to the processing of personal data in the context of the activities of an establishment of a controller or a processor in the Union, regardless of whether the processing takes place in the Union or not.
> 2. This Regulation applies to the processing of personal data of data subjects who are in the Union by a controller or processor not established in the Union, where the processing activities are related to:
>   (a) the offering of goods or services, irrespective of whether a payment of the data subject is required, to such data subjects in the Union; or
>   (b) the monitoring of their behaviour as far as their behaviour takes place within the Union.
> 3. This Regulation applies to the processing of personal data by a controller not established in the Union, but in a place where Member State law applies by virtue of public international law.

* I am grateful to Maria Chiara Malaguti and Alberto Pozzolo for comments on a first draft of this chapter.

[1] Anupam Chander and Uyên P Lê, 'Data Nationalism' (2015) 64 *Emory Law Journal* 677.

[2] Jennifer Daskal, 'The Un-Territoriality of Data' (2015) 125 *Yale Law Journal* 326: 'Balkanization of the Internet into multiple, closed-off systems protected from the exterritorial reach of foreign-based ISPs' (at p 332).

[3] For a thorough analysis of the issue I will simply refer to the chapters in this volume by Federico Fabbrini and Edoardo Celeste (Ch 2), and by Oreste Pollicino (Ch 6). Previously see Stephen J Schulhofer, 'A Transatlantic Privacy Pact?: A Sceptical View', and David Cole and Federico Fabbrini, 'Transatlantic Negotiations for Transatlantic Rights: Why an EU-US Agreement is the Best Option for Protecting Privacy against Cross-border Surveillance', both in David Cole, Federico Fabbrini and Stephen Schulhofer (eds), *Surveillance, Privacy and Trans-Atlantic Relations* (Hart Publishing, 2017).

The extremely wide territorial scope of the Regulation is justified by the statement that 'the processing of personal data should be designed to serve mankind' (Recital 4) and that '[t]he principles of, and rules on the protection of natural persons with regard to the processing of their personal data should, whatever their nationality or residence, respect their fundamental rights and freedoms, in particular their right to the protection of personal data' (Recital 2).[4]

The USA quickly responded to such stance – also to counter attempts by US firms to place their data outside the domestic territory and jurisdiction – through its 2018 CLOUD Act,[5] which in its recitals states:

> Congress finds the following:
>
> (1) Timely access to electronic data held by communications-service providers is an essential component of government efforts to protect public safety and combat serious crime, including terrorism.
>
> (2) Such efforts by the United States Government are being impeded by the inability to access data stored outside the United States that is in the custody, control, or possession of communications-service providers that are subject to jurisdiction of the United States.
>
> (3) Foreign governments also increasingly seek access to electronic data held by communications-service providers in the United States for the purpose of combating serious crime.
>
> (4) Communications-service providers face potential conflicting legal obligations when a foreign government orders production of electronic data that United States law may prohibit providers from disclosing.
>
> (5) Foreign law may create similarly conflicting legal obligations when chapter 121 of title 18, United States Code (commonly known as the 'Stored Communications Act'), requires disclosure of electronic data that foreign law prohibits communications-service providers from disclosing.

[4] One can find the idea of an EU sovereignty in the field of data protection already in the CJEU decision in the USA-EU PNR controversies (Joined cases C-317/04 and C-318/04 *European Parliament v Council of the European Union* and *European Parliament v Commission of the European Communities*, decided on 30 May 2006, ECLI:EU:C:2006:346). However, the first formal declaration of EU data sovereignty is in the *Schrems* decision, widely commented on in this volume. With permission I would refer to Vincenzo Zeno-Zencovich, 'Intorno alla decisione nel caso Schrems: la sovranità digitale e il governo internazionale delle reti di telecomunicazione' (2015) 31 (4–5) *Il diritto dell'informazione e dell'informatica* 683, and to the copious literature cited therein. The English version of the article 'Around the CJEU Schrems Decision: Digital Sovereignty and International Governance of Telecommunication Networks' is available at: SSRN papers.ssrn.com/sol3/papers.cfm?abstract_id=2788789. Only a few days before this chapter was sent to the publisher the CJEU rendered its decision in the *Schrems III* case (C-311/18) declaring the so-called 'Privacy Shield' agreement between the EU and the US invalid. It is impossible to analyse the extremely lengthy (50 pages) decision by the Grand Chamber. Suffice it to point out that the gist of the case is the transfer of personal data outside the territory of the EU and the renewed affirmation of EU sovereignty over personal data collected in Europe. The implications of the decision for international economic (and political) relations can be seen in the light of the arguments set out in this chapter, without forgetting (and adapting) JH von Kirchmann's 1847 famous quote from his Berlin lecture on The Worthlessness of Jurisprudence as a Science: 'Three lines from the Court of Justice and entire libraries become waste paper'.

[5] HR 4943 – Clarifying Lawful Overseas Use of Data Act (CLOUD Act) (available at the US Congress website: www.congress.gov/bill/115th-congress/house-bill/4943).

(6) International agreements provide a mechanism for resolving these potential conflicting legal obligations where the United States and the relevant foreign government share a common commitment to the rule of law and the protection of privacy and civil liberties.

And the Act's first and foremost provision – § 2713 – determines unambiguously:

> A provider of electronic communication service or remote computing service shall comply with the obligations of this chapter to preserve, backup, or disclose the contents of a wire or electronic communication and any record or other information pertaining to a customer or subscriber within such provider's possession, custody, or control, regardless of whether such communication, record, or other information is located within or outside of the United States.

Although the preambles of the US Act and a subsequent decision of the EU Court of Justice (*Google v CNIL*)[6] declare that the aim of the two normative provisions is that of avoiding conflicts of laws, the practical result is that the same database may be subject to conflicting jurisdictions. At any rate the conflict is deeply rooted in the different views of the main international actors – EU, USA, and China – on international relations and on the role that data flows play in geopolitical strategies.[7]

Over these last years there have been growing concerns on the effects, present and future, of such conflicts, and legal scholarship has often indicated that the appropriate legal and institutional context in which to solve them is that of international trade and of global or regional trade law and negotiated agreements.[8] In this direction there are already several examples which are commonly indicated

[6] Analysed in this volume by John Quinn, Ch 4.

[7] See Henrique Choer Moraes, 'The Geoeconomic Challenge to International Economic Law: Lessons from the Regulation of Data in China' (available on SSRN at: papers.ssrn.com/sol3/papers.cfm?abstract_id=3479504) who speaks of a 'clash of models'.

[8] The literature from the international trade law perspective has considerably grown in these last years. For a first selection, without any pretence of completeness, see: Susan Ariel Aaronson and Patrick Leblond, 'Another Digital Divide: The Rise of Data Realms and its Implications for the WTO' (2018) 21 *Journal of International Economic Law* 245; Ike Brannon and Hart Schwartz, 'The New Perils of Data Localization Rules' (2018) 41(2) *Regulation* 12; Mira Burri, 'The Governance of Data and Data Flows in Trade Agreements: The Pitfalls of Legal Adaptation' (2017) 51 *UC Davis Law Review* 65 (2017); Chan-Mo Chung, 'Data Localization: The Causes, Evolving International Regimes and Korean Practices' (2018) 52 *Journal of World Trade* 187; Dan Ciuriak, Maria Ptashkina, 'Towards a Robust Architecture for the Regulation of Data and Digital Trade' (July 2019) available on SSRN at: papers.ssrn.com/sol3/papers.cfm?abstract_id=3423394; Bret Cohen, Britanie Hall and Charlie Wood, 'Data Localization Laws and Their Impact on Privacy, Data Security and the Global Economy' (2017) 32 *Antitrust* 107; Alyssa Coley, 'International Data Transfers: The Effect of Divergent Cultural Views in Privacy Causes Deja Vu' (2017) 68 *Hastings Law Journal* 1111; Victoria Conrad, 'Digital Gold: Cybersecurity Regulations and Establishing the Free Trade of Big Data' (2018) 10 *William & Mary Business Law Review* 295; Morgan A Corley, 'The Need for an International Convention on Data Privacy: Taking a Cue from the CISG' (2016) 41 *Brook Journal of International Law* 721; Henry Gao, Digital or Trade? The Contrasting Approaches of China and US to Digital Trade (2018) 21 *Journal of International Economic Law* 297; Susannah Hodson, 'Applying WTO and FTA Disciplines to Data Localization Measures' (2019) 18 *World Trade Review* 579; Jane Kelsey, 'How a TPP-Style E-commerce Outcome in the WTO would Endanger the Development Dimension

as models. In this chapter, I will attempt to highlight that although certain world or multilateral trade institutions (eg the WTO or the OECD) may be the most productive through which to work out accepted and effective solutions, the basic principles of international trade that have been elaborated over the last 75 years are not generally applicable to FFD because of certain unique features which require different approaches and solutions.

As such, the chapter is structured as follows: I will first analyse FFD from the point of view of general and regional international trade law agreements. I will then critically evaluate their application to the extremely vast – if not fuzzy – notion of 'data' and the possibility that it may be the object of 'trade'. I then present the argument that the 'Most Favoured Nation' (MFN) and 'National Treatment' (NT) principles appear impracticable when applied to data. I conclude with some suggestions of tentative solutions and on the fora where they could be reached.

II. The International Trade Frame of Reference

If one tries to set a few firm points in the debate on the free-flow of data, one must necessarily consider, in the first place, decisions taken in the WTO and regional agreements context.

This appears reasonable: data are essential for economic activities, both to record the present and the past of contractual relations, and to understand and forecast the future.

of the GATS Acquis (and Potentially the WTO)' (2018) 21 *Journal of International Economic Law* 273; Joshua P Meltzer, 'A New Digital Trade Agenda', Overview paper of the E15 Expert Group on the Digital Economy (August 2015) (available on-line at: www.e15initiative.org/wp-content/uploads/2015/07/E15-Digital-Economy-Meltzer-Overview-FINAL.pdf); Andrew D Mitchell and Neha Mishra, 'Data at the Docks: Modernizing International Trade Law for the Digital Economy' (2018) 20 *Vanderbilt Journal of Entertainment & Technology Law* 1073; Andrew D Mitchell and Neha Mishra, 'Regulating Cross-Border Data Flows in a Data-Driven World: How WTO Law Can Contribute' (2019) 22 *Journal of International Economic Law* 389; Shin-yi Peng and Han-wei Liu, 'The Legality of Data Residency Requirements: How Can the Trans-Pacific Partnership Help' (2017) 51 *Journal of World Trade* 183; Jaromir Pumr, 'Digital Platforms as Big Data Harvesters in the Digital Economy – Competition Overview' (2020) 16 *Common Law Review* 40; John Selby, 'Data Localization Laws: Trade Barriers or Legitimate Responses to Cybersecurity Risks, or Both' (2017) 25 *International Journal of Law & Information Technology* 213; Nivedita Sen, 'Understanding the Role of the WTO in International Data Flows: Taking the Liberalization or the Regulatory Autonomy Path?' (2018) 21 *Journal of International Economic Law* 323; Johannes Thierer, 'Privacy as an Obstacle: Data Privacy Laws under the GATS' (2018) *Freilaw: Freiburg Law Students Journal* 8; Benjamin Wong, 'Data Localization and ASEAN Economic Community' (2020) 10 *Asian Journal of International Law* 158; Svetlana Yakovleva, 'Should Fundamental Rights to Privacy and Data Protection Be a Part of the EU's International Trade Deals?' (2018) 17 *World Trade Review* 477; Svetlana Yakovleva and Kristina Irion, 'The Best of Both Worlds? Free Trade in Services, and EU Law on Privacy and Data Protection' (2016) *European Data Protection Law Review* 191 (available on SSRN at: papers.ssrn.com/sol3/papers.cfm?abstract_id=2877168); Peter K Yu, 'Data Exclusivities and the Limits to Trips Harmonization' (2019) 46 *Florida State University Law Review* 641. One can refer also to the special issue of (2019) 21 *Digital Policy, Regulation and Governance*, devoted to 'Digital Trade vs Cyber Nationalism'.

However, in an 'Industry 4.0' context, data is collected for a multiplicity of other reasons, mainly to monitor constantly one's devices and to collect surrounding information. At any rate, we are quite often confronted with a constant and uninterrupted flow of data. Halting it prevents the functioning of analytics based on real-time input and immediate response (eg data from the 'black box' of an automobile).

Therefore, one can easily detect a few loopholes, with the first being that generally, data flows are not the object of an international trade transaction (goods bought or sold; services requested or provided), but are *ancillary* aspects of any economic activity, in the sense that enterprises have always collected data on their clients and providers and on the contracts they have with them. The second, and consequential, problem is that data flows are not easily classifiable as goods or services, and therefore there is uncertainty whether they fall under the General Agreement on Tariffs and Trade (GATT) or under the General Agreement on Trade in Services (GATS).[9] Could one claim that the first applies when the core business is the trade of goods; the second, when the core business in the provision of services? Or is this a case of international barter (or countertrade)?[10]

Further, in many online services, data (personal and metadata) are the consideration for the services provided. Can one apply to this flow the provisions which can be found in international trade treaties or in the IMF Agreement which regulate restrictions on payments and currency exports?[11]

Some provisions are even more specific and are generally cited by the literature on the issue:

a) The 1997 Annex to the WTO Protocol on market access to basic telecommunications states (§ 5) that members are granted access to and use of public telecommunications networks on non-discriminatory terms for the supply of

[9] Martina Ferracane, 'Data Flows and National Security: A Conceptual Framework to Assess Restrictions on Data Flows under GATS Security Exception' (2019) 21 *Digital Policy, Regulation and Governance* 44 simulates a WTO dispute on data flow restrictions. One has, however, to point out that while GATT has been an overall success for international trade of industrial products, GATS has substantially failed in its objectives for the reasons clearly and authoritatively set out by Michael J Trebilcock, *International Trade Law* (Edward Elgar, 2015) who points out (see section III below) the extreme difficulty of applying the MFN and NT principles to trade in services (pp 125 ff). Also, in the framework of GATS – highlighting several stumbling blocks – see Andrew D Mitchell and Neha Mishra, 'Data at the Docks: Modernizing International Trade Law for the Digital Economy', cited at n 8 above.

[10] See Viviane de Beaufort, Edouard Devilder and Christian Sylvain, 'Competitiveness of European Companies and International Economic Countertrade Practices' (2014) (1) *International Business Law Journal* 1; or Robert Howse, 'Beyond the Countertrade Taboo: Why the WTO Should Take Another Look at Barter and Countertrade' (2010) 60 *University of Toronto Law Journal* 289. UNCITRAL in 1993 issued a 'Legal Guide on International Countertrade Transactions'. From an economic perspective see also Dalia Marin, Monika Schnitzer (eds), *Contracts in Trade and Transition. The Resurgence of Barter* (MIT Press, 2002).

[11] See Article VIII, § 2(a) of the IMF Articles of Agreement: 'no member shall, without the approval of the Fund, impose restrictions on the making of payments and transfers for current international transactions.'

various services including 'data transmission, typically involving the real-time transmission of customer-supplied information between two or more points'.

b) The same provision states (letter c) that service suppliers may use telecommunication networks for the movement of information within and across borders and for the access to information contained in databases.

c) However (letter d), members may take measures 'to ensure the security and confidentiality of messages' provided this does not constitute a means of unjustifiable discrimination or a 'disguised restriction on trade in services'.[12]

The provisions in the WTO Telecommunications Annex are substantially repeated in Chapters 13 and 14 of the 'Comprehensive and Progressive Agreement for Trans-Pacific Partnership', which replaced the original Trans-Pacific Partnership Agreement after the USA withdrew its signature in 2017. In particular, Article 14.13 of the Agreement, under the heading 'Location of Computing Facilities' states that:

1. The Parties recognise that each Party may have its own regulatory requirements regarding the use of computing facilities, including requirements that seek to ensure the security and confidentiality of communications.
2. No Party shall require a covered person to use or locate computing facilities in that Party's territory as a condition for conducting business in that territory.[13]

At a regional level one can mention the Asia-Pacific Economic Cooperation (APEC) and the Cross-Border Privacy Rules (CBPR) System.[14] Although the guidelines are not binding, they provide useful indications on how to balance the different interests ie on the one hand protecting personal information from misuse and unwanted intrusions; on the other hand, enabling global organisations to collect, access, use and process data in the member countries. The system is based on four steps: (*i*). self-assessment by organisations engaged in cross-border flow of data; (*ii*). compliance review by APEC; (*iii*). recognition, acceptance and listing in a compliance directory; and (*iv*). procedures for enforcement and dispute resolution.

The 2019 US-Mexico-Canada Trade Agreement (USMCA), which has (partially) replaced the North American Free Trade Agreement (NAFTA) among

[12] In a 2004 paper, Kent Bressie, Michael Kende and Howard Williams, 'Telecommunications trade liberalization and the WTO' (available on-line at: www.hwglaw.com/wp-content/uploads/2004/09/69A7C2994A9A82580D112146E5FB0E0C.pdf) express the view that 'WTO commitments act to stimulate foreign investment in the sector by opening up the market, acting as a credible commitment to reforming the domestic telecommunications sector and providing recourse to foreign investors through the World Trade Organization's dispute resolution system'. Reviewed after 15 years, the optimistic outlook does not appear to have been confirmed.

[13] Susannah Hodson, 'Applying WTO and FTA Disciplines to Data Localization Measures' (cited at n 8 above) sees the CPTPP as a significant improvement in respect of GATS.

[14] The current text (updated as of November 2019) states in its preambles that 'APEC plays a critical role in the Asia Pacific region by promoting a policy framework designed to ensure the continued free flow of personal information across borders while establishing meaningful protection for the privacy and security of personal information'.

the same three countries, devotes Chapter 19 to 'Digital Trade'[15] and explicitly refers to the APEC-CBPR, with some important specifications – such as designating restrictive measures based on policy objectives as not compliant if they are 'at the detriment of service suppliers of another Party' (Article 19.11, fn 5). The Agreement replicates in Article 19.12 and under the same heading the provision one has already seen in the 'Comprehensive and Progressive Agreement': 'No Party shall require a covered person to use or locate computing facilities in that Party's territory as a condition for conducting business in that territory.'

Another text that should be considered is the EU-Canada Comprehensive Economic and Trade Agreement (CETA), which contains numerous provisions concerning cross-border flow of information in terms not dissimilar to those that have been indicated above.[16]

[15] 'Article 19.8: Personal Information Protection

1. The Parties recognize the economic and social benefits of protecting the personal information of users of digital trade and the contribution that this makes to enhancing consumer confidence in digital trade.
2. To this end, each Party shall adopt or maintain a legal framework that provides for the protection of the personal information of the users of digital trade. In the development of this legal framework, each Party should take into account principles and guidelines of relevant international bodies, such as the *APEC Privacy Framework* and the *OECD Recommendation of the Council concerning Guidelines governing the Protection of Privacy and Transborder Flows of Personal Data (2013).*
3. The Parties recognize that pursuant to paragraph 2, key principles include: limitation on collection; choice; data quality; purpose specification; use limitation; security safeguards; transparency; individual participation; and accountability. The Parties also recognize the importance of ensuring compliance with measures to protect personal information and ensuring that any restrictions on cross-border flows of personal information are necessary and proportionate to the risks presented.
4. Each Party shall endeavor to adopt non-discriminatory practices in protecting users of digital trade from personal information protection violations occurring within its jurisdiction.
5. Each Party shall publish information on the personal information protections it provides to users of digital trade, including how:

   (a) a natural person can pursue a remedy; and
   (b) an enterprise can comply with legal requirements.

6. Recognizing that the Parties may take different legal approaches to protecting personal information, each Party should encourage the development of mechanisms to promote compatibility between these different regimes. The Parties shall endeavor to exchange information on the mechanisms applied in their jurisdictions and explore ways to extend these or other suitable arrangements to promote compatibility between them. The Parties recognize that the *APEC Cross-Border Privacy Rules* system is a valid mechanism to facilitate cross-border information transfers while protecting personal information.'

[16] Eg Article 13.15 on 'Transfer and processing of information': '1. Each Party shall permit a financial institution or a cross-border financial service supplier of the other Party to transfer information in electronic or other form, into and out of its territory, for data processing if processing is required in the ordinary course of business of the financial institution or the cross-border financial service supplier. 2. Each Party shall maintain adequate safeguards to protect privacy, in particular with regard to the transfer of personal information. If the transfer of financial information involves personal information, such transfers should be in accordance with the legislation governing the protection of personal information of the territory of the Party where the transfer has originated.'

Or Article 15.3, at para 3: 'Each Party shall ensure that enterprises of the other Party may use public telecommunications transport networks and services for the movement of information in its territory

III. A Critical Appraisal of the International Trade Approach

The first necessary remark is that 'data' (and therefore FFD) is an extremely vague notion which can be filled with many – and not necessarily consistent – meanings.[17] But the first, and preliminary, objection is that in a digital environment everything is 'data', and 'data' is produced, collected, processed and delivered through telecommunication networks. Any present-day communication – whether for personal, professional, commercial, institutional, cultural purposes – is made through the transmission and reception of data. From this perspective, it would appear that FFD has to do much more with the general fundamental right of communication guaranteed by the UN Charter and by the 1969 New York Covenant on Civil and Political Rights, than with international trade. The interaction between these two spheres is widely discussed and very good reasons have been set out to keep them separated if one does not wish to jeopardise international trade relations. At any rate, this requires distinguishing – a difficult process as we shall see – between the different kinds of 'data' and their actual inherence with international trade. The question of FFD brings us thus to establish, what 'data' are we concerned with?

This raises the question if it is possible to distinguish between 'aggregated' data, which provides an overall view of a certain situation at a certain time (or over a certain period); and 'granular' data which enables us to understand the situation of a particular natural person or of a legal entity.

The former appears to be less problematic if and when such aggregated data are held and made available by public institutions (typically those in charge of national statistics). The latter instead raises concerns not only for the protection of personal data issues, but also because such granular data are quite often collected in real time and allow for a constant monitoring of what is going on (a financial crisis, a sanitary epidemic, etc) in a different country. This has very little to do with international trade and very much with geo-politics and diplomatic relations.

A further related issue is that of 'trade'. When we talk about FFD are we considering 'data' as a commodity which is collected or delivered across borders? Or is data an ancillary aspect of any transaction? If the latter is free, the former should also be. Or is data the consideration for services that are rendered through digital networks?

or across its borders, including for intra-corporate communications of these enterprises, and for access to information contained in data bases or otherwise stored in machine-readable form in the territory of either Party'. This is a template one finds replicated in the recent (June 2020) 'Free trade agreement between the European Union and the Socialist Republic of Viet Nam'.

[17] On the distinction between data in motion, data at rest and metadata, see Tim Maurer et al, 'Technological Sovereignty: Missing the Point?' in Markus Maybaum, Anna-Maria Osula and Lauri Lindstrom (eds), *2015 7th International Conference on Cyber Conflict: Architechtures in Cyberspace* (NATO CCD COE Publications, 2015) at p 56 [available on-line at: ccdcoe.org/sites/default/files/multimedia/pdf/Art%2004%20Technological%20Sovereignity%20-%20Missing%20the%20Point.pdf].

This requires distinguishing between the many uses and purposes of 'data'.

Firstly, in any economic transaction the parties collect data on the performance of the transaction, on the counterpart, and on other surrounding circumstances. For example, in the sale of machinery or in the opening of a line of credit, it is obvious that this data flows together with the core of the transaction, which cannot stand without the parties receiving, communicating and processing such data. To use a Latin expression, such flows are *naturalia negotia*, and therefore there is no need to change existing trade agreements and practices.

A different problem arises when data flows within the same entity or a group of entities. The typical example is that of the sales of a foreign subsidiary or the information concerning employees belonging to the same multinational group. As we have seen, there are relevant normative provisions that allow this, but again it does not raise significant doubts and appears to be an inherent aspect of international trade.

Much more to the point is when the collection of data is the core business of the enterprise (as in search engines or social media platforms). In these cases, there is a service which is provided without any monetary payment but in exchange for personal and non-personal data, and therefore there is a genuine international trade issue which concerns the freedom to provide services and the limitations which may be attached. One should note that in these cases the concern is not so much about the nature of the service provided, but about the counterparty: the users from and through whom data is collected. If the service were paid for with a monetary compensation there would hardly be a problem, in the sense that it would be considered like any other contract for the provision of services. The fact that data – both personal and non-personal – are involved creates the political and economic concerns which have been presented at the beginning of this chapter and which need to be tackled in this section.

However, there are many activities in which the collection and processing of data is an important aspect of the goods or of the services provided. The obvious examples are given by the data collected by the 'black box' of a car and transferred to the producer, or the data collected by online hotel or plane reservation platforms. In general, all the Internet-of-Things (IoT) devices collect data during their functioning, whether in a house (domotics) or in an urban context (smart cities) or in a business organisation (Industry 4.0). Clearly, restrictions to FFD amount to the restriction of the international trade of those goods or services.

The EU approach, which is followed in other countries, is that of establishing limitations concerning 'personal data', ie data which is directly or indirectly referable to an individual. The best example is Regulation 2018/1807 'on a framework for the free flow of non-personal data in the European Union', which should have been fully implemented by May 2020. According to such legislation, '"data" means data other than personal data as defined in point (1) of Article 4 of Regulation (EU) 2016/679' (ie the GDPR). This classification is however rather unrealistic. When any entity (a private individual, a business entity, an organisation, a public entity) collects data, it is quite impossible to distinguish between 'personal' data and 'non-personal' data because data describe complex situations that have a common link. In the simple data concerning the sale of an object that must be delivered, one has a name: that of the buyer, but also the data concerning the object sold, the address, the carrier, the route etc. Furthermore, there is a fundamental misunderstanding when the GDPR builds its system on 'personal' data, imagining that the data belongs to one and only one 'data holder'. Generally, most of the data individuals generate are relational, in the sense that they express a relationship between two or more individuals or entities. In a contract it makes little sense stating that one party has some kind of entitlement over 'its' data, and the other party over 'its' data. All the data is shared and belongs (in an a-technical sense) to all the parties in the relationship. If one reconstructs the relationship between user and provider of on-line digital services (eg a search engine) as a contract (services in exchange of data), it is clear that the 'personal data' provided by the individual and all the metadata belong to both parties. Furthermore, the procedures to anonymise data in such a way that it is impossible to trace back the natural person to which it is referable are complex and uncertain in their result, in the sense that existing programs are able to reverse the process leading to the identification of the subject.

As has already been mentioned, the relationship between international trade law and fundamental human rights is highly problematic. On the one hand, one can point out that developed economies cannot ignore the political, economic and social plight of the countries with which they trade. These developed economies are taking advantage and are exploiting the poverty, not only economic, of millions of individuals. On the other side, one is reminded (since Smith and Ricardo) that international trade thrives on such differences – especially on the difference in the cost of labour and on comparative advantages – and behind the human rights stance there are strong protectionist pressures which result in leaving the poor even more poor.

But in the case of personal data the main issue is not that of ensuring that people living in distant countries are granted an acceptable level of protection that is considered a human right in the West. One therefore, is not talking of (authentic or pretended) 'bad conscience' of producers and consumers in developed countries. The issue is that of avoiding that fundamental rights that are already recognised and guaranteed are jeopardised by international trade and its freedom.

FFD becomes therefore a concern under two novel aspects: firstly, allowing producers of goods and providers of services access to a jurisdiction in which personal data are protected requires a prior balancing of the trade-offs between consumer welfare and citizens' rights; secondly, it raises political and international concerns inasmuch as other countries or powerful multinational enterprises have access to and at their disposal the informational database of the citizens of a different nation, in order to direct their international and business policies.

If one considers that the data can be extracted from a nation – not only from its citizens – as a strategic digital resource, rather than in an international trade context it would appear more appropriate to classify it as a national resource that can be exploited by foreign entities only on the basis of extremely detailed conditions, such as those that allow mining, oil extraction or off-shore platforms. From this perspective one way out might be that of verifying the applicability of so-called countertrade practices and principles when services (telecommunications) or goods (with an embedded digital online memory) are traded in exchange for access to data.

IV. Impracticability of the MFN, NT and TBT Principles

The argument that FFD does not properly fit within international trade is reinforced if one tries to apply the two main pillars of international trade law which have guaranteed its unparalleled success over the last 75 years.

The first is the 'Most Favoured Nation' (MFN) principle, engraved in Article I of the GATT Treaty. In substance, it means that if two countries have reached a tariff agreement on the import/export of certain products, the same treatment must be applied 'immediately and unconditionally' to like products from a third country. The provision is replicated for services, in Article II of the later GATS Treaty. The first stumbling-block is, as has already been mentioned, the dubious nature of data as a 'product' or 'service', and therefore the assimilation of FFD to the international circulation of goods and of services. Furthermore, it is rather problematic – if one gives importance to words – trying to identify 'like products' of data. More to the point is the notion of 'like services and service supplies', set in Article II of the GATS Treaty.[18] Again, FFD is not in itself a service; it is quite often an activity collateral to some other production of goods or provision of services.

However, the main obstacle to the application of the MFN principle is that, as FFD data is allowed on the basis of reciprocity and of mutual concessions, the application of the MFN principle is unworkable because it would circumvent the whole system, without bringing any advantage to trade or to international cooperation. As a matter of fact, the application of the MFN principle would be a major obstacle to agreements on free-flow of data.

The National Treatment principle does not fare well in FFD, because the concern – whether individual or national – is not how data is processed within the territory of the country, but if and how it is (or can be) processed once it is taken abroad. Therefore, the objections are raised over the external – and not the domestic – obligations that bind the data processor in its own jurisdiction.

Further, reservations have been raised over data protection laws (noticeably the GDPR) being a form of Technical Barriers to Trade (TBT), contrary to the

[18] The 'services' approach is favoured by Svetlana Yakovleva and Kristina Irion, 'The Best of Both Worlds? Free Trade in Services, and EU Law on Privacy and Data Protection', cited at n 8 above.

principles set out in the Tokyo Round.[19] Again, inasmuch as data protection rules are applied in a non-discriminatory way, there appears to be no violation. The 'barrier' is not to enter the market but to export the results of the activity in the form of data. This brings us back to the notion of national informational resources and the possibility for third parties to exploit them. The provisions on 'data localisation' – which we have seen are waived in the 'Comprehensive and Progressive Agreement for Trans-Pacific Partnership' and in the US-Mexico-Canada Trade Agreement (USMCA) – which require that data should be processed only in the country where they are collected, could be classified as TBTs.[20]

V. Some Tentative Solutions

If traditional and well-oiled international trade law principles appear to be inadequate to tackle FFD,[21] can one suggest some viable alternatives? The points and legal references that follow are only an attempt to sketch a different path which follows – albeit with some *Realpolitik* – issues that inevitably will turn up.[22]

[19] This is among the conclusions of Svetlana Yakovleva and Kristina Irion, 'The Best of Both Worlds?', cited n 8 above; see also Benjamin Wong, 'Data Localization and ASEAN Economic Community', cited at n 8 above.

[20] One could, however, express some scepticism over some economic analysis (Ike Brannon and Hart Schwartz, 'The New Perils of Data Localization Rules', cited at n 8 above) which purports to predict the losses in case of a broad data-localisation obligation.

[21] Quite obviously not everybody shares the same view: see Lurong Chen et al, 'The Digital Economy for Economic Development: Free Flow of Data and Supporting Policies', Policy Brief Under T20 Japan Task Force 8: Trade, Investment and Globalization, available on-line at: t20japan.org/policy-brief-digital-economy-economic-development/, according to whom 'a systematic formation of policies for the flow of data and data-related businesses can be developed based on an analogy with trade in goods. On this basis, the brief classifies a series of data-related policies based on the standard microeconomic theory, and provides a starting point for policy making'.

[22] Further suggestions, some similar to those here presented, some diverging, can be found in Susan Ariel Aaronson, 'Data Is Different: Why the World Needs a New Approach to Governing Cross-border Data Flows', CIGI Papers No 197 – November 2018 (available on-line at: www.cigionline.org/publications/data-different-why-world-needs-new-approach-governing-cross-border-data-flows). For more policy indications see Nigel Cory, Robert D Atkinson and Daniel Castro, 'Principles and Policies for "Data Free Flow With Trust"', Information Technology & Innovation Foundation Paper (27 May 2019) (available on-line at: itif.org/publications/2019/05/27/principles-and-policies-data-free-flow-trust) according to whom '1. The digital economy's foundation is cracking as some countries try to impose their rules on others, and some erect barriers and turn inward. 2. To maximize the innovation and productivity benefits of data, countries that support an open, rules-based trading system need to agree on core principles and common rules. 3. Rather than tell firms where they can store or process data, countries should hold firms accountable for managing data they collect, regardless of where they store or process it. 4. Countries should revise inefficient processes and outdated legal agreements governing law enforcement access to data stored in other jurisdictions. 5. Countries should adopt policies with appropriate checks and balances for ISPs to block data flows involving illegal distribution of unlicensed content. 6. For data to flow "with trust," countries must support the key technology people and businesses rely on to ensure its confidentiality: encryption'.

Sovereignty. Although sovereignty is a disputed issue,[23] this chapter posits that that each country retains sovereignty over telecommunication networks established in its territory and holds the right to regulate the data – whether personal or not – that are produced on its territory. The starting point could be similar to that expressed in Article 1 of the 1944 Chicago Convention on civil aviation. One may venture that one of the reasons for present-day 'data nationalism' is the uncertain status of data and consequently of FFD. The reference to civil aviation is relevant because telecommunications networks share many common features with air, sea and space activities,[24] with the further complexity that the routes that data follow are not predetermined in transport, but can vary according to technical features, typically the congestion of the network. This raises issues on what we mean by 'transit' (guaranteed by Article V of the GATT treaty) in FFD. It is well known that the path a communication takes through the Internet depends on a series of factors which are generally autonomous from the decision of the sender. Can one apply customary international rules on passage? Do states have a sovereign right to control (and eventually block or 'seize') communications that pass through their territory?[25]

Reciprocity. A second element that can be usefully extracted from the international transport models is that of reciprocity, which enhances mutual trust and the search for solutions that keep up with the very rapid evolution of technology, social and economic uses of data. Concessions are therefore easier to obtain and grant, promoting templates that can be easily adopted elsewhere.[26]

Opt-out approach. From a procedural point of view, it would appear preferable if, instead of having to negotiate each aspect of the agreement, the parties were faced with an extremely broad template which envisages full FFD. Discussions would therefore be centred on the specific aspects that should be kept out of the agreement or should be dependent on specific conditions.

[23] I have tried to present the various arguments, in favour and against, also from an international law perspective in my article 'Around the CJEU Schrems decision', cited at n 4 above.

[24] 'It seems logical to assimilate it to the high seas, international airspace and outer space': Wolff Heintschel von Heinegg, 'Legal Implications of Territorial Sovereignty in Cyberspace' in Christian Czosseck, Rain Ottis, Katharina Ziolkowsky (eds), *2012 4th International Conference on Cyber Conflict* (NATO CCD COE Publications, 2012) at p 9 [available on-line at: ccdcoe.org/sites/default/files/multimedia/pdf/1_1_von_Heinegg_LegalImplicationsOfTerritorialSovereigntyInCyberspace.pdf] at p 9; see also Patrick W Franzese, 'Sovereignty in Cyberspace: Can It Exist?' (2009) 64 *Air Force Law Review* 1 (at p 40f). The similarity is used also to attempt to establish jurisdiction in private international law issues: see William Guillermo Jimenez and Arno R Lodder, 'Analyzing Approaches to Internet Jurisdiction Based on Model of Harbors and the High Seas' (2015) 29 *International Review of Law, Computers & Technology* 266.

[25] See Wolff Heintschel von Heinegg, 'Legal Implications of Territorial Sovereignty in Cyberspace', n 24 above, who suggests that this might be restricted on the basis of 'customary or conventional rules of international law' (at p 11). For some possible technological solutions in order to avoid 'passage' through certain countries see Tim Maurer et al, 'Technological Sovereignty', n 17 above (at pp 58 ff).

[26] See Oreste Pollicino, Marco Bassini, 'The Law of the Internet between Globalisation and Localisation' in Miguel Maduro, Kaarlo Tuori and Suvi Sankari (eds), *Transnational Law: Rethinking European Law and Legal Thinking* (Cambridge University Press, 2014), 346 (advocating, at pp 372f, the principle of mutual recognition). See also Orla Lynskey, in this volume, Ch 12.

Extraterritoriality. Just like in the law of the sea one has territorial waters and the high seas, one has to imagine the data regime when the data are outside a national jurisdiction.[27] The are some indications as to networks in one of the most ancient and long-lasting international treaties, the 1884 Convention for the Protection of Submarine Telegraph Cables. More important is the status of satellites under international space law, considering that increasingly satellites are used to receive, process and store data which must be easily and quickly retrievable at a global level (the 'cloud' metaphor is indicative).[28]

VI. FORA

New issues such as FFD require that one should try to think out of the box. Lawyers have an innate path dependency – which explains why Roman law is still so strong – which preserves them and their role in society. Clearly one should not start everything from scratch and re-invent the wheel. However, an evolutionary and adaptive approach appears to be more rewarding than simply putting data into a Procrustean bed and bending it to a pre-digital notion. To do this the fora where appropriate solutions can be forged are very important and all can give a converging contribution.

WTO. It has been pointed out why well-established principles of international trade are difficult to adapt to FFD, and the rather poor results provided by the GATS treaty were highlighted, together with the paralysis of the Doha Round. However, if one looks at FFD in a broader trade perspective one can easily understand that in order to find an agreement there is a natural tendency to find a quid-pro-quo. This was the sense of the draft of the Trans-Atlantic Trade and Investment Partnership (TTIP) between the EU and the USA before it was dumped in 2016 by all the candidates (both Democrat and Republican) for the US presidency. The provisions on cross-border information flows and localisation of infrastructures – which clearly favoured American big-tech companies[29] – were balanced with greater access of

[27] The issue of 'digital extraterritoriality' is discussed, and challenged, in this volume by Angela Aguinaldo and Paul De Hert, Ch 10, who appropriately analyse the applicability to digital communications of the 1927 landmark decision of the Permanent Court of International Justice in the Franco-Turkish dispute concerning the steamship *Lotus*. However, seen from the perspective of 'harmful acts' that warrant a military reaction, the conclusion might significantly differ (see Wolff Heintschel von Heinegg, 'Legal Implications of Territorial Sovereignty' cited at n 24 above; and very recently François Delerue, *Cyber Operations and International Law* (Cambridge University Press, 2020), at pp 214 ff.

[28] One could add the billions of billions of data lost in the 'datasphere': see Jean-Sylvestre Bergé, Stéphan Grumbach and Vincenzo Zeno-Zencovich, 'The "Datasphere", Data Flows beyond Control, and the Challenges for Law and Governance' (2018) 5 *European Journal of Comparative Law & Governance* 144; analysed also by Omri Ben-Shahar, 'Data Pollution' (2019) 11 *Journal of Legal Analysis* 104.

[29] See the joint 'European Union-United States Trade Principles for Information and Communication Technology Services' statement of 4 April 2011 at: 2009–2017.state.gov/p/eur/rt/eu/tec/171020.htm.

EU exports to the US. Trade negotiations highlight common interests and a practical, rather than ideological, terrain of discussion.[30]

OECD. The Organization for Economic Cooperation and Development has devoted numerous documents and analysis to the FFD, starting from the 2014 'Principles for Internet Policy-Making'.[31] More recently it has tried to indicate how to bridge the differences in what it classifies as the 'four broad approaches' to the regulation of cross-border data flows.[32] The role of FFD in broader context has been set out in the February 2020 report on 'Going Digital. Integrated Policy Framework',[33] where great attention is devoted to the relationship between personal data protection and international data-driven innovation and the role that the OECD guidelines on the 'Transborder Flows of Personal Data' may have.[34] Clearly the role of the OECD in this field, as in many others, is mostly one of expert suasion. However, the circular process of formation of its guidelines and policies (from national experts to the institution, and from there to its Members) should not be underestimated.

G20 Summits. To these one should add – because of its high political level – the G20 Summits. In particular, the 2019 Osaka summit issued a final statement which expressly tackles the FFD issue, under the chapter devoted to 'Innovation: Digitalization, Data Free Flow with Trust':

> Cross-border flow of data, information, ideas and knowledge generates higher productivity, greater innovation, and improved sustainable development, while raising

[30] In favour of the WTO as the forum in which to tackle the issues of cross-border flow of information, see Susan Ariel Aaronson, 'What Are We Talking About When We Discuss Digital Protectionism?', ERIA Paper, 14 July 2017 (available on SSRN at: papers.ssrn.com/sol3/papers.cfm?abstract_id=3032108).

[31] Available on-line at: www.oecd.org/sti/ieconomy/oecd-principles-for-internet-policy-making.pdf. The document indicates among its objectives the promotion and protection of the global free flow of information and the cross-border delivery of services.

[32] See the document on 'Trade and cross-border data flows' prepared by the Working Party of the Trade Committee (December 2018) (available on-line at: www.oecd.org/officialdocuments/publicdisplaydocumentpdf/?cote=TAD/TC/WP(2018)19/FINAL&docLanguage=En). The four approaches are: 'At one extreme, there is the absence of cross-border data flow regulation, usually because there is no data protection legislation at all (largely in least developed countries). While this implies no restrictions on the movement of data, the absence of regulation might affect the willingness of others to send data. The second type of approach does not prohibit the cross-border transfer of data nor does it require any specific conditions to be fulfilled in order to move data across borders, but it provides for ex-post accountability for the data exporter if data sent abroad is misused. A third type of approach conditions the flow of data by permitting transfers only to countries that have received an *adequacy* determination (i.e. a public or private sector finding that the standards of privacy protection in the receiving country are adequate), and/or in the event that appropriate private sector safeguards, such as contractual mechanisms, are provided, or in the case of some narrow exceptions. The last broad type of approach relates to systems that only allow data to be transferred on a case-by-case basis and subject to a review and somewhat discretionary approval by relevant authorities. This approach relates not only to personal data for privacy reasons but also to a more sweeping category of data referred to as "important data", including in the context of national security'. The report contains numerous very useful tables and charts.

[33] Available at: www.oecd-ilibrary.org/docserver/dc930adc-en.pdf?expires=1584271633&id=id&accname=guest&checksum=06106FF6E578EB42FB6AB8C166B7EE2B.

[34] See the 'Recommendation of the Council concerning Guidelines Governing the Protection of Privacy and Transborder Flows of Personal Data' (2013) (available at: www.legalinstruments.oecd.org/public/doc/114/114.en.pdf).

> challenges related to privacy, data protection, intellectual property rights, and security. By continuing to address these challenges, we can further facilitate data free flow and strengthen consumer and business trust. In this respect, it is necessary that legal frameworks, both domestic and international, should be respected. Such data free flow with trust will harness the opportunities of the digital economy. We will cooperate to encourage the interoperability of different frameworks, and we affirm the role of data for development. We also reaffirm the importance of interface between trade and digital economy, and note the ongoing discussion under the Joint Statement Initiative on electronic commerce, and reaffirm the importance of the Work Programme on electronic commerce at the WTO.[35]

ITU. Because of its high technical expertise and its constant interaction with the WTO, the International Telecommunications Union (ITU) is another forum which appears to be indispensable in order to set out rules in the field of FFD. One has repeatedly noted that although the provision of telecommunication services and the collection and processing of data are strongly inter-related, they follow different logics and models: the former are the object of the activity; the latter are its result. They are kept together by the technology and by the standards which ITU helps set at an international level. The involvement of ITU is also important because private parties are important stakeholders in its legal process.

VII. Conclusion

In conclusion, free-flow of data presents too many novel aspects and a mixture of competing interests (individual rights, international trade, national and security exigencies)[36] all of which suggest that it would be preferable reasoning from a clean slate on which one should write appropriate rules extracted from existing models rather than bending and distorting the highly successful international trade laws for purposes and situations which are quite dissimilar in form and in substance.

[35] For a first comment, with interesting charts and economic data, see Tetsuro Fukunaga, 'DataFree Flow with Trust' and Data Governance' (available at: pecc.org/resources/digital-economy/2616-data-free-flow-with-trust-and-data-governance/file); and Junichi Sugawara, 'Launch of 'Osaka Track' on Digital Rules. Many difficulties lie ahead for WTO e-commerce negotiations', a Mizuho Research Institute paper (2 July 2019) (available on-line at: www.mizuho-ri.co.jp/publication/research/pdf/eo/MEA190726.pdf).

[36] Similar concerns are expressed by Mira Burri, 'The Governance of Data and Data Flows in Trade Agreements: The Pitfalls of Legal Adaptation', cited at n 8 above, who points out (at p 130) that the traditional 'analog regulatory venues' are at odds 'with the unpredictable, scruffy, dynamic, and open innovation of digital platforms and data that flows regardless of state borders'. 'Beyond the province of the economy and even in seemingly technical decision-making – such as for classification or localization requirements for foreign operators – essential rights and values like freedom of expression, privacy, fairness, equality of opportunity, and justice, will be affected'.

PART IV

Prospects

12

The Extraterritorial Impact of Data Protection Law through an EU Law Lens

ORLA LYNSKEY

I. Introduction

The initial impetus for early data protection frameworks, most notably the OECD Privacy Guidelines, was to secure unimpeded 'transfers' of personal data across territorial boundaries. This is true also for the EU data protection framework which seeks to ensure, as one of its core objectives, the free movement of personal data.[1] However, EU data protection legislation specifies that this free flow of personal data shall be between EU Member States,[2] and explicitly differentiates between data flows within the Union and those beyond the EU's borders.

Aspects of the data protection framework have therefore been characterised as data localisation measures. Chander and Lê, for instance, regard the EU's rules as part of a second generation of Internet border control measures that 'seeks not to keep information out, but rather to keep data in'.[3] Such localisation measures are increasingly prevalent; however, the justifications offered for data localisation are wide-ranging, as they suggest. Of note is the fact that protectionist motivations for such measures are often attributed to the EU. During his second term of office, President Obama implied that it is commercial rather than fundamental rights objectives that underpin EU data protection policy.[4] More recently, Fan and Gupta cite the General Data Protection Regulation (GDPR) as the most

[1] Article 1(1) and (3) of the General Data Protection Regulation (EU) 2016/679 (GDPR).

[2] See, for instance, recital 3 GDPR.

[3] Anupam Chander and Uyên P Lê, 'Data Nationalism' (2015) 64 *Emory Law Journal* 677, 679.

[4] Speaking of data protection, President Obama stated 'oftentimes what is portrayed as high-minded positions on issues sometimes is designed to carve out their commercial interests'. Liz Gannes, 'Obama Says Europe's Aggressiveness Toward Google Comes from Protecting Lesser Competitors', *Vox – recode*, 13 February 2015. Available at: https://www.vox.com/2015/2/13/11559038/obama-says-europes-aggressiveness-towards-google-comes-from.

prominent example of a barrier to cross-border data flows in a *Harvard Business Review* piece on 'The Dangers of Digital Protectionism'.[5]

The justification offered for these measures with extraterritorial impact is, as we shall see, that they are necessary in order to ensure the continued protection of the fundamental rights of EU residents when their data are processed by entities beyond the EU's borders. This chapter seeks to supplement this justification by adding another layer to the story, which is that the extraterritorial impact of EU data protection law is entirely consistent with the broader corpus of EU law. It will demonstrate this internal consistency, first, by showing that this differentiation between EU and non-EU data transfers can be justified on the basis of general principles of EU law. This claim will be illustrated by reference to the example of cross-border data transfers post-Brexit. Second, it will illustrate that the mechanisms used to ensure extraterritorial impact of data protection law are also utilised in other areas of EU law. These extraterritorial developments therefore extend beyond the sphere of data.

This consistency across EU law, with other substantive legal fields and with the general principles of EU law, provides an additional lens through which to view the extraterritorial impact of EU data protection law. In particular, it detracts from claims of protectionism by demonstrating how this impact is congruous with core principles of the legal framework. Such consistency does not, however, provide a response to claims of data protection imperialism; nor does it legitimise the extraterritorial impact of the data protection framework. At most, consistency might bolster the authority to adopt such measures but a different benchmark is needed to assess their legitimacy. Before proceeding in this way, the scene will be set by identifying the key extraterritoriality mechanisms in the EU data protection framework and highlighting the critique of such extraterritoriality.

II. Extraterritorial Impact in EU Data Protection Law

A. Mechanisms of Extraterritorial Impact in EU Data Protection Law

While acknowledging that there remains 'reasonable disagreement about how a particular jurisdictional trigger should be characterised', Scott makes an explicit distinction between measures which are extraterritorial in nature and those

[5] Ziyang Fan and Anil Gupta, 'The Dangers of Digital Protectionism', *Harvard Business Review*, 30 August 2018. Available at: www.hbr.org//2018//08//the-dangers-of-digital-protectionism (all links last verified on 20 May 2020 unless otherwise indicated).

which involve a 'territorial extension'.[6] Measures which are extraterritorial by nature are those whose application is not dependent on a territorial connection between the regulated activity and a Member State. Rather, such measures may rely on a connecting factor other than territory (such as nationality) to exert jurisdiction. In contrast, she suggests that

> a measure is considered to give rise to territorial extension where its application is triggered by the existence of a territorial connection with the EU, but where an assessment of compliance with the law requires an evaluation of foreign conduct and/or third country law.[7]

As Kuner notes, in the data protection context:

> There are different varieties or degrees of extraterritoriality, which range from the direct application of EU law to parties or conduct in third countries, to 'territorial extension', meaning the application of a measure triggered by a territorial connection but with the regulator required as a matter of EU law to take into account conduct or circumstances abroad.[8]

While Scott's distinction between 'extraterritoriality by nature' and 'territorial extension' is compelling, this chapter will consider these mechanisms collectively and simply refer to the 'extraterritorial impact' of EU law. Three such mechanisms merit mentioning here:

First, there is explicit or direct extraterritoriality. This stems from Article 3(2) GDPR. As Svantesson observes, while Article 3 GDPR purports to deal with the 'territorial scope' of the GDPR, this should not be taken literally. Rather than referring to the largely stable and undisputed territory of the EU, the provision 'outlines what types of contact with the EU's territory will activate the application of the GDPR, and it does so in a manner that is partly territoriality-dependent and partly territoriality-independent'.[9] Article 3(2) indicates two circumstances in which the GDPR will apply to a data controller or processor without an establishment within the EU's territory. As a preliminary step, it must be ascertained that the processing relates to an individual in the EU, even if on a temporary basis. As a second step, there must be either targeting of the data subject by offering them goods or services, or monitoring of their behaviour. The GDPR recitals suggest that to determine whether a non-EU controller or processor is 'targeting' an EU resident, a number of factors might be relevant that indicate the activity is directed towards EU residents (accepting EU currencies; offering delivery within the EU, etc).[10]

[6] Joanne Scott, 'The Global Reach of EU Law' in Marise Cremona and Joanne Scott (eds), *EU Law Beyond EU Borders: The Extraterritorial Reach of EU Law* (OUP, 2019) 29.

[7] Ibid, 22.

[8] Christopher Kuner, 'The Internet and the Global Reach of EU Law' in Marise Cremona and Joanne Scott (eds), *EU Law Beyond EU Borders: The Extraterritorial Reach of EU Law* (OUP, 2019) 124.

[9] Dan Svantesson, 'Article 3: Territorial Scope' in Christopher Kuner, Lee Bygrave and Christopher Docksey (eds), *The EU General Data Protection Regulation (GDPR): A Commentary* (OUP, 2020) 74, 76.

[10] European Data Protection Board (EDPB), 'Guidelines 3/2018 on the territorial scope of the GDPR (Article 3)', 12 November 2019, 15–16.

Monitoring of behaviour occurring within the EU also triggers the GDPR's application to non-EU controllers and processors. The European Data Protection Board has suggested that monitoring alone may not suffice. It indicates that monitoring 'implies that the controller has a specific purpose in mind for the collection and subsequent reuse of the relevant data about the individual's behaviour within the EU' and that online collection or personal data analysis does not automatically count as monitoring.[11] It can be seen that Article 3(2) therefore explicitly seeks to bring non-EU controllers and processors within the reach of EU data protection law.

The legitimacy of this approach has been questioned. Svantesson notes that it is possible to argue that Article 3

> goes too far, thereby giving the GDPR a scope of application that is difficult to justify on the international stage, as the GDPR may end up applying in situations in relation to which the EU may be argued to lack a legitimate interest to apply its laws and to which it only has a weak connection.[12]

Exacerbating this is the fact that it may not be possible to ensure the actual enforcement of the GDPR in these situations, leading to selective enforcement, which would also raise 'rule of law concerns and could arguably undermine the GDPR's international legitimacy'.[13]

A second source of indirect extraterritoriality also stems from Article 3 GDPR and the CJEU's case law in relation to its predecessor provision (Article 4 of the Data Protection Directive (DPD)). Article 4 DPD provided for its application where, amongst other conditions, 'the processing is carried out in the context of the activities of an establishment of the controller on the territory of the Member State'.[14] In *Google Spain*, the CJEU held that although Google Inc, the data controller for Google's search engine activities, did not have an establishment in the EU, the processing did not have to be carried out *by* the establishment in the EU; it merely had to be carried out in the context of its activities.[15] This allowed the Court to find that the activities of Google's establishment in Spain selling advertising were 'inextricably linked' to its search engine processing activities, given that the advertising revenue subsidised the provision of the latter.[16] This broad interpretation – bringing a non-EU controller within the grasp of EU data protection law – was justified on the basis that a more restrictive interpretation would

[11] Ibid, 18.

[12] Dan Svantesson, 'Article 3: Territorial Scope' in Christopher Kuner, Lee Bygrave and Christopher Docksey (eds), *The EU General Data Protection Regulation (GDPR): A Commentary* (OUP, 2020) 95.

[13] Ibid.

[14] Article 4(1)(a), Directive 95/46/EC of the European Parliament and of the Council of 24 October 1995 on the protection of individuals with regard to the processing of personal data and on the free movement of such data [1995] OJ L 281/31.

[15] C-131/12, *Google Spain SL, Google Inc v Agencia Española de Protección de Datos (AEPD)* ECLI:EU:C:2014:317, para 52.

[16] Ibid, paras 55 and 56.

jeopardise the objective of ensuring effective and complete fundamental rights protection[17] and the EU legislature's aim to prevent circumvention of the rules.[18] Thus, in this case, a territorial trigger (processing in the context of Google Spain's establishment) sufficed to regulate conduct outside the EU.[19]

In the more recent *Google v CNIL* judgment, the CJEU held that, in general, effective and complete protection of fundamental rights does not require a search engine operator subject to a successful de-referencing request by a data subject to de-reference this content on *all* versions of its search engine, including those beyond the EU.[20] The ramifications of this judgment are discussed elsewhere.[21] Suffice it to note here that it follows from the case law of the CJEU that there is potential for jurisprudentially developed extraterritorial impacts of EU data protection law, but the Court appears to be increasingly cognisant of the principle of comity.[22]

A third way in which the EU data protection regime has extraterritorial impact is through the suite of mechanisms governing transfers of personal data from within the EU to non-EU states (third countries) set out in Chapter V GDPR. Like the 1995 Directive, the GDPR incorporates an 'adequacy' assessment system whereby data transfers from within the EU to 'third-countries' outside the EU/EEA are only possible when an 'adequate' level of protection can be guaranteed in that third country. The European Commission can deem a given third country (including territories or sectors within that country) to be adequate with an 'adequacy decision'.[23] However, data transfers can also take place in a less systemic way if those involved in the data processing put in place 'appropriate safeguards' incorporating enforceable rights and effective remedies for individuals. This could occur, for instance, through the use of Commission-approved standard contractual clauses (SCCs) between the transferor and the recipient of the data or by resorting to a set of rules that are binding within a corporate entity.[24] More ad hoc data transfers can take place in specific situations enumerated in Article 49 GDPR.

The overarching aim of these mechanisms is to ensure that once transferred outside the EU, personal data continues to benefit from an appropriate level of protection. As stated in Article 44 GDPR, each provision of Chapter V is to be applied to ensure that the level of protection offered by the GDPR 'is not undermined'. As is much-discussed, 'adequate' has been interpreted by the CJEU in

[17] Ibid, para 53.

[18] Ibid, para 54.

[19] Joanne Scott, 'The New "EU" Extraterritoriality' (2014) 51 *Common Market Law Review* 1343, 1363.

[20] *Google LLC v Commission nationale de l'informatique et des libertés (CNIL)*, ECLI:EU:C:2019:772, para 64.

[21] See Quinn, Chapter 4 of this book.

[22] C-507/17, *Google LLC v CNIL* (n 20 above) paras 59 and 60.

[23] Article 45 GDPR.

[24] Article 46 GDPR.

Schrems to require protection 'essentially equivalent' to that offered by the EU.[25] In *Schrems*, which concerned the validity of the Commission decision enabling data transfers between the EU and 4,000 or so private sector companies in the US, the Court invalidated that Commission decision on the narrow ground that the decision itself did not state that the US framework ensured an adequate legal of protection.[26] Nonetheless, as Kuner notes, 'there is no doubt that the judgment is based on a condemnation of US intelligence gathering practices and their effect on fundamental rights under EU data protection law'.[27] It therefore followed from *Schrems*, and now the GDPR, that Commission 'adequacy' decisions will be determined on the basis of a holistic interrogation of the entirety of a third-country legal framework, including relevant legislation 'concerning public security, defence, national security and criminal law'.[28]

In order to meet this benchmark of adequacy, or essential equivalence, non-EU states find their domestic law and policy in the data protection arena heavily influenced by EU law. This is what Bradford has famously labelled 'The Brussels Effect': the way in which, under certain conditions, EU regulations become entrenched in non-EU legal frameworks leading to a Europeanisation of significant aspects of global commerce, such as the determination of data protection standards.[29] This Europeanisation of data protection standards therefore leads to another form of de facto extraterritorial influence of the EU rules. Similarly, Scott refers to the 'territorial extension' of EU law to describe situations where the EU does not adopt extraterritorial legislation but where the existence of a territorial connection with the EU is used to influence conduct that is occurring outside the EU.[30]

In order to illustrate the extraterritorial leverage of Chapter V of the GDPR in practice, the case of cross-border data flows post-Brexit will be considered. This example is chosen as it vividly illustrates that non-EU Member States may be held to a higher standard of data protection and privacy than EU Member States before data transfers are permitted. However, as will be shown subsequently, this ostensible double standard is consistent with, and can be explained by, general principles of EU law.

[25] C-362/14, *Maximillian Schrems v Data Protection Commissioner*, 6 October 2015, ECLI:EU:C:2015:650 *(Schrems)*, paras 97 and 98.

[26] Ibid.

[27] Christopher Kuner, 'Reality and Illusion in EU Data Transfer Post *Schrems*' (2017) 18 *German Law Journal* 882, 890.

[28] Article 45(2)(a) GDPR.

[29] See, Anu Bradford, 'The Brussels Effect' (2012) 107 *Northwestern University Law Review* 1, Columbia Law and Economics Working Paper No 533. Available at SSRN: https://papers.ssrn.com/sol3/papers.cfm?abstract_id=2770634.

[30] Joanne Scott, 'Extraterritoriality and territorial extension in EU Law' (2014) 62 *American Journal of Comparative Law* 87.

B. Extraterritorial Impact in Action: Brexit and Transnational Data Flows

Following the UK's exit from the EU in January 2020, and at the scheduled end of the transition period (31 December 2020), the UK will become a 'third country' for the purposes of EU data protection law. At the time of writing, the future arrangements between the UK and the EU remain in flux. Given this uncertainty, 'to assume a hard Brexit provides a secure foundation for an analytical inquiry, since this is the outer boundary of the range of possibilities'.[31] This analysis will therefore proceed from the assumption that the UK secures no form of bespoke trading relationship with the EU and engages with the EU on the basis of the World Trade Organization rules.

As a third country, the UK will no longer benefit from the free flow of personal data between EU Member States, and personal data flows between the UK and the EU will need to comply with the requirements of Chapter V GDPR. The UK Government has repeatedly stated that it seeks to secure 'unhindered' data flows between the EU and the UK. As the (then) Minister of State for Digital and Culture, Matt Hancock, told a House of Lords Select Committee, unhindered data flows are important not only for data-heavy businesses and law enforcement but they also increasingly underpin any form of trade.[32]

One might assume, given the current regulatory alignment between the UK and the EU on data protection law, that an adequacy assessment would be easily forthcoming. Indeed, the UK Prime Minister indicates that an adequacy assessment should be 'technical' and 'confirmatory of the reality that the UK will be operating exactly the same regulatory frameworks as the EU at the point of exit'.[33] Indeed, external observers might find it counter-intuitive, even hypocritical, that on the eve of the end of the transition period the UK is de facto 'adequate' as an EU Member State while the following day it is not. Yet, it is questionable whether the UK will be deemed 'adequate' once the transition period ends.

It is worth recalling that although there is political support on both sides for an adequacy decision (for instance, the European Commission made a commitment in the Political Declaration that it would endeavour to adopt an adequacy decision during the transition period, should the applicable conditions be met), these decisions should ultimately be apolitical in nature. The CJEU has shown its willingness to exercise oversight of the Commission's use of its powers in this context by declaring two consecutive adequacy decisions concerning the US to be invalid for their failure to comply with EU law.[34] In *Schrems* the Court

[31] Eilís Ferran, 'The UK as a Third Country Actor in EU Financial Services Regulation' (2017) 3(1) *Journal of Financial Regulation* 40, 40.

[32] House of Lords, Select Committee on the European Union, 'Corrected oral evidence: The EU Data Protection Package', 1 February 2017, p 2.

[33] Boris Johnson, UK/EU relations: Written statement – HCWS86, 3 February 2020.

[34] Schrems C-311/18, *Data Protection Commissioner v Facebook Ireland Limited and Maximillian Schrems (Schrems II)*, ECLI:EU:C:2020:559.

emphasised that the standard of review would be strict, given the 'important role played by the protection of personal data in light of the fundamental right to respect for private life' and the large number of individuals whose fundamental rights were at stake.[35]

These strict standards are anchored in EU primary law and cannot be circumvented. Moreover if, for instance, the UK were to seek a bespoke international agreement with the EU in the area of law enforcement and judicial cooperation, this would not escape such strict judicial review, as *Opinion 1/15* on the EU-Canada PNR Agreement demonstrates. In that Opinion, the Court conducted a forensic analysis of the compatibility with Articles 7 and 8 EU Charter of an international agreement providing for passenger name record data processing for security purposes.[36] Taking a proverbial red pen to the international agreement, it indicated each of the agreement's provisions that required amendment.[37] This might be contrasted, for instance, with the Court's requirement only of 'equivalence' in the context of financial services regulation where, as Ferran notes, 'the focus on substantive outcomes in practice as well as on paper has gone some way to allay fears that blockages would be caused by undue attention to differences in line-by-line detail'.[38]

The possibility that a potential adequacy agreement would not survive judicial scrutiny is already alluded to in a Commission Recommendation of February 2020.[39] It envisages that any security partnership between the EU and the UK should provide for its suspension 'if the adequacy decision is repealed or suspended by the Commission or declared invalid by the CJEU'.[40] It also provides that this partnership should provide for automatic termination if the UK denounces the ECHR.[41] It is recalled that pursuant to the Withdrawal Act 2018, the EU Charter is 'not part of domestic law on or after exit day'.[42]

There are two key impediments to a finding of 'adequacy' for the UK. First, adequacy assessments are dynamic in nature. Domestic legal and policy developments can therefore entail a shift from being adequate to inadequate. Thus, although the UK and the EU start in perfect alignment, this can quickly change: for instance, the UK Government has made explicit its desire to 'develop

[35] *Schrems* (n 25 above) para 78.

[36] *Opinion 1/15*, EU-Canada Passenger Name Record Agreement ECLI:EU:C:2016:656.

[37] For critical analysis of this see Christopher Kuner, 'International agreements, data protection, and EU fundamental rights on the international stage: Opinion 1/15, *EU-Canada PNR*' (2018) 55 *Common Market Law Review* 857.

[38] Eilís Ferran, 'The UK as a Third Country Actor in EU Financial Services Regulation' (2017) 3(1) *Journal of Financial Regulation* 40, 60.

[39] Recommendation for a Council Decision authorising the opening of negotiations for a new partnership with the United Kingdom of Great Britain and Northern Ireland, COM(2020) 35 final.

[40] Ibid, para 113.

[41] Ibid, para 113.

[42] Section 5(4), European Union (Withdrawal Act) 2018 (c 16).

separate and independent policies' in areas including data protection.[43] The GDPR provides EU Member States with a 'margin for manoeuvre' in law that sets out the circumstances for specific processing operations.[44] Yet, as has been noted by one authoritative data protection practitioner:

> the UK GDPR's potential for modification is better described as permitting a '*coach and horse*' to be driven through it. This is because the (European Withdrawal Act) powers available to Ministers can permit variation to any *obligation* in the UK GDPR (including to Principles, definitions, rights, security and transfer arrangements). Such fundamental changes to the data protection regime cannot be applied by Member States to the GDPR.[45]

Indeed, through the Data Protection, Privacy and Electronic Communications (Amendments etc) (EU Exit) Regulations 2019 the UK's Data Protection Act 2018 has been amended and a new 'UK GDPR' has been introduced. While the latter tailors GDPR provisions to a purely domestic context (for instance, replacing references to 'the EU' with 'the UK'), it also brings into force a number of notable changes relevant to cross-border data flows between the UK and the EU. For instance, the UK GDPR gives the Secretary of State the power to determine or revoke adequacy.[46] The relevant procedure foresees no role for the UK's Information Commissioner's Office (ICO) or for Parliamentary scrutiny, rendering adequacy decisions vulnerable to politicisation.[47] Yet, although the UK will merely be required to have 'due regard' to CJEU jurisprudence pursuant to the Withdrawal Agreement,[48] deviations from its adequacy assessments may be difficult. The UK has, for instance, now entered into a controversial data-sharing agreement with

[43] Johnson statement to Parliament: /www.parliament.uk/business/publications/written-questions-answers-statements/written-statement/Commons/2020-02-03/HCWS86/. Further statements from EU Chief Negotiator on Brexit, Michel Barnier, indicate the extent of this divergence. He stated that the UK 'insists on lowering current standards and deviating from agreed mechanisms of data protection – to the point that it is even asking the Union to ignore its own law and the jurisprudence of the European Court of Justice on passenger data ("PNR rules"). That is of course impossible'. European Commission, 'Remarks by Michel Barnier following Round 3 of negotiations for a new partnership between the European Union and the United Kingdom', Brussels, 15 May 2020'. Available at: ec.europa.eu/commission/presscorner/detail/en/SPEECH_20_895.

[44] Recital 10 GDPR.

[45] Chris Pounder, 'Draft Brexit Data Protection Regulations would undermine adequacy determination for the UK', 18 January 2019, at: amberhawk.typepad.com/amberhawk/2019/01/draft-brexit-data-protection-regulations-would-undermine-adequacy-determination-for-the-uk.html.

[46] The Data Protection, Privacy and Electronic Communications (Amendments etc) (EU Exit) Regulations 2019 (SI 2019/419), Schedule 1, para 38(3)(a).

[47] Chris Pounder, 'Draft Brexit Data Protection Regulations would undermine adequacy determination for the UK', 18 January 2019. amberhawk.typepad.com/amberhawk/2019/01/draft-brexit-data-protection-regulations-would-undermine-adequacy-determination-for-the-uk.html.

[48] Article 4(5) of the Withdrawal Agreement requires the UK to have 'due regard' to relevant CJEU case law handed down at the end of the transition period. Council of the EU, Agreement on the withdrawal of the United Kingdom of Great Britain and Northern Ireland from the European Union and the European Atomic Energy Community [2019] OJ C 384 I/01.

the US for law enforcement purposes.[49] However, in *Schrems II* the CJEU declared that the EU-US Privacy Shield was invalid on the grounds, amongst others, that the processing of data by US Intelligence Services was not limited to what was strictly necessary and the safeguards in place were not essentially equivalent to those required by the EU Charter.[50] While this assessment of the adequacy of the safeguards offered by the US would not directly bind the UK, the Commission (and the Court, if asked) would take into account 'the rules for onward transfer of personal data to another third country or international organisation' which are in place in the UK when making an adequacy assessment.[51] This has been confirmed by the Court in *Opinion 1/15*.[52] In practice, this means that in reality, to secure a stable adequacy finding, the UK would need to continue in lockstep with the EU in recognising the adequacy of other third countries' data protection frameworks. Failure to do so would jeopardise its own 'adequacy' status.

Secondly, while the UK was an EU Member State, it was not possible for the EU to prohibit or limit data flows to the UK on the basis of its national security policies. This is because Article 4(2) of the Treaty on European Union explicitly states that 'national security remains the sole responsibility of each Member State', and activities outside of the scope of EU law fall outside of the material scope of the GDPR and its predecessor, the 1995 Directive.[53] However, as the Court has recently confirmed in *Schrems II*, Article 4(2) TEU concerns only Member States of the Union.[54] Pursuant to Article 45(2)(a) GDPR, the Commission must take account of 'relevant legislation' in third countries, including national security legislation, when assessing adequacy.

This may be the most significant challenge to a finding of adequacy for the UK. In *Tele2 Sverige and Watson*,[55] the Court of Justice concluded that even when serving the justified objective of fighting serious crime, general and indiscriminate data retention legislation exceeds what is necessary and is therefore disproportionate. On this basis, the UK's data retention legislation was deemed incompatible with EU law.

The legislation in question was repealed just weeks after the judgment and replaced by the Investigatory Powers Act 2016 (IPA). However, this replacement Act continues to rely upon the use of bulk (ie, general and indiscriminate) communications data by the security and intelligence agencies (SIAs). For instance, section 87 of the Act provides the Secretary of State with the power to require telecommunications operators to retain electronic communications

[49] US Department of Justice, 'U.S. And UK Sign Landmark Cross-Border Data Access Agreement to Combat Criminals and Terrorists Online', 3 October 2019. Available at: www.justice.gov/opa/pr/us-and-uk-sign-landmark-cross-border-data-access-agreement-combat-criminals-and-terrorists.

[50] *Schrems II* (n 34 above) paras 184 and 185.

[51] Article 45(2)(b) GDPR.

[52] *Opinion 1/15* (n 36 above) para 214.

[53] Article 2(2)(a) GDPR.

[54] *Schrems II* (n 34 above) para 81.

[55] C-203/15 and C-698/15, *Tele2 Sverige AB v Post- och telestyrelsen* and *Secretary of State for the Home Department v Tom Watson and Others*, ECLI:EU:C:2016:970.

metadata of all customers for up to 12 months.[56] The legality of the predecessor to the Investigatory Powers Act 2016 is also challenged before the European Court of Human Rights. A finding of incompatibility with Article 8 ECHR would be highly relevant for an adequacy assessment.[57] Moreover, although the status of the *Tele2 Sverige and Watson* findings might be queried, given that they were not referred to by the CJEU in *Schrems II*,[58] these provisions of the UK IPA are clearly at odds with the findings of the Court in *Tele2 Sverige and Watson* regarding general and indiscriminate data retention. This has led the UK's Investigatory Powers Tribunal (IPT) to query whether the '*Watson* requirements' should be applied to the national security context and, in particular, whether a domestic law requirement imposed upon electronic communications service providers to provide such data to SIAs is within the scope of Union law. The IPT clearly indicated its position in a preliminary reference to the CJEU where it stated that the application of the *Watson* requirements to the national security context would 'frustrate the measures take to safeguard national security by SIAs, and thereby put the national security of the United Kingdom at risk'.[59] Similar queries have been raised by other national courts and referred to the CJEU.[60] Yet, even if the CJEU ultimately concludes that the *Watson* requirements do *not* apply to the national security context, this will be of little avail to the UK once it is outside of the EU. This is because the Court may use them to indirectly assess the compatibility with the EU Charter of the national security regimes of third countries for adequacy assessments. This may result in the paradoxical situation that third countries will be held to higher data protection standards in the national security context than EU Member States.

This mechanism is an example of 'territorial extension' yet, as Scott notes, although territorial extension

> has an external dimension in that it makes compliance with EU law conditional upon conduct or circumstances abroad, it would be misleading to assume on this basis that it

[56] Similarly, section 136 allows the Secretary to issue 'bulk acquisition warrants'. These bulk acquisition warrants require telecommunications operators to disclose general or specified electronic metadata they possess or can access (including metadata outside the UK) to intelligence agencies.

[57] *Big Brother Watch and Others v United Kingdom*, Applications nos 58170/13, 62322/14 and 24960/15, judgment of 13 September 2018.

[58] Similarly, Christakis, commenting on *Schrems II* observes that '*Schrems II* does not include the harsh criticism against surveillance appearing in *Schrems I* where the CJEU clearly stated that "legislation permitting the public authorities to have access on a generalised basis to the content of electronic communications must be regarded as compromising the essence of the fundamental right to respect for private life …".' Theodore Christakis, 'After Schrems II: Uncertainties on the Legal Basis for Data Transfers and Constitutional Implications for Europe', *European Law Blog*, 21 July 2020. Available at: europeanlawblog.eu/2020/07/21/after-schrems-ii-uncertainties-on-the-legal-basis-for-data-transfers-and-constitutional-implications-for-europe/.

[59] C-623/17, *Privacy International v Secretary of State for Foreign and Commonwealth Affairs and Others*, 22 January 2018, [2018] OJ C 22/41.

[60] See, for instance, Case C-520/18, *Ordre des barreaux francophones et germanophone and Others v Conseil de ministres*, application for preliminary ruling from the Cour constitutionelle (Belgium), August 2018.

> operates exclusively, or even principally, in pursuit of external as opposed to global or internal objectives.[61]

As will be suggested in the next section, the EU's current stance on data transfers outside of the EU is compatible with emerging general principles of EU law, such as mutual trust. Moreover, the extraterritorial mechanisms of data protection law outlined above are also evident in other areas of EU law. This suggests that, contrary to popular perception, data protection law is not exceptional in this regard and the ostensible 'double standard' between EU and non-EU Member States finds its logic in the broader EU legal order.

III. An EU Law Rationale for Extraterritorial Impact

A. Mutual Trust and the Differentiated Treatment of Non-EU States

Irion observes that the

> reception of the *Schrems I* and *II* rulings can have a flavor of differential treatment afforded to a third country as compared to an EU Member State, even though the divisive rationale of Article 4(2)TEU is deeply engrained in the foundations of EU law.[62]

For instance, from a UK perspective, the adequacy system may lead to two perceived injustices: first, that, it may lose its presumption of adequacy overnight once the transition period ends despite adopting the GDPR; and, second, that its national security legislation will be taken into account when a blind eye was turned to this as an EU Member State. The latter objection might be explained briefly by reference to the EU's competences. As noted above, whether the CJEU has any competence to assess the compatibility of the national security legislation of Member States with the EU Charter is heavily contested, whereas the 'competence' issue is not an obstacle in relation to third countries, although it may pose issues of legitimacy and comity challenges.[63]

However, the overnight shift from being 'presumed adequate' to needing to prove adequacy can be explained by other factors. It is suggested that when looked

[61] Joanne Scott, 'The Global Reach of EU Law' in Joanne Scott and Marise Cremona, *EU Law Beyond EU Borders: The Extraterritorial Reach of EU Law* (OUP, 2019), 29.

[62] Kristina Irion, 'Schrems II and Surveillance: Third Countries' National Security Powers in the Purview of EU Law', *European Law Blog*, 24 July 2020, www.europeanlawblog.eu/2020/07/24/schrems-ii-and-surveillance-third-countries-national-security-powers-in-the-purview-of-eu-law/.

[63] Criticism of this approach is implicit in Propp and Swire's statement that the CJEU in *Schrems II* 'confirmed that EU privacy protections travel abroad with personal data originating in the territory of the EU, even when a foreign state's national security organs subsequently claim access to that data', an approach they label 'a nakedly extraterritorial assertion of EU jurisdiction'. Kenneth Propp and Peter Swire, 'Geopolitical implications of the European Court's *Schrems II* Decision', *LawFare*, 17 July 2020. Available at: www.lawfareblog.com/geopolitical-implications-european-courts-schrems-ii-decision.

at through an EU law lens, the presumed adequacy of data protection offered by EU Member States can be explained by the concept of mutual trust.

Those familiar with EU law will be aware of the foundational concept of mutual recognition, originating in the jurisprudence on the free movement of goods.[64] Mutual recognition, a deregulatory form of negative integration, requires a Member State to accept goods that have been made in accordance with the regulatory rules of another EU Member State, subject to some limited exceptions.[65] Mutual recognition is often juxtaposed with the harmonisation or approximation of laws, a form of positive integration which renders mutual recognition redundant. However, in other fields of EU law where, similarly to data protection,[66] there is approximation or harmonisation of domestic law, the CJEU has developed a (partial) principle of 'mutual trust'. Maiani and Migliorini suggest that, in the abstract, trust-based mechanisms are founded on the same basic logic:

> in dealing with a person or situation falling *a priori* under its jurisdiction, Member State A must or may recognise the decision previously adopted by Member State B, or acknowledge the competence of Member State B, subject to exceptions designed to protect competing interests.[67]

Therefore, when outlined in this way, mutual trust implies a type of mutual recognition of decisions or judgments.

The concept of mutual trust has been invoked with relative frequency in the area of freedom, security and justice (AFSJ).[68] When it comes to the execution of European Arrest Warrant requests, for example, the CJEU initially held that it was not open to domestic courts (in that case, Spain) to refuse to execute a European Arrest Warrant on grounds deriving from the national Constitution that were not set out in the EU Framework Decision. The CJEU has subsequently only recognised heavily constrained exceptions to this automatic execution of warrants.[69] Similarly, in European Asylum law, which is itself heavily harmonised,

[64] Case 120/78, *Rewe v Bundesmonopolverwaltung für Branntwein ('Cassis de Dijon')* ECLI:EU:C:1979:42.

[65] Paul Craig and Gráinne de Burca, *EU Law: Text, Cases and Materials* (OUP, 2015) 608.

[66] The GDPR is, it is suggested, an instrument of maximum harmonisation. Although there are many references to national law in the GDPR, thus leaving scope for Member State divergence, the GDPR remains a directly applicable Regulation. Moreover, the Court held in relation to the DPD in *ASNEF* that the Directive was an instrument of maximum harmonisation.

[67] Francesca Maiani and Sara Migliorini, 'One principle to rule them all? Anatomy of mutual trust in the law of the area of freedom, security and justice' (2020) 57 *Common Market Law Review* 7, 26.

[68] John Spencer, 'EU Criminal Law' in Catherine Barnard and Steve Peers, *European Union Law*, 2nd edn (OUP, 2017), 5.2, p 782.

[69] C-404/15, *Aranyosi and Căldăraru v Generalstaatsanwaltschaft Bremen*, ECLI:EU:C:2016:198. In that case the Grand Chamber held that where there 'objective, reliable, specific and properly updated evidence' indicating that the detention conditions in the issuing state might entail a breach of the Article 4 EU Charter prohibition on inhumane and degrading treatment, the court in the executing state could seek reassurances from the issuing state and if these were not received within a reasonable time, it could consider whether to postpone the surrender procedure (paras 89–98).

Article 78(2)(a) TFEU refers to a 'uniform status of asylum … valid throughout the Union'. Presently, under the Dublin III Regulation, Member States recognise the negative asylum decisions of other EU Member States. However, positive asylum decisions are not yet mutually recognised, which, as Maiani and Migliorini note, 'reflects a lack of mutual trust between the Member States that is paradoxical, given the breadth and depth of harmonization in this area'.[70]

While the execution of European arrest warrants and negative asylum assessments may seem a far cry from data protection law, Spencer observes that the justification for such a system, whereby EU Member States enforce each other's judgments and orders more or less automatically, is mutual trust: 'the legal systems of all Member States can be trusted to act decently and fairly'.[71] The logic underpinning this quasi-automatic reception is that as

> the 'issuing' State is bound by the same fundamental rights standards as the 'requested' State, any legal obligation that the person concerned may wish to raise before the authorities of the requested State can be safely taken up in the legal system of the issuing State.[72]

It is thus the presumed mutual respect for fundamental rights that facilitates these trust mechanisms.

Similarly, in data protection law, although there is no reference to mutual trust in the GDPR or the 1995 Directive, it is the assumed mutual respect for fundamental rights standards (provided for in EU secondary legislation) that facilitates the 'free movement' of personal data within EU Member States, without need for formal adequacy findings. In *Opinion 2/13*, when the CJEU delivered its opinion on the draft agreement negotiated with the Council of Europe regarding the EU's accession to the ECHR, this was made more explicit. According to the Court in that Opinion, the EU's legal structure is founded on the fundamental premise that 'each Member State shares with all the other Member States, and recognises that they share with it, a set of common values'. This, in turn, justifies the existence of mutual trust between the Member States.[73] Mutual trust, described by the Court as a principle, requires 'each of those Member States, save in exceptional circumstances, to consider all the other Member States to be complying with EU law, and particularly with the fundamental rights recognised by EU law'.[74] As a result, it is only in exceptional circumstances that a Member State may check whether another Member State has actually observed the fundamental rights guaranteed

[70] Francesca Maiani and Sara Migliorini, 'One principle to rule them all? Anatomy of mutual trust in the law of the area of freedom, security and justice' (2020) 57 *Common Market Law Review* 7, 25.

[71] John Spencer, 'EU Criminal Law' in Barnard and Peers (eds), *European Union Law*, 2nd edn (OUP, 2017), 5.2, 782.

[72] Francesca Maiani and Sara Migliorini, 'One principle to rule them all? Anatomy of mutual trust in the law of the area of freedom, security and justice' (2020) 57 *Common Market Law Review* 7, 36.

[73] *Opinion 1/15* (n 36 above) para 168.

[74] Ibid, para 191.

by the EU in a specific case.[75] It was the potential for the ECHR to upset this balance that ultimately constituted one of the reasons why the CJEU considered the draft agreement to be incompatible with EU law.[76]

The contours of the principle of mutual trust have yet to refined.[77] Moreover, it has been suggested that 'in its present state of development, it is not a self-standing principle', rather 'it applies *through* the legislation and consists of a bundle of interpretative doctrines designed to maximize the *effet utile* of the latter'.[78] This may be so. Yet, the fact remains that this concept explains the ostensible injustice in the UK's shift from being (presumed) adequate to potentially inadequate at the end of the transition period, even were the law in the UK not to change at all. Indeed, rather than exposing the adequacy regime for data transfers to third countries as illegitimate, it may shine further light on the flaws of the principle of mutual trust in the human rights context. As astutely observed by Maiani and Migliorini, this principle instructs

> national authorities taking rights-affecting measures (e.g. the surrender of a person or the seizure of assets) *not* to do what fundamental rights law, generally, requires of them: to assess the consequences of said measures in a careful, individualised manner and to provide an effective remedy including full human rights review.[79]

We might therefore most accurately conclude that the UK never did offer an 'adequate' level of data protection for data flowing to it from other EU Member States and that this will simply be recognised at the end of the transition period.

B. Consistently 'Extraterritorial': The Parallels with Other Bodies of EU Law

Just as an alternative explanation for the strict adequacy mechanism can be found when looking to the broader body of EU law, so too can some insights into the extraterritorial mechanisms of EU data protection law. In particular, this sub-section suggests that while the mechanisms for extraterritorial influence in EU data protection law (outlined in section II.A above) have attracted widespread attention, and often criticism, this pattern of cross-border influence is

[75] Ibid, para 192.

[76] Ibid, para 194 and 195. Eleanor Spaventa, 'Fundamental Rights in the European Union' in Barnard and Peers, *European Union Law*, 2nd edn (OUP, 2017) 260.

[77] John Spencer, 'EU Criminal Law' in Catherine Barnard and Steve Peers, *European Union Law*, 2nd edn (OUP, 2017), 5.2, p 782. Spencer queries, for instance, 'Is it a given: a state of affairs the existence of which must be officially assumed? Or is just an aspiration, meaning that the courts of an executing state are free, in a given case, to refuse to recognize a judgement or order if they feel that to do so would be unjust?'.

[78] Francesca Maiani and Sara Migliorini, 'One principle to rule them all? Anatomy of mutual trust in the law of the area of freedom, security and justice' (2020) 57 *Common Market Law Review* 7, 36.

[79] Ibid.

not exclusive to EU data protection law. A cursory examination of other fields of EU law demonstrates that such patterns were already visible in these areas of law and policy before they emerged in data protection law.

Writing in 2014, Scott examined existing patterns of extraterritorial reach in EU law in a range of different fields. Scott categorised the triggers for such extraterritorial reach as either 'established' or 'novel'. She presents the following table to illustrate this.

	Triggers		
Established	Conduct	Nationality	Presence
Novel	Effects	Anti-Evasion	Transacting with EU person or property

(Scott, 'The New EU "Extraterritoriality"' (2014) 51 *Common Market Law Review* 1343, 1347, *Table 1: Triggers Old and New in EU Law*).

The 'established' triggers that launch the application of EU law and delimit its scope of application are quite familiar. They are: first, that a person engages in conduct in the EU (conduct); second, that a person holds the nationality of an EU Member State (nationality); and, third, that a person is legally or physically present in the EU (presence). As Scott notes, these three triggers are founded on the principles of territoriality and nationality that are well-established in customary international law.[80] However, what is much less clear, as she notes, is whether the novel forms of triggers that she identifies should be viewed as territorial or not.[81]

Scott provides examples of each of the novel triggers drawn from various aspects of financial services regulation. A recurring example she uses is that of the EU's Regulation on derivatives: the European Market Instruments Regulation (EMIR). This instrument imposes clearing and risk-mitigation obligations on those concluding certain forms of derivatives contracts. This Regulation includes elements of all three novel triggers.

With regard to effects, Scott claims that it constituted the 'first clear and express embodiment of the effects doctrine contained in EU legislation'. Even in the context of contracts concluded exclusively by third-country entities, this Regulation may impose legal obligations where the contract concluded has a direct, substantial and foreseeable effect within the EU.[82] Similarly, in order to tackle regulatory evasion, EMIR also requires third-country entities to comply with the Regulation's clearing and risk-mitigation obligations where necessary or appropriate to prevent the evasion of any of the Regulation's provisions.[83]

[80] Joanne Scott, 'The New "EU" Extraterritoriality' (2014) 51 *Common Market Law Review* 1343, 1347.

[81] Ibid, 1345.

[82] Ibid, 1357.

[83] Ibid, 1359.

Finally, the Regulation attaches a clearing obligation to third-country entities when they enter into a relevant contract with an EU financial counterparty, thus transacting with an EU person or property.[84]

While some procedural aspects of the GDPR bear strong resemblances to financial services regulation,[85] from a substantive perspective they also share some common traits. One might observe that just as the provision of financial services is characterised by complexity and often opacity, so too is personal data processing. Moreover, like financial markets, data processing operations are of a 'truly global nature' and EU governments and residents are vulnerable 'in the face of high risk or systematically risky behaviour that takes places elsewhere'.[86] For present purposes however, what is notable is that, according to Scott, the presence of these novel extraterritorial triggers in EU legislation was confined to the financial services domain.[87] Yet, in the intervening period, EU data protection law has developed in a way that incorporates some of these triggers, as can be seen by reference to the three extraterritorial mechanisms outlined above.

The inclusion of non-EU data controllers and processors within the material scope of the GDPR when they offer goods or services to data subjects in the EU, for instance, could clearly be categorised as an extension of scope to entities transacting with persons in the EU. The same might be said of such entities who monitor the behaviour of EU residents while in the EU, albeit that those being monitored might not so readily recognise this as a transaction. It might also be argued that these mechanisms could be justified on the basis of their effects within the EU on EU residents, although this is not explicitly stated.[88]

The judicial extension of the scope of application of the data protection rules to apply to Google Inc, a non-EU entity, in *Google Spain* was explicitly motivated, in part, by the aim of preventing the circumvention of the data protection rules. This therefore arguably constitutes an 'anti-evasion' measure, albeit a non-legislative one. What is perhaps interesting is that although many commentators had hoped the Court's findings would be limited to situations where there was no data controller established in the EU,[89] the Court nevertheless applied this same *Google Spain* logic in the intra-EU context in *Wirtschaftsakademie Schleswig-Holstein*,[90] where the 'anti-evasion' justification does not hold.[91] Another way,

[84] Ibid, 1360.

[85] Orla Lynskey, 'The "Europeanisation" of Data Protection Law' (2017) 19 *Cambridge Yearbook of European Legal Studies* 252.

[86] Joanne Scott, 'The New "EU" Extraterritoriality' (2014) 51 *Common Market Law Review* 1343, 1365.

[87] Ibid, 1346.

[88] This could, for instance, be contrasted with the financial regulation instruments which explicitly require that the effects must be 'direct, substantial and foreseeable'.

[89] See, for instance, Dan Svantesson, 'Article 4(1)(a) "establishment of the controller" in EU data privacy law – time to rein in this expanding concept?' (2016) 6 *International Data Privacy Law* 210, 216.

[90] C-210/16, *Unabhängiges Landeszentrum für Datenschutz Schleswig-Holstein v Wirtschaftsakademie Schleswig-Holstein GmbH*, ECLI:EU:C:2018:388, paras 57 to 64.

[91] This issue has likely subsequently been rectified by Article 56 GDPR which provides for the establishment of a lead authority for the purposes of the enforcement of cross-border data processing.

however, of viewing the *Google Spain* judgment is as being concerned with the effects of data processing operations by non-EU data controllers on EU data subjects, with the Court seeking to ensure the 'effective and complete protection' of these individuals.

Applying this categorisation to cross-border data transfers, we can indirectly see that each of the three triggers – effects, anti-evasion, transacting with an EU person or property – is present. The rules on cross-border data transfers are perhaps best categorised as anti-evasion rules. Recital 101 on general principles for international data transfers provides that the level of protection for individuals provided by the GDPR 'should not be undermined' when personal data are transferred from the Union to controllers, processors or other recipients in third countries or to international organisations. As Kuner notes, the 'prevention of circumvention of the law is the most frequently cited policy underlying regulation of international data transfers under data protection law'.[92] Indeed, in *Schrems* the CJEU indicated that an adequate level of protection should be understood to mean one which is 'essentially equivalent' to that guaranteed within the EU. The Court justified this strict standard on the grounds that the high level of protection provided by the legislative framework (at that time, the 1995 Directive), read in light of the Charter, 'could easily be circumvented by transfers of personal data from the European Union to third countries'.[93] The CJEU reiterated this in *Opinion 1/15* in the context of the EU-Canada PNR agreement and the logic was extended to standard contractual clauses in *Schrems II*.[94]

Stepping back, we can therefore see that this phenomenon of increased extraterritorial impact is not exclusive to data protection law; rather it is an emerging trend across fields of EU law. Such consistency across EU law provides a counter-argument to claims of data exceptionalism. It does not, however, necessarily legitimise the extraterritorial impact of EU law. As Murray and Reed suggest, in cyberspace there are often competing, and sometimes conflicting, claims of jurisdiction over the same conduct. Not all such claims are equally legitimate and they therefore propose criteria against which to assess legitimacy.[95] These are: the extent to which the law is perceived as being addressed to a cyberspace user; how far the law's provisions are congruent with the rest of the environment in which the cyberspace user acts; and the perceived fairness and justice of the

[92] Christopher Kuner, 'Article 44: General principles for transfer' in Christopher Kuner, Lee Bygrave and Christopher Docksey (eds), *The EU General Data Protection Regulation (GDPR): A Commentary* (OUP, 2020) 755, 757 (citing Christopher Kuner, *Transborder Data Flow Regulation and Data Privacy Law* (OUP, 2013) 107–13).

[93] *Schrems* (n 25 above) para 73.

[94] *Opinion 1/15* (n 36 above) para 214; *Schrems II* (n 34 above) para 96.

[95] Chris Reed and Andrew Murray, *Rethinking the Jurisprudence of Cyberspace* (Edward Elgar, 2020), 177.

law's claims to obedience.[96] Through such contextual assessments it is possible to make a more nuanced assessment of the *legitimacy* of particular extraterritorial mechanisms.

IV. Conclusion

The motivation for, and legitimacy of, the extraterritorial dimensions of EU data protection law are highly contested. This chapter seeks to make a modest contribution to this debate by drawing attention to two important factors. First, this extraterritorial impact is not exclusive to EU data protection law: rather, 'novel extraterritorial triggers' are visible in other areas such as financial services regulation. Second, the differentiation between EU and non-EU Member States, even those with close legal alignment with the EU such as post-Brexit UK, can be explained by factors beyond protectionism. In particular, the concept of mutual trust, prominent in the AFSJ, offers an explanation for the current assumption that the UK offers an adequate level of data protection. This assumption falls away once the UK no longer adheres to Article 2 TEU and shares 'a set of common values' with the other EU Member States. This consistency across domains of EU law may legitimise these measures from an internal EU law perspective; however it, of course, may not legitimise the extraterritoriality of EU data protection law in the eyes of external observers.

[96] Ibid.

13

Digital Sovereignty in the EU: Challenges and Future Perspectives

EDOARDO CELESTE

I. Introduction

In October 2019, at the annual Digital Summit in Dortmund, the German Federal Minister for Economic Affairs, Peter Altmaier, in partnership with the French Minister of Finance, Bruno Le Maire, officially launched Gaia-X, the project of a European data infrastructure.[1] In an economy currently dominated by American and Chinese tech giants, Germany and France are investing in the creation of a federated cloud 'made in Europe'.[2] According to the supporters of this initiative, only in this way will Europe eventually regain its 'digital sovereignty' and ultimately preserve its values in the digital ecosystem.[3]

Back in 2017, French President, Emmanuel Macron, stressed the importance of regaining sovereignty in the digital sector as one of the key policies to 'refound' the EU.[4] German Chancellor Angela Merkel, in her speech at the Internet Governance Forum 2019, reiterated the centrality of digital sovereignty in the

[1] Bundesministerium für Wirtschaft und Energie, 'Pressemitteilung zur deutsch-französischen Zusammenarbeit für eine sichere und vertrauenswürdige Dateninfrastruktur', www.bmwi.de/Redaktion/DE/Pressemitteilungen/2019/20191029-pressemitteilung-zur-deutsch-franzoesischen-zusammenarbeit-fuer-eine%20sichere-vertrauenswuerdige-dateninfrastruktur.html, accessed 21 May 2020. On the mission and activities of the Digital Summit, see 'Digital-Gipfel', www.de.digital/DIGITAL/Redaktion/DE/Dossier/digital-gipfel.html, accessed 21 May 2020.

[2] Federal Ministry for Economic Affairs and Energy (BMWi), 'Project GAIA-X – A Federated Data Infrastructure as the Cradle of a Vibrant European Ecosystem' (2019), www.bmwi.de/Redaktion/EN/Publikationen/Digitale-Welt/project-gaia-x.pdf?__blob=publicationFile&v=; Federal Ministry for Economic Affairs and Energy (BMWi), 'Digital Sovereignty in the Context of Platform-Based Ecosystems' (2019), www.de.digital/DIGITAL/Redaktion/DE/Digital-Gipfel/Download/2019/digital-sovereignty-in-the-context-of-platform-based-ecosystems.pdf?__blob=publicationFile&v=7.

[3] Federal Ministry for Economic Affairs and Energy (BMWi), 'Project GAIA-X – A Federated Data Infrastructure as the Cradle of a Vibrant European Ecosystem' (n 2 above); see also Bundesministerium für Wirtschaft und Energie, 'GAIA-X', www.bmwi.de/Redaktion/DE/Dossier/gaia-x.html, accessed 22 May 2020.

[4] 'Les 6 piliers du plan de Macron pour "refonder l'Europe"' (*L'Obs*, 26 September 2017), www.nouvelobs.com/politique/20170926.OBS5171/les-6-piliers-du-plan-de-macron-pour-refonder-l-europe.html, accessed 9 July 2020.

European digital policy agenda, but at the same time earnestly highlighted that this concept may have various meanings and be interpreted in different ways.[5] Like other neologisms combining the adjective 'digital' with a previously existing and well-established concept, the expression 'digital sovereignty' presents a high evocative power and, simultaneously, scarcely defined contours.[6] At first sight, it could look like an oxymoronic expression. The adjective 'digital' evokes the idea of a borderless virtual space, an un-territorial[7] or post-territorial[8] dimension where states, 'weary giants of flesh and steel, [...] have no sovereignty'.[9] Sovereignty instead is a concept that historically emerged and evolved in association with the idea of territory, people and power.[10]

This chapter aims to reconstruct the meaning of digital sovereignty, and to understand the significance, rationale and challenges of this concept as a core value inspiring recent policy in the EU. The chapter will be articulated in two parts. The first part (section II) conceptualises the notion of digital sovereignty. In particular, it analyses the historical evolution of the concept of sovereignty in general, contextualises its application in the digital ecosystem, and provides a definition of 'digital sovereignty'. The second part of the chapter (section III) then looks at how this concept has been articulated in the EU. It explains that the rationale underlying the idea of digital sovereignty in the EU lies in the need to preserve the European 'DNA' of values and rights. European data are mostly processed by foreign companies and stored outside the EU. This circumstance poses serious risks in terms of potential fundamental rights violations. The chapter thus illustrates a series of initiatives that has emerged at Member State and Union level that seeks to regain digital sovereignty in the EU. The last section finally highlights the risks associated with this tendency, warning that digital sovereignty claims can easily degenerate into forms of sovereigntism (section IV). It will be argued that EU rights and values can continue to be upheld without resorting

[5] 'Rede von Bundeskanzlerin Angela Merkel zur Eröffnung des 14. Internet Governance Forums 26. November 2019 in Berlin', www.bundeskanzlerin.de/bkin-de/aktuelles/rede-von-bundeskanzlerin-angela-merkel-zur-eroeffnung-des-14-internet-governance-forums-26-november-2019-in-berlin-1698264, accessed 22 May 2020.

[6] Cf Edoardo Celeste, 'Digital Constitutionalism: A New Systematic Theorisation' (2019) 33 *International Review of Law, Computers & Technology* 76.

[7] See Jennifer Daskal, 'The Un-Territoriality of Data' (2015) 125 *Yale Law Journal* 326.

[8] See Paul De Hert and Johannes Thumfart, 'The Microsoft Ireland Case and the Cyberspace Sovereignty Trilemma. Post-Territorial Technologies and Companies Question Territorial State Sovereignty and Regulatory State Monopolies' (July 2018) Vol 4 No 11 Brussels Privacy Hub Working Paper, papers.ssrn.com/abstract=3228388, accessed 22 May 2020.

[9] John Perry Barlow, 'A Declaration of the Independence of Cyberspace' (1996) www.eff.org/cyberspace-independence, accessed 11 December 200.

[10] FH Hinsley, *Sovereignty*, 2nd edn (Cambridge University Press, 1986) 88; for a historical perspective on the concept of sovereignty see also Jens Bartelson, *A Genealogy of Sovereignty* (Cambridge University Press, 1995); for a comprehensive overview of the contemporary meaning of the notion of sovereignty, including in the context of the digital ecosystem, see Richard Rawlings, Peter Leyland and Alison Young (eds), *Sovereignty and the Law: Domestic, European and International Perspectives* (Oxford University Press, 2013).

to counterproductive 'arm-wrestling' with foreign countries, by respecting the principles of international comity, peacefully cooperating and respecting pluralism.

II. Conceptualising Digital Sovereignty

In the existing literature as well as in policy documents, the concept of digital sovereignty has not received a univocal definition. This is partially due to the fact that the notion of sovereignty itself has evolved throughout history and has never been definitively defined.[11]

A. What is Sovereignty?

The core idea of sovereignty lies in the concepts of supremacy of power over a territory and independence.[12] In Latin, *superanus* literally meant who stands 'above'.[13] In the Middle Ages, the sovereign was the person who held supreme power over a territory. However, at that time, sovereignty was not synonymous with absolute power, but only denoted a 'relative pre-eminence'.[14] Paradigmatic examples are the kings of England – who were at the same time vassals of the kings of France – and the catholic bishops, whose jurisdiction trumped that of temporal authorities in religious matters.[15]

Subsequently, the concept of sovereignty constantly evolved. Sovereignty gradually started to denote a form of power that is not only supreme, but also absolute, original, indivisible and inalienable.[16] Traditionally, the Peace of Westphalia, terminating the Thirty Years War in 1648, marks the start of the modern idea of sovereignty, intended as supreme authority of a state within its own territory and independence from the interference of other sovereign entities.[17]

[11] See Hent Kalmo and Quentin Skinner (eds), *Sovereignty in Fragments: The Past, Present and Future of a Contested Concept* (Cambridge University Press, 2010).

[12] See Andrew Keane Woods, 'Litigating Data Sovereignty' (2018) 128 *Yale Law Journal* 328.

[13] 'Sovereign, n. and Adj.', www.oed.com/view/Entry/185332#eid21519750, accessed 26 May 2020.

[14] 'sovranità', *Dizionario di filosofia Treccani* (2009), www.treccani.it//enciclopedia/sovranita_(Dizionario-di-filosofia), accessed 26 May 2020; on the possibility of conceiving a form of sovereignty in the Middle Ages, cf Francesco Maiolo, *Medieval Sovereignty: Marsilius of Padua and Bartolus of Saxoferrato* (Eburon, 2007) 19 ff; on the same point, talking of 'proto-sovereignty' and with reference to the Renaissance, see also Bartelson (n 10 above) 88 ff.

[15] Further on the point see George W White, *Nation, State, and Territory: Origins, Evolutions, and Relationships* (Rowman & Littlefield 2004) 124 ff; Joseph Canning, *Ideas of Power in the Late Middle Ages, 1296–1417* (Cambridge University Press, 2014).

[16] A major impulse in this direction was brought by Bodin: see CH McIlwain, 'Sovereignty Again' (1926) 6 *Economica* 253; see also Stewart Motha, 'Sovereignty', *The New Oxford Companion to Law* (Oxford University Press, 2008), www.oxfordreference.com/view/10.1093/acref/9780199290543.001.0001/acref-9780199290543-e-2052, accessed 25 May 2020; Hinsley (n 10 above) ch 3.

[17] Daniel Philpott, 'Sovereignty' in Edward N Zalta (ed), *The Stanford Encyclopedia of Philosophy* (2016), plato.stanford.edu/archives/sum2016/entries/sovereignty/, accessed 25 May 2020.

The following centuries saw philosophers debating on the questions of who or which entity really holds sovereignty, and what the limits of their supreme power are.[18] The apex of the conceptual parabola of the concept of sovereignty was also the prelude to its descending phase. Before World War II, the German legal theorist Carl Schmitt still regarded the essence of sovereignty as lying in the power to suspend statutory guarantees and declare a state of emergency: sovereign was the entity who takes the 'decision on the exception'.[19] The atrocities of the first half of the Twentieth century inexorably led to a rethinking of the idea of sovereignty.[20] The sovereign state could no longer risk being totally unbound, but should be subject to internal and external limitations.[21]

B. Sovereignty in the Digital Society

The decline – or one would more correctly say, the evolution – of the traditional conception of sovereignty has undoubtedly been exacerbated by the advent of digital technologies. In 1996, John Perry Barlow published the famous *Declaration of the Independence of Cyberspace*, championing the idea that the virtual world was merely the 'home of Mind', a new *sanctum sanctorum* of culture and freedom where states could not exercise their power, and their legal system would not apply.[22] The traditional idea of state sovereignty, intended as supreme power of the state over a territory and independence from other sovereign entities, apparently found an insurmountable limit in the intangibility of the new space that digital technologies created. Cyberspace itself allegedly emerged as an independent, sovereign entity.[23]

In reality, as the scholarship promptly remarked, this cyber-anarchist view was merely utopian.[24] First of all, digital technologies still relied on physical apparatuses, tangible properties that the 'giants of flesh and steel' could physically

[18] For a comprehensive and concise overview, see Philpott (n 17 above); see also Dieter Grimm, *Sovereignty: The Origin and Future of a Political and Legal Concept* (Columbia University Press, 2015) chs 2 and 3.

[19] Stewart Motha, 'Sovereignty', *The New Oxford Companion to Law* (Oxford University Press, 2008), www.oxfordreference.com/view/10.1093/acref/9780199290543.001.0001/acref-9780199290543-e-2052, accessed 26 May 2020.

[20] See Philpott (n 17 above).

[21] On the point see Philpott (n 17 above); see also Rawlings, Leyland and Young (n 10 above); Anne Peters, 'Humanity as the A and Ω of Sovereignty' (2009) 20 *European Journal of International Law* 513.

[22] Barlow (n 9 above).

[23] For a comprehensive, but concise overview of the scholarship in favour of cyberspace sovereignty, see Dan Jerker B Svantesson, 'Sovereignty in International Law: How the Internet (Maybe) Changed Everything, but Not for Long' (2014) 8 *Masaryk University Journal of Law and Technology* 137, 144 ff.

[24] See Tim Wu, 'Cyberspace Sovereignty? – The Internet and the International System' (1997) 10 *Harvard Journal of Law & Technology* 647;Jack L Goldsmith, 'Against Cyberanarchy' (1998) 65 *University of Chicago Law Review* 1199; Jack Goldsmith and Tim Wu, *Who Controls the Internet? Illusions of a Borderless World* (Oxford University Press, 2008).

control.[25] Secondly, nation states soon understood that the Internet was not *terra nullius*. Nothing prevented them from regulating the conduct of individuals over Internet, and that this was even desirable, not to say necessary.

As seen in the previous chapters of this book, recent examples include the scope of application of the General Data Protection Regulation (GDPR) or the US CLOUD Act.[26] Article 3(2) GDPR provides that the new pan-European data protection legislation applies to data controllers and processors which are *not* established in the EU, if they process data related to the offer of goods or services to data subjects in the EU or monitor the behaviour of individuals located in the EU.[27] The US CLOUD Act empowers law enforcement authorities to request data in the 'possession, custody and control' of a US company, notwithstanding the fact that such information may be stored in servers located outside the US.[28] These two pieces of legislation demonstrate how nation states found alternative ways to exercise their sovereign power, which are not primarily based on the concept of territory.

Interestingly, this phenomenon of adaptation of the notion of territorial sovereignty to a globalised and borderless world has never been described in terms of digital sovereignty; nor has it been considered as a fully legitimate extension of the sovereign power of the state over the digital territory. The legal scholarship persists in studying this centrifugal tendency as a form of regulatory overreaching or jurisdictional trawling.[29] As we have seen in the previous chapters of this book, the traditional indissoluble bond between sovereignty and territory rightly imposes to categorise this phenomenon as *extra*-territorial.[30] Interestingly, De Hert and Thumfart regarded it as a form of 'hyper-sovereignty', classifying it as a reaction to cyberanarchy. This phenomenon would entail an exorbitant use of sovereign power, generating what Lessig called 'competition among sovereigns',[31] and unavoidably leading to an erosion of the rule of law both at national and international level.[32] Although the authors in this case recognise a scission between digital ecosystem and territory, their *post*-territorial conception does not lead them to reconceptualise the core tenets of contemporary sovereignty, and especially its rooting in a territory.

[25] What Svantesson calls 'sovereignty over the technology' in opposition to 'sovereignty over conduct'. See Svantesson, 'Sovereignty in International Law' (n 23 above).

[26] On these respective topics, see chapters by Fabbrini and Celeste (Ch 2), Lynskey (Ch 12) and Smith (Ch 8) in this book.

[27] See also Christopher Kuner, 'Extraterritoriality and Regulation of International Data Transfers in EU Data Protection Law' (2015) 5 *International Data Privacy Law* 235.

[28] See also Halefom H Abraha, 'How Compatible Is the US "CLOUD Act" with Cloud Computing? A Brief Analysis' (2019) 9(3) *International Data Privacy Law* 207.

[29] See Dan Jerker B Svantesson, 'Internet & Jurisdiction Global Status Report 2019' (2019) www.internetjurisdiction.net/news/release-of-worlds-first-internet-jurisdiction-global-status-report.

[30] In this book, see Fabbrini and Celeste, Ch 2.

[31] Lawrence Lessig, *Code: And Other Laws of Cyberspace, Version 2.0* (Basic Books, 2006) ch 15.

[32] De Hert and Thumfart (n 8 above).

This conceptual inability to severe the link between state sovereignty and territory was certainly one of the factors that pushed nation states to find a natural alternative to solve the dilemma of regulating the digital society in the re-territorialisation of the digital ecosystem. For example, recently, as Quinn examined in detail in Chapter four of this book, the CJEU demanded that Google delist search results from its website by virtue of a person's right to be forgotten, and to limit such a delisting to the territory of the EU, encouraging the use of geo-blocking technologies.[33] Erecting frontiers in a space that originally emerged as borderless has appeared as a sound solution to forestall the risk of anarchy, and at the same time to prevent one or a few powerful states from imposing a digital monarchy or oligarchy:[34] a phenomenon that from a cyber-libertarian point of view is negatively denoted as 'Internet balkanisation'.[35]

Recently, this tendency to reassert boundaries in the digital ecosystem has been accompanied by states' attempts to regain control over data and digital infrastructures. Several states have adopted data localisation laws, requiring controllers to physically store data within the territory of the state.[36] New initiatives have emerged to create national or regional digital infrastructures, as shown in the Gaia-X example presented in the Introduction (section I).[37] Interestingly, it is only in this specific context that explicit claims to digital sovereignty have emerged. States, particularly in Europe, are invoking this concept to trigger centripetal and centralist trends on data and digital infrastructures, in this way seeking to regain independence from foreign service providers and increase their capabilities of controlling these strategic assets.

C. Defining Digital Sovereignty

As the concept of sovereignty has evolved over time and its meaning has never been set in stone, a canonical definition of *digital* sovereignty similarly does not exist. The emergence of this expression is quite recent – no academic articles

[33] See ECJ, *Google Spain SL v Agencia Española de Protección de Datos (AEPD)* C-131/12, ECLI:EU:C:2014:317; ECJ, *Google LLC v Commission nationale de l'informatique et des libertés (CNIL)* C-507/17, ECLI:EU:C:2019:77. See also, in this volume, Fabbrini and Celeste (Ch 2), Pollicino (Ch 6), and Quinn (Ch 4).

[34] See Lessig (n 31 above) 302 ff, who talks of 'no law rule' and 'one law rule'.

[35] Cf Milton Mueller, *Will the Internet Fragment? Sovereignty, Globalization and Cyberspace* (Polity Press, 2017).

[36] See Edoardo Celeste and Federico Fabbrini, 'Competing Jurisdictions: Data Privacy Across the Borders' in Grace Fox, Theo Lynn and Lisa van der Werff (eds), *Data Privacy and Trust in Cloud Computing* (Palgrave, 2020); John Selby, 'Data Localization Laws: Trade Barriers or Legitimate Responses to Cybersecurity Risks, or Both?' (2017) 25 *International Journal of Law and Information Technology* 213; Neha Mishra, 'Data Localization Laws in a Digital World: Data Protection or Data Protectionism?' (Social Science Research Network, 2015) SSRN Scholarly Paper ID 2848022: papers.ssrn.com/abstract=2848022, accessed 8 November 2019.

[37] See also below in this chapter.

including this word have been found before 2011 – and it is still not common in the academic milieu.[38] Digital sovereignty appears as the last offspring of the family of concepts applying the notion of sovereignty to the technological world. The expression 'technological sovereignty' had already emerged in the 1960s.[39] 'Data sovereignty' is the most used concept of the family both in academic and commercial articles, but it now appears to be conceived as a component of the notion of digital sovereignty.[40] This trend is not surprising, as our vocabulary changes following the evolution of technology, and reflects the relative importance that these innovations play within society.[41]

In the documents presenting the project Gaia-X published by the German Federal Ministry for Economic Affairs and Energy, digital sovereignty is depicted as 'an aspect of general sovereignty',[42] and is defined as:

> the 'possibility of independent self-determination by the state and by organisations' with regard to the 'use and structuring of digital systems themselves, the data produced and stored in them, and the processes depicted as a result.'[43]

Data sovereignty would then be in turn an integral part of the concept of digital sovereignty, denoting the ability to have 'complete control over stored and processed data and also the independent decision on who is permitted to have access to it'.[44]

If one compares these definitions with the core elements of modern sovereignty – intended as supreme power of the state over a territory and its independence from external entities – one can notice a series of similarities and differences. In terms of general architecture, digital sovereignty does not subvert the core tenets of traditional sovereignty, preserving its conceptual genes.[45] Yet, the concept of digital sovereignty articulates the notion of sovereignty in the context of the digital ecosystem. The definition quoted above does not explicitly mention the idea of territory. Digital sovereignty denotes a form of control

[38] For a discourse analysis of the literature on digital sovereignty see Stephane Couture and Sophie Toupin, 'What Does the Notion of "Sovereignty" Mean When Referring to the Digital?' (2019) 21 *New Media & Society* 2305.

[39] Couture and Toupin (n 38 above).

[40] Couture and Toupin (n 38 above); on the use of the concept of data sovereignty as an aspect of digital sovereignty see Federal Ministry for Economic Affairs and Energy (BMWi), 'Project GAIA-X – A Federated Data Infrastructure as the Cradle of a Vibrant European Ecosystem' (n 2 above).

[41] See, eg, in relation to the concept of digital constitutionalism, Edoardo Celeste, 'The Scope of Application of Digital Constitutionalism. Output from an Empirical Research' (Nexa Research Papers 2017): www.nexa.polito.it/nexacenterfiles/E.%20Celeste%20-%20Research%20Paper.pdf.

[42] Federal Ministry for Economic Affairs and Energy (BMWi), 'Digital Sovereignty in the Context of Platform-Based Ecosystems' (n 2 above) 6.

[43] Federal Ministry for Economic Affairs and Energy (BMWi), 'Project GAIA-X – A Federated Data Infrastructure as the Cradle of a Vibrant European Ecosystem' (n 2 above) 7, quoting the Digital Summit Focus Group 'Digital Sovereignty in a Connected Economy' (2018).

[44] Federal Ministry for Economic Affairs and Energy (BMWi), 'Project GAIA-X – A Federated Data Infrastructure as the Cradle of a Vibrant European Ecosystem' (n 2 above) 7.

[45] Cf Celeste, 'Digital Constitutionalism' (n 6 above).

over digital assets, which can be material and immaterial entities, thus potentially 'located' in a space that transcends physical boundaries. Moreover, digital sovereignty is not only a prerogative of states, but also of private 'organisations' that are vested with this power. States alone cannot cope with the challenges of a globalised world; regional and international organisations, such as the EU, necessarily emerge to complement states' functions.[46] Finally, although the element of 'control' is still rooted in the concept of digital sovereignty, particular emphasis is placed on the ability to be 'independent' from external interference. In the Gaia-X documents, for instance, digital sovereignty is defined as '*independent self*-determination'. The prominence given to this aspect of sovereignty should not be underestimated because it reflects the peculiar context in which the concept of digital sovereignty has emerged: the European appeal to regain independence in the digital field. The next section will analyse how claims to digital sovereignty have surfaced in the EU and what their rationale is.

III. Digital Sovereignty in the EU

Today, digital technologies are an integral part of the everyday life of individuals, companies and institutions in Europe, but the market for digital products and services is dominated by American and Chinese multinational corporations.[47] Multiple risks are identified in the European inability to fully control its data and digital infrastructures. Regaining sovereignty of its portion of the digital ecosystem is seen in the EU as a potential solution to preserve its unique DNA of rights and values. To this purpose, a series of initiatives has emerged both at Member State and Union level. However, as we will see in the following sections, this phenomenon risks degenerating into economically and legally counter-productive sovereigntist arm-wrestling.

A. Preserving the European DNA

Digital sovereignty claims originally materialised in Europe in response to the perceived excessive role of foreign technology companies.[48] What is traditionally defined as 'external' sovereignty, the capability of a state to exercise its power without interference by other entities, is perceived to be under threat in the European

[46] See, eg Petra Dobner and Martin Loughlin (eds), *The Twilight of Constitutionalism?* (Oxford University Press, 2010) pt 1; Anne Peters, 'Compensatory Constitutionalism: The Function and Potential of Fundamental International Norms and Structures' (2006) 19 *Leiden Journal of International Law* 579.

[47] In relation to the cloud sector, see, eg, Will Bedingfield, 'Europe Has a Plan to Break Google and Amazon's Cloud Dominance', *Wired UK*, 27 January 2020: www.wired.co.uk/article/europe-gaia-x-cloud-amazon-google, accessed 5 June 2020.

[48] See Pierre Bellanger, *La souveraineté numérique* (Stock, 2014).

digital society. Products and services offered by non-European multinationals dominate the market, consequently imposing their values and rules. European individuals and institutions are left at the mercy of technology firms from China and the US.

This condition is regarded negatively for a series of reasons, both generally and specifically related to the two countries dominating the technological sector: China and the US. First of all, data and digital infrastructures are seen as assets of critical importance for European economic development.[49] Therefore, heavily relying on non-European service providers could increase the risk of an excessive dependency on those countries[50] – a consideration that today, in the current trade war between the US and China, seems to be more concrete than ever.[51]

Secondly, foreign countries may not offer an adequate level of protection to European personal data. According to the GDPR, this is one of the conditions among others for authorising the transfer of European personal data to third countries.[52] However, looking beyond this normative requirement, even in cases where this criterion is ostensibly met, European personal data could be exposed to risks. As a paradigmatic example, one can mention the existence of the US mass surveillance programme unveiled by Edward Snowden in 2013, which also involved data of millions of European users[53] – a factor that certainly enhanced the level of suspicion that EU Member States currently harbour towards the level of data protection offered by the US.[54] China, on the other side, is generally mistrusted as a non-democratic country, and the recent adoption in 2017 of a new National Intelligence Law, obliging Chinese companies to collaborate with Chinese intelligence agencies, certainly does not help.[55] Finally, the Cambridge Analytica scandal implicating Facebook in 2018 also illustrates that a concrete threat for data protection could come not only from foreign law enforcement and intelligence agencies, but also from private corporations.[56]

[49] See European Commission, 'A European Strategy for Data', COM(2020) 66 final, www.ec.europa.eu/info/sites/info/files/communication-european-strategy-data-19feb2020_en.pdf.

[50] See Federal Ministry for Economic Affairs and Energy (BMWi), 'Project GAIA-X – A Federated Data Infrastructure as the Cradle of a Vibrant European Ecosystem' (n 2 above).

[51] For a comprehensive view on the latest news on the issue, see 'US-China Trade Dispute', *Financial Times*, www.ft.com/us-china-trade-dispute, accessed 5 June 2020.

[52] For a succinct, but comprehensive overview see Celeste and Fabbrini, 'Competing Jurisdictions' (n 36 above).

[53] See Ioanna Tourkochoriti, 'The Snowden Revelations, the Transatlantic Trade and Investment Partnership and the Divide between U.S.-E.U. in Data Privacy Protection' (2014) 36 *University of Arkansas at Little Rock Law Review* 161.

[54] See Edoardo Celeste and Federico Fabbrini, 'Targeted Surveillance: Can Privacy and Surveillance Being Reconciled?' in Sergio Carrera, Deirdre Curtin and Andrew Geddes (eds), *20 Year Anniversary of the Tampere Programme. Europeanisation Dynamics of the EU Area of Freedom, Security and Justice* (European University Institute, 2020).

[55] See Yuan Yang, 'Is Huawei Compelled by Chinese Law to Help with Espionage?', *Financial Times* (5 March 2019), www.ft.com/content/282f8ca0-3be6-11e9-b72b-2c7f526ca5d0, accessed 1 December 2019; Celeste and Fabbrini, 'Competing Jurisdictions' (n 36 above).

[56] See Patrick Greenfield, 'The Cambridge Analytica Files: The Story so Far', *The Guardian* (25 March 2018), www.theguardian.com/news/2018/mar/26/the-cambridge-analytica-files-the-story-so-far> accessed 30 April 201S9.

Thirdly, and more generally, a heavy reliance on foreign service providers may expose Europeans to potential fundamental rights infringements. Before the *Schrems* decision, for instance, where the Court of Justice of the EU (CJEU) invalidated the agreement allowing the transfer of EU personal data to selected American companies, EU data subjects did not have any right to judicial redress before US courts in case of infringement of their data protection rights.[57]

From these considerations, it is possible to argue that the main rationale behind digital sovereignty claims in the EU lies in the desire to preserve European core values, rights and principles. By invoking control over personal data and digital infrastructures, the EU is seeking to maintain its fundamental values of respect for democracy and human rights unaltered in the face of the challenges of the global digital society.[58] In a communication released in February 2020, the EU Commission stressed the difference between the American, Chinese and European strategies in the context of the data economy. The US would be characterised by the predominant role of private actors; in China, the government would play an incisive oversight role; the 'European way', conversely, would combine the need to preserve a free-flow of data and competition among economic players with high standards of protection in terms of privacy, security, ethics and fundamental rights in general.[59]

According to the Commission, this can be achieved through the creation of a 'European data space', where an adequate level of digital infrastructure allows for the processing a data-driven economy, and EU law and its fundamental rights are respected and enforced effectively.[60] The next sub-section will explore which measures have been concretely suggested to be implemented both at national and EU level.

B. Member States' and Union Initiatives

Measures invoked in the name of digital sovereignty have in common the exercise of a centripetal force on data and digital infrastructures by states or supranational organisations. At first sight, they could be seen as the opposite of extraterritorial measures.[61] States do not seek to extend their jurisdiction over data or

[57] ECJ, *Maximillian Schrems v Data Protection Commissioner* C-362/14, judgment of 6 October 2015, ECLI:EU:C:2015:650; see David Cole, Federico Fabbrini and Stephen J Schulhofer (eds), *Surveillance, Privacy, and Transatlantic Relations* (Hart Publishing, 2017) ch 11.

[58] See European Commission (n 49 above); see also Christopher Kuner, 'The Internet and the Global Reach of EU Law' in Marise Cremona and Joanne Scott (eds), *EU Law Beyond EU Borders: The Extraterritorial Reach of EU Law* (Oxford University Press, 2019) para 4.

[59] European Commission (n 49 above) 3.

[60] European Commission (n 49 above) 4–5; cf Selby (n 36 above), who considers local law enforcement as one of the drivers of digital sovereignty claims.

[61] See Bertrand de La Chapelle and Paul Fehlinger, 'Jurisdiction on the Internet: From Legal Arms Race to Transnational Cooperation' in Giancarlo Frosio (ed), *Oxford Handbook of Online Intermediary Liability* (Oxford University Press, 2020), www.cigionline.org/sites/default/files/gcig_no28_web.pdf, accessed 8 June 2020.

digital infrastructures located abroad by stretching the scope of their regulation; they rather attempt to re-attract such data and digital infrastructures into their classical jurisdictional boundaries by requiring their 'physical' return to their territories.

A paradigmatic example is represented by so-called data localisation, or data residency initiatives, whereby a state or a supranational organisation requires personal data to be stored within its territory.[62] In 2014, for instance, the CJEU in *Digital Rights Ireland* invalidated the Data Retention Directive.[63] The Directive provided for the retention of communications metadata for law enforcement purposes. In other words, service providers were required to store all data relating to one person's communications, such as time, location or receiver of a phone call, but excluding its content, for a specific amount of time in order to allow law enforcement authorities to access it for the prosecution of a criminal offence. The CJEU invalidated the Data Retention Directive on a series of grounds, including its failure to require communications providers to store metadata within the EU.[64] Article 8 of the Charter of Fundamental Rights of the EU enshrines a right to data protection, and at paragraph (3) explicitly vests national data protection authorities with the duty to ensure compliance with this right. According to the CJEU, the power of these oversight agencies would be irremediably restricted if telecommunication providers were able to store metadata outside the EU, and thus beyond their jurisdiction. Hence the necessity, derived *a contrario* from the judgment of the CJEU, to store metadata with the EU territory.

Digital Rights Ireland exclusively concerned the storage of users' metadata for law enforcement purposes. There is no absolute obligation to store personal data in the EU; personal data can be freely transferred outside the EU, subject to specific rules.[65] However, in *Digital Rights Ireland*, the CJEU balanced the necessity to preserve such a relatively free-flow of data with the need to ensure a high level of protection of this specific processing requirement. In particular, the CJEU's solution was justified by the particular risks that storing a significant amount of metadata outside the EU may entail in terms of security and protection, such as risks of abuse, and unlawful access and use.[66]

A similar sectoral approach was adopted in other countries, both in the EU and beyond, for analogous reasons.[67] In the EU, many Member States require financial

[62] Cf Selby (n 36 above) 214.

[63] ECJ, *Digital Rights Ireland Ltd v Minister for Communications, Marine and Natural Resources and Others* and *Kärntner Landesregierung and Others*, Joined Cases C-293/12 and C-594/12, 8 April 2014, ECLI:EU:C:2014:238; for an analysis of the case, see Edoardo Celeste, 'The Court of Justice and the Ban on Bulk Data Retention: Expansive Potential and Future Scenarios' (2019) 15 *European Constitutional Law Review* 134.

[64] *Digital Rights Ireland* (n 63 above) para 68.

[65] See GDPR, art 44 ff.

[66] *Digital Rights Ireland* (n 63 above) paras 66–68.

[67] See Anupam Chander and Uyên P Lê, 'Data Nationalism' (2015) 64 *Emory Law Journal* 677; see also Selby (n 36 above).

data to be stored on the national soil; some of them impose similar obligations on public institutions.[68] However, in contrast to these balanced solutions, other states have preferred more holistic data localisation regimes.[69] In 2014, for instance, the Russian Federation passed a bill requiring the compulsory storage of all citizens' personal data collected by electronic communication providers within the territory of the state.[70] Similarly, Chinese law imposes an obligation to store within the national territory all personal data collected by critical information infrastructures, such as healthcare, financial institutions, energy and transport companies.[71]

Similar wide-ranging data localisation measures have never been taken in Europe on a permanent basis. In 2013, in the aftermath of the Snowden revelations, the conference of the German national data protection authorities ceased issuing authorisations for data transfers from Germany to non-EU countries.[72] More recently, in 2019, the Commissioner for Data Protection and Informational Liberty of the Land of Hessen, in central Germany, temporarily prohibited the use of Microsoft Office 365 by schools.[73] The national data protection authority claimed that Microsoft's decision to store data outside the EU would have exposed personal information related to Hessian children to the risk of being accessed by US law enforcement authorities.[74] The Microsoft ban, therefore, would have been justified to preserve the State's digital sovereignty by ensuring that the level of protection accorded to data processed by Microsoft be in line with European and German fundamental rights.[75]

The recent decision of the Hessian data protection commissioner is a paradigmatic example of the challenges and the implications of claiming digital sovereignty in the EU. Non-European corporations often offer state-of-the-art

[68] See Selbey (n 36 above) 226.

[69] See Selbey (n 36 above) 215.

[70] See W Kuan Hon and others, 'Policy, Legal and Regulatory Implications of a Europe-Only Cloud' (2016) 24 *International Journal of Law and Information Technology* 251; Selby (n 36 above).

[71] On the point see Selbey (n 36 above).

[72] Chairman of the federal and national data protection authorities 2013, 'Press Release. Conference of Data Protection Commissioners Says that Intelligence Services Constitute a Massive Threat to Data Traffic between Germany and Countries Outside Europe' (24 July 2013), www.bfdi.bund.de/SharedDocs/Publikationen/Entschliessungssammlung/ErgaenzendeDokumente/PMDSK_SafeHarbor_Eng.pdf?__blob=publicationFile; See Chander and Lê (n 67 above) 692.

[73] Der Hessische Beauftragte für Datenschutz und Informationsfreiheit, 'Stellungnahme des Hessischen Beauftragten für Datenschutz und Informationsfreiheit zum Einsatz von Microsoft Office 365 in hessischen Schulen' (9 July 2019), datenschutz.hessen.de/service, accessed 30 November 2019; see also Der Hessische Beauftragte für Datenschutz und Informationsfreiheit, 'Zweite Stellungnahme zum Einsatz von Microsoft Office 365 in hessischen Schulen' (2 August 2019), datenschutz.hessen.de/pressemitteilungen/zweite-stellungnahme-zum-einsatz-von-microsoft-office-365-hessischen-schulen, accessed 30 November 2019, in which the Hessian data protection authority lifted its ban after an intense phase of dialogue with Microsoft.

[74] Der Hessische Beauftragte für Datenschutz und Informationsfreiheit, 'Stellungnahme des Hessischen Beauftragten für Datenschutz und Informationsfreiheit zum Einsatz von Microsoft Office 365 in hessischen Schulen' (n 73 above) para 2.

[75] Der Hessische Beauftragte für Datenschutz und Informationsfreiheit, 'Stellungnahme des Hessischen Beauftragten für Datenschutz und Informationsfreiheit zum Einsatz von Microsoft Office 365 in hessischen Schulen' (n 73 above) para 2.

products and services used by millions of users in the Union. Guaranteeing a high level of data protection within the EU by physically storing data in the territory of the Union implies that non-European companies desist from using their digital infrastructures located abroad. However, in this case, the main quandary is whether existing digital infrastructures in the EU are able to satisfy its internal demand. Many initiatives have emerged both at national and Union level, in advocating the creation of such an infrastructure, speak of the inadequacy of existing resources in the EU.[76] In this context, one can mention the idea – proposed since 2011 – of an EU-only cloud or even a 'Schengen' virtual area.[77] In 2016, the European Commission launched the European Cloud Initiative as a key component of its Digital Single Market Strategy.[78] This project would entail the creation of a European Open Science Cloud, a secure cloud infrastructure for researchers, and a European Data Infrastructure, which would provide the underlying super-computing solutions.

Some Member States have long tried to put in place national digital infrastructures. In 2011, the French government launched the project of a 'sovereign cloud', Andromède, subsequently giving birth to two competing platforms, Cloudwatt, managed by Orange, and Numergy, led by SFR.[79] In 2013, Deutsche Telekom presented a project to create an 'Internetz', a German-only Internet, routing all traffic data nationally.[80] More recently, the launch of the Franco-German Gaia-X project, which advocates the creation of a pan-European federated cloud infrastructure, bears witness to an acknowledgement of the necessity to leave behind a parochial approach and join the forces at EU level to deliver a broader, more scalable, and consequently potentially more successful, digital infrastructure.[81] Such a federated approach seems also to be the solution recently advocated by the EU Commission in its 2020 communication on an EU strategy for data.[82] The European data space will be the result of a plurality of EU-wide interoperable digital ecosystems, each one covering a critical sector of the European economy.[83] To achieve this result, the Commission not only plans to invest a significant amount of resources to build the necessary infrastructure in the next decade, but also aims to introduce a coherent legislative package that will complement the existing regulatory framework for data, without however imposing a rigid ex ante regulation.[84]

[76] See also European Commission (n 49 above).

[77] See C Kuner and others, 'Internet Balkanization Gathers Pace: Is Privacy the Real Driver?' (2015) 5(1) *International Data Privacy Law* 1; Kuan Hon and others (n 70 above).

[78] European Commission, 'European Cloud Initiative – Building a Competitive Data and Knowledge Economy in Europe' (2016), www.eur-lex.europa.eu/legal-content/EN/TXT/PDF/?uri=CELEX:52016DC0178&from=EN.

[79] See Bedingfield (n 47 above).

[80] See Kuan Hon and others (n 70 above).

[81] See Federal Ministry for Economic Affairs and Energy (BMWi), 'Project GAIA-X – A Federated Data Infrastructure as the Cradle of a Vibrant European Ecosystem' (n 2 above).

[82] European Commission (n 49 above) 16.

[83] European Commission (n 49 above) 12, 16.

[84] European Commission (n 49 above) 12.

C. The Risk of Digital Sovereigntism

In Europe, digital sovereignty claims have explicitly emerged in relation to a specific number of initiatives. However, if one takes a functional approach, looking at the ultimate aim of digital sovereignty claims – which is to regain control and independence in the management of the digital ecosystem – it is possible to identify a series of other mechanisms that would contribute to (re)affirm the European digital sovereignty. Chander and Lê, for example, regard the EU data protection rules limiting the transfer of personal data to third countries as a claim of digital sovereignty, even though this is not an explicit objective of the GDPR.[85] Looking beyond the EU, Jordan Fischer in this book has analysed the US attempt to adopt a federal data privacy law.[86] This bill certainly represents an attempt to respond to the Cambridge Analytica scandal and to avoid a scenario of legislative fragmentation in the US after the recent enactment of privacy legislation by California. However, one may also argue that it aims to reaffirm the American privacy values and ultimately its digital sovereignty. The broad scope of application of the GDPR and the introduction of harsh fines in case of violation of data protection rules have pushed American companies to proactively embrace the new European standards.[87] This further example of the Brussels effect in the field of data protection may be arguably be read, from an American standpoint, as a form of imperialism, and, at any rate, as a de facto erosion of their digital sovereignty.[88]

Interestingly, following this line of arguments, even an apparent expression of legislation with extraterritorial reach such as the US CLOUD act, commented on by Stephen Smith in this book, may be regarded as a form of exercise of digital sovereignty.[89] The US would aim to reassert their control over data which American multinational companies store abroad in order to comply with foreign data protection law. And of course, in the same way, one may contend that the broad scope of application of the GDPR, encompassing also companies not established within the EU territory, is equally to be regarded as a corollary of European digital sovereignty.[90]

[85] Chander and Lê (n 67 above).

[86] See Chapter 3 of this book.

[87] See Michael L Rustad and Thomas H Koenig, 'Towards a Global Data Privacy Standard' (2019) 71 *Florida Law Review* 365.

[88] On the Brussels effect in the field of data protection, see Anu Bradford, *The Brussels Effect: How the European Union Rules the World* (Oxford University Press, 2020) ch 5; on the notion of data protection imperialism see Federico Fabbrini and Edoardo Celeste, 'The Right to Be Forgotten in the Digital Age: The Challenges of Data Protection Beyond Borders' (2020) 21 *German Law Journal* 55; see also Dan Jerker B Svantesson, 'The Google Spain Case: Part of a Harmful Trend of Jurisdictional Overreach' (2015) EUI Working Papers, cadmus.eui.eu//handle/1814/36317, accessed 15 January 2020; cf Rustad and Koenig (n 87 above) who also analyse an opposite 'D.C. effect'.

[89] See Chapter 8 of this book.

[90] Cf John Quinn, Chapter 4.

Paradoxically, therefore, this functional interpretation of digital sovereignty leads to conflation of centripetal and centrifugal pressures in a single phenomenon: extraterritoriality and localisation become two sides of the same coin. Digital sovereignty emerges as a useful lens through which to interpret this complex mix of apparently opposing trends. However, by embracing this interpretation, it is apparent that the element of territory, which was central to the traditional notion of sovereignty, loses its centrality. All forms of digital sovereignty aim to gain and maintain control of the digital ecosystem. The reference to a territory becomes only one of various mechanisms that states and regional organisations may use to affirm their jurisdiction over sectors of the digital world.

Overtaking the traditional anchoring to the territory, digital sovereignty may contemplate the co-existence of a plurality of sovereignties within the same physical space. This apparent oxymoron is explained by the fact that digital sovereignty may use the territory as *one* of the mechanisms to be asserted as much as it may resort to other reference points, such as the connection with a user located in a state or the offer of goods of services to those users. This post-territorial perspective effaces the question of territorial alignment of data protection, and more broadly, digital regulation.[91] Yet, the dilemma of how to accommodate co-existing sovereignties still persists.

A series of unfettered sovereign claims would naturally tend toward a state of continuous conflict in the attempt to predominate and possibly establish a scenario of 'One Law Rule'.[92] Dis-anchoring sovereignty from territory does not escape the question of the limitations of digital sovereignty. One needs to find a peaceable and efficient way of re-composing the mosaic of sovereign claims. In line with other scholars, this chapter contends that a global digital society may continue to exist, while preserving states' interests.[93] The solution lies in preventing digital sovereignty from degenerating into a form of sovereigntism or nationalism.[94] The latter arises when digital sovereignty claims advocate unjustified forms of protectionism and isolationism.[95] Exercising an excessive centripetal force to attract data into Europe and subsidising the creation of digital infrastructures made in the EU could be legally and economically counterproductive. For example, data localisation policies may alter the global economic course by generating higher costs related to the relocation of data centres in Europe.[96] Centralising data in the EU is not always synonymous with enhanced security, since delocalisation may be

[91] On the question of territorial alignment of cyberspace, see Mueller (n 35 above) ch 4 ff.

[92] Lessig (n 31 above) 305 ff.

[93] See, in particular, Woods (n 12 above); see also La Chapelle and Fehlinger (n 61 above).

[94] Specifically in the context of data protection, see Fabbrini and Celeste, 'The Right to Be Forgotten' (n 88 above), who articulate the tension between data protection imperialism and sovereigntism; Chander and Lê (n 66 above), who describe this phenomenon in terms of 'data nationalism'.

[95] See Kuner and others (n 77 above); Christopher Millard, 'Forced Localization of Cloud Services: Is Privacy the Real Driver?' (Social Science Research Network 2015) SSRN Scholarly Paper ID 2605926; Celeste and Fabbrini, 'Competing Jurisdictions' (n 36 above).

[96] Mishra (n 36 above).

a strategy to enhance system resilience and decrease the level of vulnerability.[97] Digital sovereigntism could exacerbate political and economic tensions with third states, leading to a strenuous arm-wrestling that, ultimately, would not enhance the protection of European data and foster our economy.[98]

Defending the European DNA of values and rights is of utmost importance. Nevertheless, this should not nurture a form of legal-economic insularity; nor should it justify a revamp of European normative imperialism, overstretching the scope of application of EU law. In the global digital ecosystem, the EU should preserve its ideological genes by simultaneously considering the transnational consequences of its regulatory activity.[99] As argued by John Quinn in this volume, the *Google v CNIL* case recently decided by the CJEU went exactly in this direction, posing the fundamental questions of what would happen if the EU imposed word-wide delisting orders on search engines, and if all sovereign states exercised the same prerogative.[100] Absent a cosmopolitan solution, respecting the principles of international comity emerges as the only viable prospect.[101] In a world characterised by manifold overlapping sovereignties, the respect of regulatory choices of other countries is essential to avoid counterproductive tensions.[102] In order to reconcile multiple sovereigns in a post-territorial ecosystem, Europe should be as 'open as possible, and as closed as necessary'.[103] Only in this way will the EU preserve its unique DNA of rights and values, foster its digital economy, and pacifically prosper with its foreign allies.

IV. Conclusion

Over the past few years, a series of initiatives has been launched in the EU in the name of digital sovereignty. Data of European citizens, companies and institutions is mostly in the hands of American and Chinese technology corporations, where it may be accessed by law enforcement and intelligence authorities of these

[97] Mishra (n 36 above).

[98] In relation to cloud computing, see Celeste and Fabbrini 'Competing Jurisdictions' (n 36 above).

[99] Cf Kuner, 'The Internet and the Global Reach of EU Law' (n 58 above) para F.

[100] *Google LLC v Commission nationale de l'informatique et des libertés (CNIL)* (n 33 above); in this volume, see Quinn at Chapter 4.

[101] In this sense, Woods (n 12 above); Fabbrini and Celeste 'The Right to Be Forgotten' (n 88 above).

[102] On the point, see *Google LLC v CNIL* (n 33 above), where the CJEU demanded member states to consider the existence of different approaches to data protection and in principle limit the enforcement of the right to be forgotten to the EU territory; see also the Opinion of Advocate General Szpunar in *Google LLC v CNIL* (n 33 above), ECLI:EU:C:2019:15, at 61, who highlighted the risk of having third states demanding global delisting and ultimately limiting access and circulation of information at global level.

[103] This sentence has been originally coined for the EU open research data policy. See 'Open Access – H2020 Online Manual', ec.europa.eu/research/participants/docs/h2020-funding-guide/cross-cutting-issues/open-access-data-management/open-access_en.htm, accessed 17 June 2020.

countries. Recent scandals have shown that this situation poses significant risks in terms of potential violations of fundamental rights. Geopolitical tensions between the US and China may have considerable repercussions for the level of security and availability of digital services and infrastructures in the EU. By invoking digital sovereignty, various EU initiatives seek to exert a centripetal force on data and digital infrastructures. Imposing an obligation to store specific types of information in the EU and promoting digital products and services made in Europe would help reacquire control of European data, and at the same time enhance the degree of independence from foreign service providers. In this way, the EU would aim to preserve its unique DNA of values and rights.

Digital sovereignty is a notion that emerged in the EU in relation to a specific series of initiatives. However, this chapter has shown that this concept can be used as a lens to interpret a broader phenomenon. As illustrated in section II of this chapter, historically, the notion of sovereignty has denoted the power of the state over a territory and its independence from external actors. The advent of digital technology has accelerated the transition towards a global society where national boundaries are no longer neatly demarcated. This chapter has argued that in this post-territorial ecosystem the concept of sovereignty loses its traditional anchoring to the notion of territory. The physical location of a juridical entity becomes one of the various mechanisms by which to exercise state sovereignty. Multiple sovereignties can be deemed to coexist in the same context. Digital sovereignty claims can therefore take the form not only of localisation law, but also of legislation having an extraterritorial scope. From this perspective, the latter is not to be automatically condemned as imperialist, because territorial boundaries are no longer the exclusive parameter to consider.

However, even this post-territorial approach does not exempt us from analysing the question of the limits of digital sovereignty. On the one hand, unfettered sovereignties produce tensions between states, and ultimately risk enhancing the likelihood of having dominant players imperially regulating vast portions of the digital ecosystem. On the other hand, exercising excessively a centripetal force on data and digital infrastructures to achieve a realignment with territorial jurisdictions may lead to forms of protectionism and isolationism. Section III of this chapter has focused in particular on this last point, warning against the risk of disguising sovereigntist policies as legitimate sovereign claims.

The global digital society is an ecosystem where, as Ralf Michaels put it, 'everything has an effect on everything'.[104] The solution advanced by this chapter to accommodate multiple sovereign interests in a post-territorial world consequently pivots on the respect of the principles of international comity, peaceable cooperation, and the guarantee of pluralism. In this respect, EU law still seems to be in a transition phase, uncertain on which strategy to adopt to preserve

[104] Ralf Michaels, 'Territorial Jurisdiction After Territoriality' in Pieter J Slot and Mielle K Bulterman (eds), *Globalisation and Jurisdiction* (Kluwer Law International 2004) 123.

its DNA of values and principles in the digital ecosystem. Christopher Kuner rightly observes that 'EU law is still searching for a paradigm for its application to the Internet'.[105] Critiques of EU legislative overreaching and digital sovereigntism speak of the difficulty of finding an intermediate strategy which translates sovereign interests in a global environment.[106] However, recent developments in the case law of the CJEU show that EU law is progressively moving in the right direction.

[105] Kuner, 'The Internet and the Global Reach of EU Law' (n 58 above) 140.

[106] See Christopher Kuner, 'Data Nationalism and Its Discontents' (2015) 64 *Emory Law Journal* 2089, 2098.

INDEX

www.ingramcontent.com/pod-product-compliance
Lightning Source LLC
Chambersburg PA
CBHW071300180926
51613CB00001B/84
9781509940660